SPIRITUALITY IN
CLINICAL PRACTICE

SPIRITUALITY IN CLINICAL PRACTICE

Incorporating the Spiritual Dimension in Psychotherapy and Counseling

Len Sperry, M.D., Ph.D.

BRUNNER-ROUTLEDGE
ALERE FLAMMAM
Taylor & Francis Group

USA	Publishing Office:	BRUNNER-ROUTLEDGE *A member of the Taylor & Francis Group* 325 Chestnut Street Philadelphia, PA 19106 Tel: (215) 625-8900 Fax: (215) 625-2940
	Distribution Center:	BRUNNER-ROUTLEDGE *A member of the Taylor & Francis Group* 7625 Empire Drive Florence, KY 41042 Tel: 1-800-634-7064 Fax: 1-800-248-4724
UK		BRUNNER-ROUTLEDGE *A member of the Taylor & Francis Group* 27 Church Road Hove E. Sussex, BN3 2FA Tel: +44 (0) 1273 207411 Fax: +44 (0) 1283 205612

SPIRITUALITY IN CLINICAL PRACTICE: Incorporating the Spiritual Dimension in Psychotherapy and Counseling

1 2 3 4 5 6 7 8 9 0

Printed by Sheridan Books, Ann Arbor, MI, 2001.
Cover design by Ellen Seguin.

A CIP catalog record for this book is available from the British Library.
∞ The paper in this publication meets the requirements of the ANSI Standard Z39.48-1984 (Permanence of Paper).

Library of Congress Cataloging-in-Publication Data
Sperry, Len.
    Spirituality in clinical practice : incorporating the spiritual dimension in pyschotherapy and counseling / Len Sperry.
        p. cm
    Includes bibliographical references and index.
    ISBN 1-58391–067–0 (alk. paper)
    1. Psychotherapy—Religious aspects. 2. Counseling—Religious aspects.
3. Spirituality. I. Title.
RC489.R46 S66 2001
616.89'14—dc21   00-066762

ISBN 1-58391-067-0 (paper)

CONTENTS

About the Author   vii
Acknowledgments   ix
Preface   xi

PART I
NEW DIMENSIONS IN CLINICAL PRACTICE

Overview   1

1 The Spiritual Dimension in Psychotherapy and Counseling: 3
An Overview

PART II
PERSPECTIVES ON THE SPIRITUAL DIMENSION

Overview   21

2 Dimensional Perspectives on Spiritual Development   23

3 Developmental Models of the Spiritual Dimension   51

4 Spiritual Dynamics, Crises, and Emergencies in Psychotherapy 79

PART III
STRATEGIES FOR INCORPORATING
THE SPIRITUAL DIMENSION

Overview   103

5 Engagement and Assessment Strategies   105

6   **Spiritually-Oriented Interventions**   120
    with Individuals and Couples

7   **Incorporating Spiritual Disciplines**   147

PART IV
THE SPIRITUAL DIMENSION AND THE CLINICIAN

    Overview   167

8   **Incorporating the Spiritual Dimension**   169
    in Personal and Professional Life

    Epilogue   193

    Index   195

ABOUT THE AUTHOR

Len Sperry, M.D., Ph.D. is Clinical Professor of Psychiatry at the Medical College of Wisconsin and Professor of Health Services Administration and Psychology at Barry University. He is board certified in Psychiatry and Clinical Psychology and listed in *Best Doctors in America*. He has written widely in the area of spirituality and psychotherapy and is a Fellow of the Division of Psychology and Religion of the American Psychological Association and a member of Committee on Psychiatry and Religion of the Group for the Advancement of Psychiatry. He is the author of more than 30 books.

ACKNOWLEDGMENTS

A special note of thanks is extended to P. Scott Richards, Ph.D., Lisa Miller, Ph.D, Edward Shafranske, Ph.D., Paul Giblin, Ph.D., Everett Worthington, Ph.D., and James Oglivie, Ph.D., for their first-person accounts included in Chapter 8. Each has graciously and courageously offered to share with readers the ways in which they incorporate the spiritual dimension in their professional as well as their personal lives. I say courageously because, generally speaking, helping professionals remain reticent in discussing their personal philosophy and spiritual beliefs with students, supervisees, and colleagues at a time when trainees are increasingly eager to understand how the spiritual dimension impacts their professional and personal lives. The result is that students have little or no access to role models who incorporate the spiritual dimension in their professional and personal lives. These portraits provide a window into the lives of these highly regarded professionals. I would also like to express my appreciation to Tim Julet, acquisitions editor, and Rachel Ravitsky, production editor, at Brunner-Routledge.

ACKNOWLEDGMENTS

PREFACE

In recent years, spirituality has become increasingly important in the lives of many Americans. Just as individuals have become more sensitized to the biological dimension in their lives by their attention to diet and exercise, increasingly, many are seeking to incorporate the spiritual dimension in their daily lives as well. They may have experimented with various spiritual practices which evoked very positive religious experiences or even rather discomforting feelings or experiences. Consequently, it is not surprising that clinicians are now expected to be sensitive to spiritual, religious, ethical, and moral issues, as well as to incorporate the spiritual dimension in their professional work.

Traditionally, clinicians were trained and expected to focus principally on the psychological dimension, while leaving the spiritual dimension to clergy, chaplains, and other ministry personnel. However, the reality is that the psychological and spiritual dimensions overlap considerably. Today, many clients are insisting that clinicians deal with both the spiritual and the psychological dimensions. Accordingly, the challenge for contemporary clinicians is to become sufficiently conversant with spiritual and religious dynamics to meet client needs and expectations.

To meet this emerging need, training programs are gearing up to offer training which focuses on the spiritual dimension in psychotherapy: graduate-level courses to clinicians-in-training, and continuing education seminars for those clinicians who are already in practice. There are already a few books that address these concerns. Some are large, comprehensive texts while others are more narrowly focused. Some emphasize theory and research over practice while others are largely practice focused. Curiously, there is little or no mention of the contributions of transpersonal psychology or other Eastern approaches in these books. Currently, no text is available that provides a concise overview and integration of relevant theory and research while emphasizing strategies and interventions for incorporating the spiritual dimension in clinical practice.

Spirituality in Clinical Practice: New Dimensions in Psychotherapy and Counseling is a concise, theory-based, clinically oriented text that integrates a broad range of theoretical perspectives and clinical strategies for understanding and intervening with the spiritual, moral, and religious issues that emerge in the treatment process. It offers clinicians a broad theoretical overview of the spiritual dimension as well as effective strategies for incorporating this dimension into the practice of psychotherapy and counseling. It includes perspectives not found in other texts such as a developmental perspective integrating moral and spiritual development; the interface of spiritual development with personality functioning; and insights from object relations, self psychology, and transpersonal psychotherapy as they relate to various spiritual traditions and contemporary spiritual practices. It also emphasizes and illustrates several clinical considerations and treatment strategies including engagement strategies, ethical issues involving spirituality and religion, countertransference, assessment methods and spiritual measures, and treatment approaches for combining spiritual practices with therapeutic interventions.

There are three other unique features of the book. One is the inclusion of strategies for incorporating the spiritual dimension in the treatment of couples (Chapter 6). Another is the inclusion of Roger Walsh's multicultural, integrative model of spiritual practices derived from both Western and non-Western perspectives (Chapter 7). Unfortunately, a more comprehensive and detailed discussion of the multicultural perspective on other aspects of spirituality in clinical practice is beyond the scope of this short text. The third unique feature is a description of how prominent psychotherapists and counselors actually incorporate the spiritual dimension in their daily clinical practice and their own personal lives (Chapter 8).

Spirituality in Clinical Practice: New Dimensions in Psychotherapy and Counseling is intended as a basic text or supplemental text in seminars and courses that address spiritual issues in a psychological context, such as, 'Religious and Spiritual Issues in Psychotherapy,' 'Human Development: Psychological and Spiritual Dimensions,' 'Psychotherapy and Spirituality,' 'Psychotherapy, Spirituality and Religion,' 'Theory and Practice of Pastoral Counseling,' 'Spiritual Guidance,' and 'Psychology and Religion.' It is also intended as a professional book for practicing clinicians such as psychotherapists, spiritual directors, and pastoral counselors who need to become more familiar with the clinical aspects of the spiritual dimension. It may also be of interest to clinicians who are interested in the spiritual dimension for their own personal and spiritual growth.

A word about language usage: While terms like *spiritual counseling, spiritual psychotherapy,* and *spiritually-oriented psychotherapy* are often used interchangeably, there is little consensus about definition or scope of practice. At the same time, established professions such as spiritual direction, spiritual companionship, pastoral counseling, and pastoral psychotherapy seem to be enlarging their scope of practice. Since a new area of clinical practice appears to be emerging, it seems premature to attempt to specify either definition or scope of practice of this new area. Accordingly, the designation *spiritually-attuned psychotherapy and counseling* will be used to refer to a general set of clinical perspectives and strategies that are more inclusive than exclusive. Also, the term *treatment* is used instead of 'therapy' or the 'counseling process.' Furthermore, instead of utilizing 'psychotherapist,' 'counselor,' 'spiritual therapist,' 'pastoral counselor,' 'spiritual director,' or 'spiritual friend,' the generic designation *clinician* is used to refer to these various professionals. Similarly, there is no common consensus on the use of such terms as 'spiritual client,' 'religiously committed client,' 'spiritual person,' 'spiritual companion,' or 'directee.' Thus, the designations *client* and *spiritual seeker* are used interchangeably to refer to individuals with issues or concerns about the spiritual dimension in their lives.

I

NEW DIMENSIONS IN CLINICAL PRACTICE

Today, more and more individuals are seeking greater meaning and fulfillment in their lives, believing that spirituality is
vital for their growth and essential for helping them deal with
life's problems. Many have begun to pursue a spiritual journey and to engage in spiritual practices such as prayer and
meditation. However, they often find themselves trapped in
old feelings, attitudes, and habits that seem to undo their
progress and discourage them from this spiritual journey. Even
those who have made progress on this journey often encounter roadblocks to growth that may last for months or even
years. Not surprisingly, these spiritual seekers turn to psychotherapy and counseling for information, advice, and support.

Chapter 1, The Spiritual Dimension in Psychotherapy and
Counseling: An Overview, provides a topical introduction and
overview of the entire book. It begins by analyzing the impact that spirituality has made and will continue to make on
the practice of counseling and psychotherapy. Then it poses
and briefly addresses several questions, such as: Is spirituality

different than religion? What theoretical basis is there for this type of practice? Is it appropriate and professionally sanctioned to incorporate spirituality in psychotherapy? When is it indicated, ethical, and proper? What strategies and methods are utilized? Is special training required? Should this incorporation involve the clinician's personal life? These questions and related concerns are addressed more fully in subsequent chapters.

1

The Spiritual Dimension in Psychotherapy and Counseling: An Overview

Based on the number of magazine articles and trade books addressing the topic, it appears that many individuals are searching for ways of incorporating spirituality in their daily lives. Survey research indicates that 94 percent of Americans believe in God, nine out of ten pray, 97 percent believe their prayers are answered, and two of five report having life-changing spiritual experiences (Steere, 1997, pp. 43 & 54).

Drawing upon surveys and discussions with spiritual seekers drawn to the Omega Institute—the largest retreat center in the U.S. focusing on spirituality and wellness—Elizabeth Lesser, a cofounder of the Institute, has articulated what she calls the "New American Spirituality" (Lesser, 1999). She contrasts it with the traditional spirituality which emphasized hierarchial power and provided a clearly defined path to truth and spiritual growth with prescribed spiritual disciplines, rituals and practices. This new spirituality, which she recently renamed 21st Century Spirituality (Lesser, 2000), is based on democracy and diversity and draws from religious teaching of the Christian tradition and weaves it with the wisdom of the contemplative and Eastern traditions, feminism, and the findings of contemporary psychology, into new forms of spirituality.

She and others have noted that clients want and expect clinicians to incorporate the spiritual dimension in psychotherapy and counseling. Several questions arise: First, is spirituality different than religion? What theoretical basis is there for this type of practice? Is it appropriate and professionally sanctioned to incorporate spirituality in psychotherapy? When are there indications for it? When is it ethical and proper to offer it to clients? What strategies and methods are utilized? Is special training required? Should this incorporation involve the clinician's personal life? This book addresses these questions and related concerns. We begin by distinguishing spirituality and religion.

☐ Spirituality and Religion: Commonalities and Differences

What are the similarities and differences between spirituality and religion? Religion is born of awareness of the Transcendent together with expression of that awareness in conceptual, cultural, and social form (Ellswood, 1990). Religion is about a shared belief system (dogma) and communal ritual practice (liturgy). However, for many people today, religion carries a negative connotation: "Spirituality, as opposed to religion, connotes a direct, personal experience of the sacred unmediated by particular belief systems prescribed by dogma or by hierarchical structures of priests, ministers, rabbis, or gurus" (Berenson, 1990, p. 59).

Spirituality is about one's search for meaning and belonging and the core values that influence one's behavior. Spirituality is "harmonious interconnectedness-across time and relationships" (Hungelmann, 1985), "the human capacity to experience and relate to a dimension of power and meaning transcendent to the world of sensory reality" (Anderson, 1987), and "the experience of consciously striving to integrate one's life in terms not of isolation and self-absorption but of self-transcendence toward the ultimate value one perceives" (Schneiders, 1986).

Benner (1989) makes a helpful distinction between religion and spirituality: "Not all spirituality is religious, and not all religious spirituality is Christian." All persons are created spiritual beings as they experience a yearning for self-transcendence and surrender. This quest becomes religious in relation to some higher power and responds to this relationship with prayer and worship.

☐ Spitituality and the Changing Context of Clinical Practice

In order to effectively address the question of incorporating the spiritual dimension in clinical practice, it is useful to contextualize the matter. Four interrelated dimensions characterize the context of this question: clients, psychotherapists, professional and scientific developments, and treatment setting.

Clients

It has been observed that as many Americans have become less 'at home' in the religious traditions that have previously provided them a source of spiritual power and influence, they have become increasingly 'spiritually homeless' (Steere, 1997). Subsequently, they are searching for a sense of healing and spiritual direction from sources outside religious traditions. According to Steere, these individuals seek healing not simply for physical or emotional pain but also for a sense of wholeness and wellness. They are also seeking spiritual direction that can bring meaning, purpose, and a sense of inner fulfillment to their lives. Furthermore, because many of these individuals also manifest psychiatric symptoms and impaired functioning, they are also seeking a 'cure.' This three-pronged search for healing, spiritual direction, and cure "provides the background for a rapprochement between psychotherapy and spirituality" (Steere, 1997, p. 13) and propels these seekers into psychotherapy and counseling.

But what kind of psychotherapy or counseling are they seeking? A 1992 Gallup poll surveyed 1,000 American men and women about the context in which they would seek counseling or psychotherapy. Interestingly, 66% said they would prefer to receive counseling from a person who represented their spiritual values. Of those surveyed, 81% indicated they wanted their own spiritual values respected and integrated into the counseling process.

Psychotherapists

Whether they want the role or not, London (1985) in *The Modes and Morals of Psychotherapy*, contends that psychotherapists have, by default of religious institutions, become today's 'secular priests.' Whether they agree with this assessment or not, most practicing clinicians have had the experience of being asked for spiritual advice by clients. Clinicians may also experience some of the same spiritual hunger that others seek to satisfy. They want meaning and fulfillment in their lives, personally and professionally. They seek to achieve some measure of balance in their lives given the waves of changes that are reshaping the landscape of healthcare. They may even engage in spiritual practices like prayer, meditation, and the like. Yet, most have had no formal training in incorporating the spiritual dimension into clinical practice, and many wonder whether this function of attending to some or all of the spiritual dimension, which in the past seemed to have been discouraged, should be a legitimate part of the practice of psychotherapy. Serendipitously, some recent professional and scientific developments address these concerns. A subsequent section will detail the spiritual attitudes and practices of mental health professionals.

Professional and Scientific Developments

The relationship between spirituality and psychotherapy is not new. Historically, psychological and spiritual issues were largely the domain of the priest-healer until the eighteenth century. Ellenberger (1970) contends that dynamic psychotherapy emerged in 1775 because of the "clash between the physician Mesmer and the exorcist Gassner" (p. 53). Gassner was a priest whose fame in healing through exorcism was fatefully pitted against the psychological methods of Mesmer in a contest to treat the same client. Gassner's loss symbolized the split of religion from psychotherapy, and the denigration of religion in the psychotherapeutic context. This denigration was further reinforced by Freud and later by Albert Ellis and others. In short, religion was viewed at best as irrelevant and at worst as detrimental to mental health (Larsen & Milano, 1997).

However, this attitude has begun to change recently. The reason appears to be a combination of Western culture's hunger for the spiritual and an increasing number of studies that suggest that religion and spirituality can positively impact mental health and psychological well-being. The result is that psychotherapy and counseling are beginning to reverse their skepticism and resistance to the involvement of religious and spiritual issues in the psychotherapy and psychiatric treatment context.

Treatment Context

Steere (1997) contends that increasing numbers of the 'spiritually homeless' have so strained our current two tiered health care system—private and public sector—that a 'third tier' is evolving. He envisions the third tier will be comprised of clinicians "who choose to continue to develop and provide this dimension of spiritual presence in their work. They will do so realizing an economically driven system cannot and should not be expected to sustain it. They will do so in response to the demands for it among the spiritually homeless . . . and . . . out of their own need for a sense of spiritual presence that will not diminish or disappear" (p. 280).

Because managed care focuses more on cure than healing, it necessarily bypasses much of the spiritual dimension of psychotherapy. This is not to say that managed care organizations are impervious to the spiritual dimension, but they may be more disposed to a referral to pastoral counseling than incur the expense of a psychiatrist treating the DSM-IV (American Psychiatric Association, 1994) V-code 'Religious or Spiritual Problem' (V62.89). It remains to be seen to what extent, if any, third-party payors will sanction and support psychiatric involvement with the spiritual dimension. It probably will depend on the degree and level of incorporation.

☐ Use of Spiritual Interventions by Mental Health Professionals

A national survey indicates that a majority of American adults (63%) believe that doctors should pray with patients if the patient requests it. And, 34% believe that prayer should be a standard part of medical practice (CBS News poll reported in Shafranske, 2000). Another national survey found that 58% of psychiatrists reported that they would pray *for* a patient if requested by the patient, but only 15% would pray *with* the patient. In that same survey, psychiatrists were asked if they would use spiritual interventions if it were scientifically proven that these interventions improved patient progress. Thirty-seven percent of the psychiatrists reported they would use the intervention and 57% would recommend the patient consult with a minister or rabbi. Furthermore, 62% would recommend the use of a spiritual intervention such as meditation (Shafranske, 2000). What about other mental health professionals? Do clients expect clinicians to utilize spiritual interventions? What are beliefs and practices of mental health professionals with regard to the use of spiritual interventions? These are reasonable questions for practicing clinicians and for the graduate and continuing education programs that train them. Unfortunately, at the present time there is relatively little research that addresses such questions. What follows are the findings of some recently published surveys involving social workers, psychiatrists, and counseling, clinical, and rehabilitation psychologists.

In a study of Virginia clinical social workers in which they were asked to rate the use of twenty-five religious and spiritual interventions in their practice, these social workers rated exploring a client's spiritual background, exploring a client's religious background, clarifying spiritual values, and recommending participation in spiritual programs (i.e., meditation groups or 12-step groups) as the highest. The lowest-rated interventions were praying with clients in session, reading scripture with clients, touching clients for 'healing' purposes, and performing exorcisms (Bullis, 1996, pp. 19–20) .

In a recent national survey of psychiatrists (Shafranske, 2000), over

80% rated 'spirituality' to be important or very important in their lives as compared to 57% who rated 'religion' to be important or very important in their lives. When asked the frequency with which religious or spiritual issues were involved in their psychiatric practice, 49% reported that these issues came up often or a great deal of the time. 'Loss of purpose or meaning in life' was reported as the most common focus of treatment in such cases. When asked to rate their use and approval of thirteen different religious and spiritual interventions, these psychiatrists rated knowing patients' religious background; exploring their religious beliefs; making a referral to a chaplain, minister or rabbi; and using religious language or concepts highest, while they rated praying with a patient and recommending leaving a religion lowest.

In a national survey of clinical and counseling psychologists (reported in Shafranske, 1996), 73% rated 'spirituality' to be important or very important in their lives as compared to 48% who rated 'religion' to be important or very important in their lives. When asked to rate their use and approval of various religious and spiritual interventions, these psychologists rated knowing patients' religious background, and using religious language or concepts the highest, while they rated praying with a patient and recommending leaving a religion lowest. However, a national survey of rehabilitation psychologists reported much different findings (Shafranske, 2000). Some 80% rated 'spirituality' to be important or very important in their lives as compared to 55% who rated 'religion' to be important or very important in their lives. When asked to rate their use and approval of thirteen different religious and spiritual interventions, the rehabilitation psychologists reported findings similar to the psychiatrists surveyed by Shafranske (2000). Whether differences in personal characteristics, training, work setting, or other factors accounted for these differences between clinical and rehabilitation psychologists is not known.

These survey results suggest that mental health professionals distinguish between religion and spirituality. The studies also suggest that social workers, psychologists, and psychiatrists are willing to perform or recommend certain spiritual interventions, such as spiritual assessment. However, they are less likely to use other spiritual interventions, such as praying with patients.

☐ Spiritually-Attuned Psychotherapy and Counseling

What is spiritually-attuned psychotherapy and counseling? While it shares commonalities with traditional and contemporary psychotherapy approaches, as well as spiritual direction and pastoral counseling, it is different. It differs in a number of respects from these others orientations in terms type of clientele served, goals and purposes, the nature of the relationship with the professional, and the type of interventions utilized. A brief description of psychotherapy, spiritual direction and pastoral counseling and psychotherapy is given, followed by a general description of the parameters of spiritually-attuned psychotherapy and counseling.

Psychotherapy

Very briefly, nonspiritually-attuned forms of psychotherapy, whether traditional or contemporary, share a number of commonalities. The typical clientele include disordered clients or patients presenting with symptomatic distress and usually some degree of impairment in one or more areas of life functioning. The typical goals of treatment are the reduction of symptomatic distress and the restoration of baseline functioning (Sperry, 1999). Depending on the type of psychotherapy, personality change may or may not be a treatment goal. Increased psychological well-being, self-fulfillment, or individuation may be additional goals of some psychotherapeutic approaches. Establishing a working therapeutic relationship, sometimes called a therapeutic alliance, is central to effecting change and positive treatment outcomes. The relationship can vary from situations in which the psychotherapist functions in an expert role as in classical psychoanalytically-oriented psychotherapy to the therapist having a collaborative relationship with the client. Various psychotherapeutic interventions are utilized depending on the needs of the client or patient and the issues being addressed; and psychotropic medication or referral for a medication evaluation may be indicated. It is estimated that there are approximately 450,000 licensed mental health clinicians practicing psychotherapy in the U.S., including social workers, marriage and family counselors, mental health counselors, psychiatrists, and clinical and counseling psychologists (Simpkinson & Simpkinson, 1998). Practice patterns vary, but clients or patients are often seen for weekly sessions.

Spiritual Direction

Spiritual direction is also known as spiritual guidance, spiritual friendship, and spiritual companionship. It is practiced, in various forms, in nearly all spiritual traditions. In the Christian traditions its roots go back to the third century, and while the practice has evolved since that time in the Catholic tradition, it has vigorously developed in the various Protestant traditions in the past 30 years.

Spiritual direction can be described as the art of spiritual listening carried out in the context of a one-to-one trusting relationship. It involves a trained director who guides or is a companion for another person, listening to that person's life story with an ear for the movement of the divine. In the spiritual direction session there is typically a candle, a bible, or some other non-verbal symbol representing the Holy. Spiritual direction always occurs in the context of prayer. A priority in spiritual direction is placed on discernment. The relationship between director and directee is one of mutual engagement based on the recognition that both are walking the same spiritual journey. The role of faith in the spiritual dimension and one's relationship to a faith community are central to Christian spiritual direction (Gratton, 1992). In addition, spiritual direction involves spiritual conversion, in that it is attentive to the "dynamics of change through conversion, the radical transformation. . . . a relational, personal surrender to a personal, living God" (Galindo, 1997, p. 400).

Spiritual direction focuses on the maintenance and development of spiritual health and well-being. Spiritual direction assumes that the person is already whole, but has not yet fully embraced this truth for himself or herself. Thus, spiritual direction is not for everyone, since it presumes a moderate degree of psychological health and well-being.

A focus on developing and monitoring the directee's prayer life, including meditation or contemplation, is the central method of spiritual direction. Instruction in prayer and the prescription of rituals and other spiritual practices are other interventions. When indicated, spiritual directors may refer directees with certain psychological effects or issues for concurrent psychotherapy or will suspend spiritual direction until the course of therapy is completed. Whether one professional can effectively and appropriately provide both spiritual direction and either psychotherapy or pastoral counseling is a matter of considerable debate (cf. May, 1992).

How are spiritual directors trained and how is spiritual direction usually practiced? There are no set requirements for practicing spiritual direction. Some contend that it is a vocation rather than a profession—a special calling for which formal coursework and supervision are not essential. Others contend that specialized training in selected areas of theology and psychology are helpful or essential. Currently, there are a number of formal graduate training institutes and programs in spiritual direction but no universally recognized certification or licensure for spiritual directors. However, a professional organization called Spiritual Directors International claims a worldwide membership of 3,500 members and has approved a code of professional ethics for its members. Spiritual direction is customarily provided in a one-to-one format and usually on a monthly basis, although spiritual direction can also occur in small group settings. Some spiritual directors and guides charge a fee or request a free-will offering, while others do not.

Although there is some overlap, spiritual direction differs from pastoral counseling (Barry & Connelly, 1982). The interested reader will find a more detailed description of spiritual direction and it similarities and differences with pastoral counseling in *Spirituality and Personal Maturity* by Conn (1989).

Pastoral Counseling and Pastoral Psychotherapy

Currently, two forms of pastoral counseling are practiced: a brief, time-limited form that is problem-solving or solution focused, and a long-term form that is often psychoanalytically-oriented that focuses on personality change (Stone, 1999). Clergy and other ministry personnel who have some training in pastoral care and counseling provide a majority of short-term pastoral counseling. However, ministry personnel and others with formal supervised training in counseling and psychotherapy who are certified and/or licensed can practice what is called pastoral psychotherapy. Pastoral psychotherapy is variously defined (Wise, 1980) but tends to involve longer-term therapy, and in some instances is difficult to distinguish from psychotherapy.

Clientele for pastoral counseling are typically troubled individuals presenting with life transitions, emotional or relational crises, or seek counseling because of guilt, abuse, addictions, or low self-esteem. Pastoral counseling is well suited for such crises and concerns, and is a unique form of counseling which uses religious and spiritual resources as well as psychological understanding for healing and growth. Its primary goals are problem resolution and restoration of psychological health, however, personality change may also be a goal in pastoral psychotherapy.

As in other forms of psychotherapy, the relationship between pastoral counselor and client is important, and maintaining some measure of clinical distance is useful in diagnosis and therapy. Nevertheless, many recently trained pastoral counselors advocate a mutually collaborative relationship with the client.

Treatment interventions usually include active listening and other problem solving or solution-focused counseling methods. It may also include advice on religious or spiritual matters, such as forgiveness. Unlike spiritual direction, pastoral counseling and psychotherapy typically do not bring to bear the resources of the client's faith community for healing, growth, or integration. Furthermore, pastoral counselors are likely to refer clients with certain presentations for psychotherapy. How are pastoral counselors trained and how do they practice? Pastoral counselors are often psychologically as well as theologically trained and it is not uncommon for the pastoral counselor or psychotherapist to possess graduate degrees in ministry and in pastoral counseling or another mental health discipline. An increasing number are licenced to practice, usually in a mental health speciality. Certification is available from the American Association of Pastoral Counselors, a professional organization representing 3,000 pastoral counselors. This form of counseling usually involves the client but may include the client's spouse or even the family. Sessions are usually scheduled weekly, more likely in a counseling clinic than in a church or synagogue community.

Finally, it should be noted that because of increasing interest in spirituality and spiritual direction, more pastoral counselors are exploring ways of incorporating spiritual direction methods in order to more intentionally address the spiritual needs and issues of their clients. Some writers are wary of this endeavor, citing differences in epistemological perspectives and praxis stances between the two fields (Galindo, 1997).

☐ Comparison of the Four Orientations

Before describing some specific spiritually-attuned approaches, it might be useful to provide some side-by-side comparisons of these differing orientations. Table 1.1 summarizes the major similarities and differences of spiritually-attuned psychotherapy and counseling with psychotherapy, spiritual direction, and pastoral counseling and psychotherapy.

Figure 1.1 visually depicts the relationship of these various orientations in terms of both the spiritual and psychological dimensions. Spiritual direction (SD) in the figure is represented largely in the spiritual dimension, reflective of its primary roots in that dimension. It is also represented with some overlap in the psychological dimension since it utilizes psychological theories of development and psychotherapeutic methods. Pastoral counseling (PC) is represented as partly in the spiritual dimension, in which it also has its roots, but largely in the psychological dimension because of its heavy reliance on psychological constructs as well as intervention strategies and methods. Not surprisingly, psychotherapy (PY) , in its various traditional and contemporary forms, is represented in the psychological dimension. Finally, spiritually-attuned psychotherapy and counseling (SP) is represented centrally at the intersection of both the spiritual and psychological dimensions.

☐ Spiritually-Attuned Psychotherapy and Counseling Approaches

Although there is increasing interest in developing fully articulated approaches for incorporating the spiritual dimension in therapy, no such

TABLE 1.1. A comparison of pastoral counseling, spiritual direction, psychotherapy, and ppiritually-attuned psychotherapy and counseling

	Pastoral counseling and psychotherapy	Spiritual direction or companionship	Nonspiritually-attuned psychotherapy	Spiritually-attuned psychotherapy and counseling
Clientele	Troubled individuals often concerned with religious issues and/or desire that their values be respected	Usually relatively healthy spiritual seekers	Disordered clients or patients with symptoms and/or impairment	Varies from relatively healthy spiritual seekers to troubled or disordered individuals with spiritual or religious concerns
Goal(s)	Usually problem resolution; may also include personality change if pastoral psychotherapy is the modality	Spiritual growth, with focus on prayer relationship with God; may also focus on crisis issues that impact spiritual life	Reduce symptoms and/or impairment; personality change; self-fulfillment	Varies: may include reduction of symptom and/or impairment, help with spiritual emergencies, and spiritual growth
Relationship with therapist or director	Varies: from counselor as expert to mutual collaboration	Mutual collaboration with the recognition that the Holy Spirit is the actual director	Varies from therapist as expert to mutual collaboration with client	Usually mutual collaboration; respect for religious/spiritual values and concerns
Interventions and methods	Listening; advice; counseling interventions; may include religious or spiritual advice or practices; referral for psychotherapy	Listening, instruction in prayer and other spiritual practices; possibly referral for psychotherapy	Various psychotherapeutic interventions	Various counseling and/or psychotherapeutic interventions plus spiritual practices and interventions, including referral to clergy or chaplain

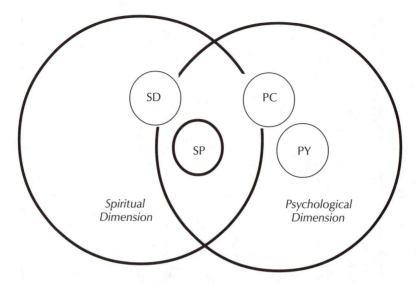

FIGURE 1.1. The relation of Spiritually-Attuned Psychotherapy and counseling (SP) to Spiritual Direction (SD), Pastoral Counseling (PC), and Psychotherapy (PY).

systems have yet been published. For illustrative purposes, this section briefly describes three somewhat different approaches for incorporating the spiritual dimension, and provides references to other efforts.

Spiritual Counseling

Various descriptions of religious and spiritual counseling can be found in the literature. Sperry (1998) describes Spiritual Counseling as an approach similar to but distinct from pastoral psychotherapy and spiritual direction. It addresses a wide range of concerns of clients including spiritual seekers and troubled individuals. It refers disordered clients and patients for appropriate treatment. It is based on a developmental rather than a pathological model of health and well-being, and it views growth in a holistic fashion including the psychological, moral, and somatic dimensions as well as the spiritual dimension.

Because of its holistic focus, special attention is directed to a comprehensive assessment of the client's spiritual development and God representation, overall health status, psychological strengths and defenses, as well as the individual's involvement in a faith community and the type and level of support it provides. The specific goal of spiritual counseling is in promoting the process of transformation or ongoing conversion in all its spiritual, psychological, moral and somatic dimensions. Various psychotherapeutic and spiritual modalities, including spiritual disciplines such as prayer, are utilized to achieve this goal.

Three phases of Spiritual Counseling can be described.

Phase One: Establishing a Therapeutic Alliance

In the first phase, the clinician focuses on establishing a therapeutic alliance and engaging the client in the treatment process. This alliance is most likely to develop in an atmosphere of caring, trust, faith, and hope. Of course, just because a client attends sessions does not mean that growth and change will occur. The client's motivation and readiness for change must be assessed and dealt with if these are insufficient. Finally, the client's expectations for the process and outcomes for psychotherapy need to be articulated and clarified. It is usually quite early in the course of treatment that the client's need for and/or desire to focus on psychospiritual issues becomes evident.

Phase Two: Conducting a Comprehensive Assessment

The second phase involves conducting a comprehensive assessment. Since religious or spiritual conversion is a holistic process, it is essential to assess the individual from a holistic perspective. This includes pertinent information on biological and somatic factors, psychological factors including affective and intellectual dimensions, social factors including family, cultural, and sociopolitical dimensions, and spiritual factors including moral and religious dimensions. Usually within the first session or two it is possible for a clinician to gather sufficient information to formulate a strategy for enhancing the process of psychospiritual growth. Data about the biological or somatic domain involves the present and past health status, treated and untreated medical conditions, and response to such treatment. In the psychological realm, it is useful to elicit the individual's self-description and self-image, and information about the presence of persistent negative affects such as anger, fear, guilt, sadness, and defensiveness, as well as psychic conflicts and traumas. In the sociocultural domain it is useful to elicit information about their family of origin and nuclear family. Constructing a genogram or family tree can prove useful in tracing generational patterns of physical, psychological, and spiritual health and pathology. A brief review of functioning in school and in the workplace is useful, as is an inquiry into social friendships and intimacies; eliciting the presence or absence of childhood 'best friends' helps to estimate the client's past and current level of social and relational functioning. Clarifying the client's attitudes and beliefs about religion and the spiritual dimension of life is also helpful. In the spiritual domain it is useful to elicit data on the individual's religious and spiritual formation from early childhood to the present, including information on denominational affiliation(s); current spiritual disciplines and practices; image(s) of God; spiritual mentors along the client's journey; and an estimation of his or her level of faith development and conscience development.

If the client has had previous traditional psychotherapy, combined psychotherapy and medication management, pastoral counseling, or spiritual direction, it is essential to review the outcomes of these efforts. The purpose of this assessment is twofold: first, to assess the client's level of conversion in each of the six domains—that is, the degree of growth or fixation—and second, to plan a strategy for healing and enhancing psychospiritual growth.

Phase Three: Planning and Implementing a Therapuetic Strategy

The third phase of spiritual counseling involves planning and implementing a strategy of healing, growth, and development. Healing is usually accomplished in terms of healing prayer and/or psychotherapeutic methods and techniques. Growth is usually accomplished with the prescription of spiritual disciplines and practices or through various psychotherapeutic and spiritual interventions (Sperry, 1999).

Spiritual Psychotherapy

Karasu (1999) describes a form of spiritual psychotherapy characterized by transformation, self-transcendence, and expanded consciousness in which treatment is targeted primarily to the spiritual dimension. It is based on a model of normative health rather than pathology and eliminates and transcends formal diagnoses. The goal of this form of spiritual psychotherapy is salvation and healing rather than cure, and its aim is harmony among body, mind, and soul. Karasu carefully distinguishes his version of spiritual psychotherapy from religious counseling, existential therapies, and analytic psychotherapies. Those practicing spiritual psychotherapy must have a life philosophy consistent with transformation and spiritual enlightenment and engage in spiritual practices. The therapist's role is not that of teacher, transference object, cognitive modifier or empathic self object. Rather, it is a redemptive one "not geared to common sin and guilt, but to a more benevolent restitution and liberation" (Karasu, 1999, p. 158). In short, the therapist assists the client in seeking "the self beyond itself. . . . self transcendence" (Karasu, 1999, pp. 160–161).

Christotherapy and Other Approaches

Tyrell (1982) describes an approach to healing and facilitating psychological and spiritual maturity he calls Christotherapy. It blends counseling and spiritual direction. This approach can be utilized as a therapeutic approach or as a self-therapy. It is described as applicable for a wide range of emotional problems and addictive behaviors. A unique aspect of this approach is that it emphasizes spiritual, moral, and psychological conversion or transformation.

Recently, a number of articles and books have been published about the need for spiritually-attuned psychotherapy. Some of these publications have suggested strategies for incorporating spiritual dimension into psychotherapy. The interested reader is referred to books by Richards and Bergin (1997), Miller (1999), Steere (1997), and Cornett (1998).

Spiritual Issues, Crises and Emergencies

As individuals are encouraged to discuss spiritual matters, a clinician's skill in differentiating healthy from pathological religious experiences becomes important. Three common diagnostic considerations are: the differential diagnosis of psychosis, depression, and other psychiatric disorders, from 'mystical voices and visions,' 'dark night of the soul,' and other 'spiritual emergencies.' Spiritual emergencies is a term being used to describe a range of intense energy experienced as various emotional and somatic symptoms. Grof and Grof (1989) and Gersten (1998) differentiate 'legitimate' spiritual emergencies from the manifestations of mania, dissociative disorders, and borderline personality disorder. As mentioned earlier, the DSM-IV (American Psychiatric Association, 1994) focuses more on 'spiritual crises' as brief reactive responses to specific religious and spiritual experiences and provides the V-Code: 'Religious or Spiritual Problem' (V62.89). Chapter 4, Spiritual Issues, Crises, Emergencies and Personality Dynamics, details these matters.

☐ Concluding Note

Today, more and more individuals are seeking greater meaning and fulfillment in their lives. They believe spirituality is vital for growth and essential for dealing with life's problems. Many have begun to pursue a spiritual journey and have started practicing spiritual disciplines such as prayer and meditation. But while these individuals ardently desire to lead a more spiritually-meaningful life, they often find themselves trapped in old feelings, attitudes, and habits that seem to undo their progress and discourage them from this spiritual journey. Thus, the ideal of a more spiritual existence seems less and less attainable. Even those who have made progress on this journey often encounter roadblocks to growth that may last for months or even years.

Spirituality has already begun to impact the practice of counseling and psychotherapy. Today, clinicians are experimenting with different ways of incorporating the spiritual dimension in their professional work, and also in their personal lives. While it is not yet clear how managed care and third-party payers will respond to these developments, the genie is already 'out of the bottle' and the spiritual dimension in clinical practice may not easily be contained.

☐ References

American Psychiatric Association (1994). *Diagnostic and statistical manual of mental disorders* (4th ed.). Washington DC: Author.

Anderson, D. (1985). Spirituality and systems therapy. *Journal of Pastoral Psychotherapy, 1,* 19–32.

Barry, W., & Connolly, W. (1982). *The practice of spiritual direction.* New York: Seabury.

Benner, D. (1989). Toward a psychology of spirituality: Implications for personality and psychotherapy. *Journal of Psychology and Theology, 8,* 19–30.

Berenson, D. (1990). A systemic view of spirituality: God and Twelve Step programs as resources in family therapy. *Journal of Strategic and Systemic Therapies, 9,* 59–70.

Bullis, R. (1996). *Spirituality in social work practice.* Philadelphia: Taylor & Francis.

Conn, J. (1989). *Spirituality and maturity.* New York: Paulist Press.

Cornett, C. (1998). *Soul of psychotherapy: Recapturing the spiritual dimension in therapeutic encounters.* New York: Simon & Shuster.

Ellenberger, H. (1970). *The discovery of the unconscious: The history and evolution of dynamic psychiatry.* New York: Basic Books.

Ellswood, R. (1990). Religion. In R. Hunter (Ed.) *Dictionary of pastoral care and counseling.* Nashville: Abingdon Press.

Galindo, I. (1997). Spiritual direction and pastoral counseling. *Journal of Pastoral Care, 51*(4), 395–402.

Gersten, D. (1998). *Are you getting enlightened or losing your mind? How to master everyday and extraordinary spiritual experiences.* New York: Random House/Three Rivers Press.

Gratton, C. (1992). *The art of spiritual guidance: A contemporary approach to growing in the spirit.* New York: Crossroad.

Grof, C., & Grof, S. (Eds). (1989). *Spiritual emergency.* Los Angeles: Tarcher.

Hungelmann, J. (1985). Spiritual well-being in older adults: Harmonious interconnectedness. *Journal of Religion and Health, 24,* 147–153.

Karasu, T. (1999). Spiritual psychotherapy. *American Journal of Psychotherapy, 53*(2), 143–162.

Larsen, D., & Milano, M. (1997). Making the case for spiritual intervention in clinical practice. *Mind/Body Medicine: A Journal of Clinical Behavioral Medicine, 2*(1), 20–30.

Lesser, E. (1999). *The new American spirituality: A seeker's guide.* New York: Random House.

Lesser, E. (2000, Spring). Insider's guide to 21st-century spirituality. *Spirituality and Health: The Soul/Body Connection,* 46–51.

Lipp, M. (1986). *Respectful treatment: The human side of medical care* (2nd ed.). New York: Elsevier.

London, P. (1985). *The modes and morals of psychotherapy* (2nd ed.). New York: Hemisphere.

May, G. (1992). *Care of mind, care of soul: A psychiatrist explores spiritual direction.* San Francisco: HarperCollins.

Miller, W. (Ed.). (1999). *Integrating spirituality into treatment: Resources for practitioners.* Washington, DC: American Psychological Association.

Richards, P., & Bergin, A. (1997). *A spiritual strategy for counseling and psychotherapy.* Washington, DC: American Psychological Association.

Schneiders, S. (1986). Theology and spirituality: Strangers, rivals, or partners? *Horizons, 13,* 253–274.

Shafranske, E. (1996). Religious beliefs, affiliations, and practices of clinical psychologists. In E. Shafranske (Ed.), *Religion and the clinical practice of psychology* (pp. 149–162). Washington, DC: American Psychological Association.

Shafranske, E. P. (2000). Religious involvement and professional practices of psychiatrists and other mental health professionals. *Psychiatric Annals, 30*(8), 525–532.

Simpkinson, A., & Simpkinson, C. (1998). *Soul work: A field guide for spiritual seekers.* San Francisco: HarperCollins.

Sperry, L. (1998). Spiritual counseling and the process of conversion. *Journal of Christian Healing, 20*(3 & 4), 37–54.

Sperry, L. (1999). *Cognitive behavior therapy of DSM-IV personality disorders.* Philadelphia: Brunner/Mazel.

Steere, D. (1997). *Spiritual presence in psychotherapy: A guide for caregivers.* New York: Brunner/Mazel.

Stone, H. (1999). Pastoral counseling and the changing times. *Journal of Pastoral Care, 53,* 47–56.

Tyrell, B. (1982). *Christotherapy II.* Ramsey, NJ: Paolist Press.

Wise, C. (1980). *Pastoral psychotherapy.* New York: Jason Aronson.

II

PERSPECTIVES ON THE SPIRITUAL DIMENSION

Part II provides a detailed description and discussion of several developmental models and perspectives regarding the spiritual dimension and the process of spiritual growth and development. Furthermore, it describes a number of common spiritual issues, crises and emergencies that are associated with the spiritual dimension.

There are five basic dimensions of human experience: psychological, social, moral, somatic, and spiritual. A basic premise of this book is that the spiritual dimension is central to and integrally related to the other four dimensions. The professional literature describes several perspectives for conceptualizing the spiritual dimensions and the process of spiritual growth and development. Chapter 2, Dimensional Perspectives on Spiritual Development, described six such perspectives: Object-Relations, Transpersonal, Self-Transformation, Self-Transcendence, Character, Conversion, and the Ethical perspective as they relate to the process of spiritual development.

Chapter 3, Developmental Models of the Spiritual Dimension, describes seven developmental stage models that directly or indirectly address the spiritual dimension. These include Psychosocial Development, Moral Development, Faith Development, Self Development, Spiritual Development, Spiritual Growth, and the Full Spectrum models. Some of these models have generated considerable research support while others are theoretical models which spiritually-attuned therapists have found clinically useful.

As individuals are encouraged to discuss spiritual matters, a clinician's skill in differentiating healthy from pathological religious experiences becomes important. Three common diagnostic considerations are: the differential diagnosis of psychosis, depression, and other psychiatric disorders, from 'mystical voices and visions,' the 'dark night of the soul,' and other 'spiritual emergencies.' Spiritual emergencies is a term being used to describe a range of intense energy experienced as various emotional and somatic symptoms. It is critically important that clinicians can differentiate 'legitimate' spiritual emergencies from the manifestations of mania, dissociative disorders, and borderline personality disorder. DSM-IV focuses more on 'spiritual crises' as brief reactive responses to specific religious and spiritual experiences and provides the V-Code: 'Religious or Spiritual Problem' (V62.89).

Chapter 4, Spiritual Dynamics, Crises and Emergencies in Psychotherapy, further explores spiritual emergencies, religious/ spiritual disorders and problems, and related spiritual issues. It also describes a number of personality types and their characteristic God representations, prayer styles, and other spiritual behaviors.

Dimensional Perspectives on Spiritual Development

This chapter introduces five basic dimensions of human experience and describes the spiritual dimension as central to human experience. Next, it briefly reviews the results of research on the positive impact of the spiritual dimension on health and well-being. The moral dimension is then described as the 'neglected' dimension in not only the psychological and behavioral sciences but also in spiritual theology. Then, six perspectives or frames of reference for understanding the spiritual dimension and the process of spiritual development are discussed.

☐ The Dimensions of Human Experience

Historically, human experience has been described in terms of several dimensions. These have included the spiritual or religious, the moral, the social, the biological or somatic, and the psychological dimensions. While human experience has always been considered holistically from an Eastern perspective, it is only recently that it has begun to be viewed in this fashion from a Western perspective. Because of its allegiance to the scientific method and the law parsimony, or Ockham's Razor (i.e., the simplest explanation is preferable to a more elaborate one), Westerners have been content to explain all of human experience in terms of a single dimension. For example, in the early twentieth century, scientists were content to conceptualize the theory and practice of medicine in terms of a single dimension of human experience—the biological or somatic dimension.

Similar efforts have been made to conceptualize individual human behavior or social and organizational processes in terms of either the psychological or the social dimension. Efforts to combine the dimensions of
the psychological and the somatic were called 'psychosomatic' medicine,
while efforts to combine the psychological and social dimensions were
called the 'psychosocial.'

Contemporary efforts in psychiatry and professional psychology to more
adequately understand and change human behavior, and even organizational behavior, have led to the adoption of the biopsychosocial model.
First proposed by George Engel in 1977, this model describes a way of
conceptualizing human behavior in terms of three dimensions of human
experience rather than previous models based on only one or two dimensions. Due to increasing scientific knowledge and clinical necessity over
the past twenty years, the fields of psychiatry, family medicine and internal medicine have come to adopt the biopsychosocial model as the theoretical and clinical basis for professional practice. Very recently, and based
on scientific as well as political and economic considerations, the American Psychological Association officially adopted the biopsychosocial model
as the basis for clinical practice.

The Centrality of the Spiritual Dimension

Five dimensions of human experience are commonly posited: psychological, social, moral, spiritual or religious, and somatic or biological
(Wilber, 1999). Figure 2.1 diagrams the interrelationship among the five
basic dimensions of human experience. The spiritual dimension is placed
at the core of the diagram to illustrate the belief that the spiritual dimen-

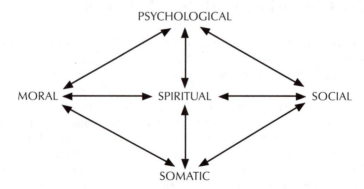

FIGURE 2.2. The centrality of the spiritual dimension among the dimensions of human
experience.

sion is foundational to all the other dimensions of human experience. This core may or may not involve any formal affiliation with a religious tradition, but it reflects the beliefs, effects, and behaviors associated with the basic spiritual hunger or desire for self-transcendence that all individuals experience.

☐ Research on the Spiritual Dimension and Health and Well-Being

Currently, there is considerable interest in examining the impact of the spiritual dimension on the psychological, social and somatic dimensions. Considerable research is underway or has already been reported on the so called 'health effects' of religious and spiritual behaviors and physical health and psychological and relational well-being. Based on over 200 published studies, it appears that higher levels of spirituality are related to lower risk for disease, fewer medical and psychiatric problems and higher levels of psychosocial functioning. (Koenig, 1998; Levin, 1994; Levin & Chatters, 1998; Worthington, Kurusu, McCullough, & Sandage, 1996). Interestingly, this finding seems to hold regardless of gender, ethnicity, the severity or type of the disease, or how the concept of spirituality is measured or defined or the type of research design used (Levin, 1994).

Looking more specifically at the somatic, psychological, and social dimensions, the following findings or results have been reported.

The Somatic Dimension

Religious and spiritual commitment is related to a lower prevalence of illnesses, including heart disease, hypertension, stroke, and most cancers. Such individuals tend to live longer, have stronger immune systems, and respond better to treatment after being diagnosed with a disease. If they are undergoing surgery they tend to have lower rates of postoperative mortality and faster recovery time from hip fractures and open-heart surgeries. Finally, they have a reduced likelihood of perceived disability.

The Psychological Dimension

Individuals with higher levels of spiritual and religious commitment tend to report higher levels of well-being and life satisfaction. They experience less anxiety, including less fear of death, and less worry and neurotic guilt. They have less depression and substance abuse and dependence, and report fewer suicidal impulses and less likelihood of committing suicide. Finally, they tend to show more empathy and altruism.

The Social Dimension

Commitment and social involvement, which includes attendance at religious or spiritual services and activities, tends to have a prophylactic effect on health and well-being. Individuals who engage in spiritual practices such as prayer, meditation, reading sacred writings, and seeking spiritual counsel and support from religious leaders and community during stressful times tend to adjust better to crises and problems. Religious commitment tends to be negatively correlated with depression. Attendance at religious services is related to greater marital satisfaction and adjustment, less divorce, less use or abuse of alcohol or drugs, and lower rates of premarital sex, teenage pregnancy, and delinquency. There is also less clinical depression among the spiritually- or religiously-engaged elderly.

Parenthetically, this same line of research also studied the impact of the spiritual dimension on the moral dimension. Religious commitment is positively associated with moral behavior, in terms of individuals adhering to higher moral standards and curbing personal desire, to promote the welfare of others. With regard to the other dimensions, these findings seem less surprising and newsworthy. Why is this? An examination of the tenuous relationship among the moral dimension with both the psychological and the spiritual dimensions suggests an explanation.

☐ The 'Neglected' Moral Dimension in Psychotherapy

There is almost no mention of morality or the moral dimension in recent psychological literature. In a sense, it seems to be a neglected topic. Why has the moral dimension in psychology and psychotherapy been the 'neglected' dimension? A brief review of the history of psychology and psychotherapy provides an answer. As psychology evolved as a discipline and field of inquiry, it attempted to distinguished itself from its roots in moral philosophy. While moral philosophy emphasized the common good, values and virtue, rational judgement, and will or the volitional aspects of character, psychology increasingly focused on individuality, behavior, emotion and nonrationality, value-neutrality, and the unconscious aspects of personality.

The most effective strategy psychology utilized for both distinguishing and distancing itself from its roots in the field of philosophy was by differentiating the study of personality from the study of character. Gordon Allport was one of many academic psychologists to banish character from American psychology. His famous dictim: "Character is personality evaluated, and personality is character *devalued*" (italics added, Allport, 1937, pp. 252) suggests psychology's disdain for the concept of character. As a result of this focus, psychology succeeded in establishing a scientific and, presumably, a value-free foundation distinct from a philosophical foundation for understanding human behavior and actions. For all practical purposes, the concept of character, once a staple of everyday conversation, has been almost entirely replaced with the concept of personality (Taylor, 1995).

From the late 1950s through the early 1970s the profession of psychology endeavored to reformulate psychotherapy into the same scientific, value-free framework as the rest of psychology. Unfortunately, many psychotherapists have become increasingly dissatisfied with this supposedly value-free, scientific view of psychotherapy as represented by the DSM-IV, clinical practice guidelines, and treatment outcome measures. Critiques of psychotherapy's value-free stance are long standing. They include Philip Rieff's provocative analysis in *Freud: The Mind of a Moralist* (1959) and *Triumph of the Therapeutic* (Rieff, 1966), as well as Jerome Frank's *Psychotherapy and the Human Predicament* (1978).

Frank observed that all psychotherapies share a value system which accords primacy to self-fulfillment and views individuals as the center of their moral universe. He believes that this value system can easily become a source of misery in itself because of its unrealistic expectations for personal happiness and because it downplays traditional values such as "the redemptive power of suffering, acceptance of one's lot in life, adherence to tradition, self-restraint and moderation" (Frank, 1978, pp. 6–7).

More recently, Philip Cushman (1990, 1995) suggests that the goal of attaining and maintaining an "autonomous self" may be misguided. Furthermore, Cushman contends that such a preoccupation with an inner self which is self-soothing, self-loving, and self-sufficient eventually leads to an 'empty self.'

Furthermore, there is mounting concern that traditionally practiced psychotherapy tends to foster individual self-fulfillment over community well-being. For example, James Hillman and Michael Ventura in *We've Had a Hundred Years of Psychotherapy and the World's Getting Worse* (1992) contend that psychotherapy has been so successful that it has effectively refocused our view of the problems of daily life into personal issues and reframed our view of the communal world in terms of psychopathology. They note that therapy tends to draw sensitive, intelligent people away from the political arena into introspection and support groups. The result is that any motivation these individuals might have had to improve their local community (i.e., taking on causes such as hunger, illiteracy, homelessness, etc.) is effectively displaced. Furthermore, they note that most therapeutic approaches have little to say about character, conscience, or commitment. In others words, psychotherapy has effectively changed the moral calculus from a social ethic to an individual ethic (Richardson, Fowers, & Guignon, 1999).

Some researchers and clinicians are proposing that values and ethics can and must be integrated into a scientific understanding of psychology and psychotherapy. Rather than being viewed as "getting in the way" of a science and practice of psychotherapy, values and ethics should be recognized as integral to any science that claims to systematically study the human person. This view offers a compelling way to reconceptualize psychotherapy that retains many of its foundations, while challenging it to greater social relevance and responsibility. It acknowledges that psychology and psychotherapy are value-laden enterprises, and that it requires that mental health professionals consciously integrate values, morality, ethics, and politics into their professional efforts. The result will be a science that better reflects the fullness of human life, that is more effective in practice, and that, as a result, promises more fulfillment to psychotherapists.

Does the practice of psychotherapy make a significant and positive contribution to human welfare and the struggle for a good society? In *Re-envisioning Psychology: Moral Dimensions of Theory and Practice*, Richardson et al. (1999) present an invigorating look at psychology and psychotherapy and their societal purpose, and offer an alternative philosophical foundation—hermeneutics—from which psychotherapists can more incisively examine their work. They issue a call for a new perspective on the societal value of psychology and psychotherapy and aims to reinvigorate individual psychotherapists' belief in the larger purposes of their own work.

☐ The Relationship of the Moral and Spiritual Dimensions

It seems self-evident that the moral dimension and the spiritual dimension should be closely linked. Just as the link between the psychological and moral dimensions has been strained in psychology and psychotherapy, the link between the moral and spiritual dimensions likewise has been considerably strained. Historically, in the Christian tradition, moral and spiritual theology were a single discipline until they began to separate in the late middle ages. While several factors influenced this split, the result was that morality became the province of the commoners, while spirituality became the province of a small elite. Morality became associated with goodness, moral codes, sin, and living in the real world with daily duties and responsibilities, while spirituality was associated with holiness, altered states, contemplative prayer, and living an other-worldly existence in a monastery or cloister. In short, the moral dimension is about goodness, while the spiritual dimension is about holiness. Everyone was expected to manifest goodness but only a few would achieve holiness. It should be noted that there was no such split between morality and spirituality in the Eastern religions.

Since the late 1960s there has been a gradual 'reconciliation' not only among Western moral and spiritual theologies, but also among spiritual seekers. Now, anyone and everyone can aspire to both goodness and holiness whether or not they are living a cloistered life. Consumerism, materialism, and unbridled individualism seem to be fueling the pursuit for spiritual development. Many would say that the spiritual journey requires that the spiritual and moral dimensions be pursued simultaneously and integrated with the other three dimensions of human experience (Gelpi, 1998; Keating, 1998; Wilbur, 1998). It appears that many so-called 'New Age' spiritualities place a premium on the pursuit of holiness while downplaying the pursuit of goodness. Whether the spiritual seeker pursues the journey of both goodness and holiness, or only the holiness journey, is and should be a basic consideration in spiritually-oriented psychotherapy and counseling.

☐ Perspectives on Spiritual Development

This section describes several perspectives involving the spiritual dimension and the process of spiritual development. Table 2.1 lists these six perspectives.

TABLE 2.1. Six perspectives on spiritual development

1. Character Perspective

2. Ethical Perspective

3. Transpersonal Perspective

4. Self-Transcendence Perspective

5. Object-Relations Perspective

6. Conversion Perspective

☐   The Character Perspective

Character can be thought of as that dimension of personality which describes how individuals conduct themselves in interpersonal and organizational situations, and is shaped through the simultaneous development of self-identity and self-regulation. When this learning or socialization process is reasonably adequate and without significant developmental arrests, adaptive, creative, and socially responsible or virtuous behavior—called 'good character'—can be expected. Generally speaking, an individual with a good character or reputation is considered to be responsible, trustworthy, respectful, fair, caring, and a good citizen, which means they cooperate and play by the rules.

How is character different from personality? Currently, personality is described as the confluence of both character and temperament. Temperament refers to the more biologically or somatically determined aspects of personality, while character refers to the enduring component of personality based on learned, psychosocial influences (Sperry, 1999a). Because character is essentially learned, it follows that it can be changed through such processes as psychotherapy. Largely due to the influence of Freud and the subsequent psychodynamic revolution, psychotherapy focused primarily on the dimension of character to the point at which personality essentially became synonymous with character. Before 1980 personality was often conceptualized in "character language," such as the oral character or obsessive character. Descriptions of personality disorders in the DSM-I and DSM-II reflected this emphasis on character and psychodynamics. Within the psychoanalytic community, character reflected specific defense mechanisms. Accordingly, the defenses of isolation of affect, intellectualization, and rationalization were common in the obsessive character. Another way of specifying the characterological component of personality is with the term 'schema'. Whether in the psychoanalytic tradition or the cognitive therapy tradition, schema refers to the basic beliefs individuals use to organize their view of self, the world, and the future. While the centrality of schema has historically been more central to the cognitive tradition and the cognitive-behavioral tradition than to the psychoanalytic tradition, this apparently is changing. While classical psychoanalysts focused on libidinal drives, some modern analysts have focused instead on relational themes, emphasizing the self, the object and their interaction, and a number of ego psychology and object relations theorists have emphasized schema theory.   While the theoretical and clinical literature on character is quite extensive, the empirical literature is not. On the basis of extensive interview studies, Robert Cloninger and his colleagues concluded that individuals with mature personalities tend to be self-reliant, cooperative, and self-transcendent

(Cloninger, Svrakic, & Przybeck, 1993). In contrast, those with personality disorders were noted to have difficulty with self-acceptance, were intolerant and revengeful toward others, and felt self-conscious and unfulfilled. This suggested that the presence or absence of a personality disorder could be defined in terms of the character dimensions of self-directedness, cooperativeness, and self-transcendence. These three dimensions of character were subsequently incorporated into Cloninger's seven-factor model of temperament and character, and can also measured by the Temperament Character Inventory (TCI; Cloninger et al., 1993). Healthy personality reflects positive or elevated scores on these three character dimensions, while personality disorders reflect negative or low scores on them. Furthermore, individuals with low scores on one or more of the character dimensions and increased dysregulation of one or more of dimensions of typical temperament experience either considerable distress or impairment in life functioning or both. For example, the borderline personality disorder would likely rate high on temperament dimensions but low in the character dimensions of self-directedness and cooperativeness.

Self-Directedness

The basic concept of self-directedness refers to self-determination, which is an individual's ability to control, regulate, and adapt behavior in accord with his or her chosen goals and values. Individuals differ in their capacity for self-determination. According to Cloninger et al. (1993), individuals with moderate to high levels of self-determination are mature, effective, well-organized, exhibit self-esteem, are able to admit faults and accept themselves as they are, feel their lives have meaning and purpose, can delay gratification in order to achieve their goals, and take initiative in overcoming challenges. On the other hand, individuals with lower levels of self-determination have low self-esteem, blame others for their problems, feel uncertain of their identity or purpose, and are often reactive, dependent, and resourceless.

Self-determination can be thought of as having various subcomponents such as an internal locus of control, purposefulness, resourcefulness, and self-efficacy. Individuals with an internal locus of control tend to believe that their success is controlled by their own efforts, whereas individuals with an external locus of control tend to believe that their success is controlled by factors outside themselves. Research on locus of control indicates that those with an internal locus of control are more responsible and resourceful problem-solvers, whereas those with an external locus of control are more alienated and apathetic, tending to blame other people and chance circumstances for their problems.

Purposefulness and meaningful goal-direction are motivating forces in mature people. Such purposefulness varies widely between individuals. Initiative and resourceful problem-solving, two qualities which define effective executives, are important aspects of mature character. Self-efficacy is also related to resourcefulness and initiative in goal-directed behavior.

Self-esteem and the ability to accept one's limitations unapologetically without fantasies of unlimited ability and ageless youth are crucial aspects of the development of mature self-directed behavior. Individuals with poor adjustment and feelings of inferiority or inadequacy are often reactive and deny, repress, or ignore their faults, wishing to be best at everything always, whereas well adjusted individuals are able to recognize and admit unflattering truths about themselves. Such positive self-esteem and ability to accept individual limitations is strongly correlated with responsibility and resourcefulness. The absence of self-directedness is the common characteristic of all categories of personality disorder. Regardless of other personality traits or circumstances, a personality disorder is likely to be present if self-directedness is low.

In short, attaining self-directedness is a developmental process with several dimensions. These include: accepting responsibility for one's own choices versus blaming other individuals and circumstances; identifying individually valued goals and purposes versus having a lack of goal direction; developing problem-solving skills and resourcefulness versus apathy; self-acceptance versus self-striving; and congruent versus personal distrust.

Cooperativeness

The character factor of cooperativeness was formulated to account for individual differences in identification with and acceptance of other people. This factor is a measure of character that is related to agreeability versus self-centered aggression and hostility. Low cooperativeness scores on the TCI (Cloninger et al., 1993) contribute substantially to the likelihood of a concomitant personality disorder. In individuals who scored high or only moderately low in self-directedness, the probability of a diagnosis of personality disorder was increased by low cooperativeness. All categories of personality disorder are associated with low cooperativeness. Cooperative individuals tend to be socially tolerant, empathic, helpful, and compassionate, while uncooperative individuals tend to be socially intolerant, disinterested in other people, unhelpful, and revengeful. Cooperative individuals are likely to show unconditional acceptance of others, empathy with other's feelings, and willingness to help others achieve their goals without selfish domination. It is not surprising that social acceptance, helpfulness, and concern for the rights of others are correlated with positive self-esteem. Empathy, which is a feeling of unity or identification with others, facilitates improved communication and compassion. Helpful generativity and compassion are frequently noted as signs of maturity in developmental psychology. For instance, such compassion involves the willingness to forgive and be kind to others regardless of their behavior, rather than to seek revenge or to enjoy their embarrassment or suffering; it involves feelings of brotherly love, and the absence of hostility. Mature persons are more likely to seek mutually satisfying, 'win–win' solutions to problems rather than indulge personal gain. Finally, religious traditions also emphasize the notion of pure-hearted acceptance of principles that cannot be broken without the inevitability of grave consequences for individuals and society.

In summary, cooperativeness is a developmental process with several dimensions. These include: social acceptance versus intolerance; empathy versus social disinterest; helpfulness versus unhelpfulness; compassion versus revengefulness; and, pure-hearted principles versus self-advantage. (Cloninger, et al., 1993).

Self-Transcendence

Self-transcendence and character traits associated with spirituality are typically neglected in systematic research and omitted from personality inventories. Nevertheless, observations about self-transcendence and self-actualization abound. Specifically, the subjective experiences and changes in behavior of people who attain the state of self-transcendence as a result of insight and meditation techniques have been well documented in the transpersonal psychology literature. The stable self-forgetfulness of self-transcendent individuals has been described as the same as experienced transiently when individuals are totally absorbed, intensely concentrated, and fascinated by one thing, such that they may forget where they are and lose all sense of the passage of time. Such absorption often leads to 'transpersonal' identification with things outside of the individual self. The person may identify or feel a sense of spiritual union with anything or everything. The stable self-forgetfulness of self-transcendent people has been described as the same as experienced transiently by people when they are totally absorbed, intensely concentrated, and fascinated by one thing. In such one-pointed concentration, people may forget where they are and lose all sense of the passage of time.

Self-transcendence is considerably lower in psychiatric inpatients than in adults in the general community. Except for individuals with schizoid and schizotypal personality disorder, who tended to exhibit low scores for self-transcendence, self-transcendence was not a distinguishing factor between patients with and without other types of personality disorders. Self-transcendence can be particularly useful in distinguishing schizoid from schizotypal patients because the latter tend to endorse questions about extrasensory perception and other aspects of self-transcendence. In contrast, self-directedness and cooperativeness were low in all types of personality disorders (Svrakic et al., 1993).

Considered as a developmental process, self-transcendence has various dimensions. These dimensions can be simplified to some basic experiences and behaviors that have been described in a broad spectrum: self-forgetful versus self-conscious experience; transpersonal identification versus self-differentiation; and, spiritual acceptance versus rational materialism. Thus, it seems that psychologically healthy spiritual seekers would manifest appreciably more self-transcendence than less mature individuals.

☐ The Ethical Perspective

Psychotherapists and counselors are enjoined by the codes of ethics of their professional organizations, and in some cases by state licensing boards, to act ethically in their professional roles. Professional codes of ethics and state statutes, however, are not intended to address all possible ethical and moral matters. Since research indicates that most clients expect helping professionals to assist them with moral issues and dilemmas (Cushman, 1995), it would not be unreasonable to anticipate that spiritual seekers and other clients with religious issues may need to or want to address ethical and moral matters in the course of therapy. Many questions arise. Is it ethical for therapists and counselors to discuss such matters? Should spiritual seekers and other clients be counseled to act ethically in their professional and personal lives? Is it or might it be unethical for psychotherapists and counselors to broach some ethical matters with spiritual seekers? Obviously, there are no easy answers to these questions. An ethical perspective is much broader than the provisions of a code of ethics.

Developing an ethical perspective involves not only learning ethical theories and principles but also incorporating such principles in one's own philosophy of life and then acting on these principles in one's daily personal and professional life. It means becoming a person of good character, namely, someone who acts virtuously. In other words, developing an ethical perspective means becoming a 'virtuous therapist.'

The ethical theory that emphasizes character and virtue is *virtue ethics* (MacIntyre, 1982). Virtue ethics defines certain traits of character which are universally understood to make one a morally good person. While rule or principle ethics focus on morally good actions, virtue ethics focus on morally good character. For virtue ethics the question is not, "Is this action moral?" but is rather, "What kind of person am I becoming?" According to virtue ethics, moral virtues are states of character concerned with controlling and directing not only one's thoughts and rational processes but also one's emotions and feelings. The repeated performance of virtuous actions leads to the acquisition of virtue. The morally virtuous person aims at morally good ends rather than being clever and goal-oriented.

What, then, is a virtuous therapist? A virtuous therapist is a professional individual of good moral character whose actions reflect both the practice of virtue and an ability to incorporate professional standards in daily practice. "A morally virtuous psychotherapist would seek to be honest with her clients not merely because this behavior is itself a way toward the goal of maximizing profit—supposing that 'morality pays' by attracting clients—but because honesty itself is to be valued" (Cohen & Cohen, 1999, pp. 19–20). These authors contend that rule or principle ethics (i.e., the framework for professional codes of ethics) provide a woefully inadequate basis for the ethical practice of counseling and psychotherapy. Instead, they propose a composite ethical theory that recognizes that moral action involves not only rules or professional standards but also emotions, human relatedness, virtue, and sensitivity to the nuances of a specific individual context.

☐ The Transpersonal Perspective

Transpersonal psychology is broad term for approaches to therapy which focus on the spiritual dimension (i.e., consciousness, mystical experiences, altered states of consciousness, and on questions relating to the value of life and the meaning of existence. Transpersonal psychology is considered by many to be the 'fourth force' in psychology, following psychoanalysis, behavior therapy, and humanistic psychology. Its precursors are to be found in Eastern religions and in the West. Both Augustine and Thomas Aquinas can be considered as early thinkers who combined a psychological awareness with a spiritual and philosophical focus. More recently, William James anticipated the claims of current transpersonal psychology that altered states of consciousness can be induced and can give access to special knowledge which cannot be gained through ordinary conscious processes.

In his articulation of Analytic Psychology, Carl Jung developed several ideas that are centrally relevant to transpersonal psychology. These include the Self, the collective unconscious, archetypes, and the process of individuation. Central to Jung's approach to psychotherapy is the value and importance of the spiritual dimension of human existence. Individuation, for example, includes the re-integration of the spiritual as well as the psychic.

Other approaches included under the umbrella of transpersonal psychology are Roberto Assagioli's Psychosynthesis, Stanislav Grof's Holotropic Model, Existential Transpersonal Psychotherapy, Transpersonal Psychoanalytic Psychotherapy, and Body-Centered Transpersonal Approaches (Cortright, 1997).

Perhaps the most known and influential theorist in transpersonal psychology in the past decades is Ken Wilber. He was the first to systematically demonstrate how the consciousness of mystical states related to the consciousness of neurosis and psychosis. Wilbur has proposed and refined a spectrum model (1977, 1995, 1999; Wilbur, Engler, & Brown, 1986) which is an integrating structure in which all competing psychological systems and spiritual traditions are seen as containing partial and complimentary truths about human consciousness. It is the foundation for his theories of development, psychopathlogy, and psychotherapeutic treatment. Reasoning that consciousness is composed of many different levels and that different psychotherapies are related to specific levels of his spectrum model, Wilbur posited that traditional Western psychotherapy systems are directed to the lower levels of this spectrum with psychoses representing the most limited level of consciousness, while the middle portions of the spectrum involve the neuroses and existential levels. Spiritual systems and transpersonally-oriented approaches represent the upper levels of the spectrum where consciousness is the fullest. Based on this formulation, Wilbur concludes (some might say erroneously) that psychology and spirituality are integrally related in a single line or spectrum of consciousness.

Today, there is an emerging consensus in transpersonal psychology that "the psychological and spiritual dimensions of human experience are different, though at times overlapping, with the spiritual as foundational" (Cortright, 1997, p. 237). In its earliest formulation, transpersonal psychology assumed that the psychological and spiritual lines of development were identical or formed one continuous line or spectrum (Wilber, 1977). It was also assumed that an individual would first pursue psychological integration and then move on to spiritual integration. Usually that meant beginning in psychotherapy and when successfully completed, taking up spiritual practices and working with a spiritual guide. Basically, it was believed that only those who were sufficiently healed and psychologically integrated were capable of true spiritual development and realization.

Such beliefs do not match current research and clinical practice. Some clients with highly advanced spiritual development may function at primitive levels psychologically and interpersonally, while psychological development far exceeds spiritual development in others. Then there are other clients where spiritual and psychological development is more balanced. Similarly, history records a number of disturbed, psychotic, and neurotic saints and spiritually advanced individuals. Furthermore, to presume that all saints, sages, and shamans throughout history have somehow spontaneously achieved a working through of childhood traumas and unconscious defenses leading to a high level of psychological integration prior to their spiritual development is extremely dubious (Cortright, 1997).

Transpersonally-oriented clinicians have observed that psychological and spiritual development are composed of multiple and complex developmental pathways that mutually interact but are different. In other words, the spiritual emerges in and through psychological work rather than after it. Furthermore, clinicians espousing a transpersonal approach to psychotherapy tend to view their work within a context of spiritual unfolding since the basic assumption of transpersonal psychology is that individuals are spiritual beings rather than simply a self or psychological ego.

Another basic tenet of transpersonal psychology is that achieving psychological integration is not essential for spiritual realization, nor does spiritual realization bring about psychological integration. Nevertheless, psychotherapy can be quite helpful for those on the spiritual journey in contending with avoidances and unconscious defenses, just as the inner deepening resulting from spiritual practices can be helpful in one's psychological work. In short, each can help the other but neither one is required for the other (Cortright, 1997). Clinicians practicing transpersonal psychotherapy note that it is possible to pursue psychological wholeness and spiritual wholeness simultaneously, and that while "one or the other may predominate at times, it is a *both/and* process rather than *either/or* or even *first one/then the other*" (Cortright, 1997, p. 234). Psychotherapy may facilitate spiritual unfolding by breaking unconscious and defensive patterns and processes, and by passing through the self to find the spirit deep within, more skillfully than might spiritual practices alone. Finally, since it aims at expanding consciousness, psychotherapy can be thought of as a spiritual activity, of sorts.

Consciousness is where spirituality and psychotherapy intersect. Both are paths toward exploring, deepening, and expanding consciousness. Transpersonally-oriented psychotherapy is primarily focused on consciousness. Such therapy is the exploration of consciousness and the contents of that consciousness. It has been said that the reason most individuals seek treatment is that they are stuck and underdeveloped, meaning they cannot function with full consciousness. Such individuals have blind spots or defenses which block awareness of essential aspects of themselves: feelings, bodily sensations, thoughts, etc. This blocked awareness results in symptoms, self-defeating patterns and dis-ease with life. Consciousness involves all the dimensions of human experience: cognitive, affective, moral, somatic, and spiritual. And, the greater or more complete the level of consciousness, the greater the likelihood of psychological and spiritual change and development (Cortright, 1997).

It is a tenet of transpersonally-oriented psychotherapy that engaging the consciousness of the client is the key to change and growth. Nevertheless, the clinician's own consciousness, presence, and inner clarity "provide the guiding light for the therapeutic journey" (Cortright, 1997, p. 238). Cortright notes that the consciousness of the clinician functions like a subtle energy field in inducing the client into a deeper experience of being.

Finally, transpersonal psychotherapies tend to be experiential. "It is only the experience of spirit that satisfies the soul's quest, and only by plunging into the depth of the inner heart and feeling can the realm of spiritual being be plumbed" (Cortright, 1997, p. 239). By viewing consciousness as multidimensional, the central focus on the client's consciousness implies an experiential process that involves the whole person.

Allowing for different dimensions of human experience in the therapeutic context (i.e., the affective, moral, intellectual, and somatic dimensions) means that an openness exists to alternate modes of experiencing beyond that of a traditional psychotherapy focused primarily or only on words. Nevertheless, words are important, and the articulation of inner experience can be of inestimable value in "skillfully traversing inner worlds of feeling and meaning. Only when words become launching pads into deeper experiencing is their potential realized" (Cortright, 1997, p. 239).

According to Cortright (1997), the transpersonal paradigm has seriously challenged the distinction between psychology and spirituality, science and spirit, and the sacred and the profane. By insisting that the roots of the psyche are spiritual, that the basis of consciousness is a spiritual reality, and by adopting a wider view of the self than traditional psychology, transpersonal psychology offers a more fully integrative and inclusive view of human experience than other psychological systems. As such it has considerable value to clinicians who choose to incorporate the spiritual dimension in counseling and psychotherapy.

☐ The Self-Transcendence Perspective

The Eastern and Western spiritual traditions as well as the psychological literature have emphasized the concept of the self. For the purpose of this chapter, only the concepts of *true self, false self,* and *self-transcendence* will be discussed. False self was the term Winnicott (1960) used to described the defensive structure that develops during infancy when there is not a 'good enough mother' to provide the nurturance and to facilitative conditions necessary for the development of the true self. As noted in Chapter 2, Keating (1998) describes the false self as the self that develops to cope with the emotional trauma of early childhood. It seeks happiness in satisfying the instinctual needs of survival, esteem, and control, and bases its self-worth on cultural or group identification. In contrast the true self is one's participation in the divine life manifested in one's uniqueness. Wilber (1999) makes a similar distinction between the false self and what he calls the real self. Interestingly, Thomas Merton's (1974) notion of the false self suggests that it is a failure in self-transcendence. For most spiritual writers, the movement from the false self to the real or true self involves the process of self-transcendence.

The concept of self-transcendence has much to offer for the clinician seeking to incorporate the spiritual dimension in psychotherapy. It is a term used widely in philosophy, theology and psychology as a conceptual bridge between two seemingly contradictory constructs. For example, in theology, self-transcendence provides a way of understanding the apparent contradiction between love of self and love of others, while in philosophy it links autonomy and beneficence, and in psychology, it bridges the apparent contradiction of independence with intimacy.

Self-transcendence has been described as the most basic human desire and drive to move beyond or transcend the self (Conn, 1997; Lonergan, 1972). It is the most basic and encompassing of all human drives, and is the source of everything that is uniquely human. Theologically, this drive represents divine life within a person and is fully realized in a personal relationship with God. Psychologically, self-transcendence differs from both self-sacrifice—when understood as a denial or other negation of the true self—and self-fulfillment—when understood as a collection of desires to be filled. "In contrast, the experience of self-transcendence supports the gospel's paradoxical view that authentic self-realization results not from a self-centered effort to fulfill one's every wish, but from a movement beyond oneself in an attempt to realize the good of others" (Conn, 1998, p. 324).

Self-transcendence is reflected in all the dimensions of human experience: affective, cognitive, moral, and spiritual or religious. Conn notes that the desire for self-transcendence "because it is conscious, also delineates the self by specifying distinct levels of consciousness . . . all interrelated as successive phases in the unfolding of the single desire of the human spirit for self-transcendence. From bodily nerves and psychic images, through sensitivity and intelligence to free choice and love, the radical desire for self-transcendence unifies the self in its heuristic dynamism and integrate it in its realization" (Conn, 1998, p. 325). Thus, in addition to cognitive self-transcendence there is affective self-transcendence. It is present when individuals break out of their social isolation and act spontaneously for themselves as well as for others. "Affective self-transcendence thus grounds the real possibility of achieving moral self-transcendence in decisions to act for value. And, finally, beyond cognitive, affective and moral self-transcendence, there is the possibility of religious self-transcendence" (Conn, 1998, p. 326).

What are the implications of self-transcendence for clinical practice? Self-transcendence is distinctly relational and this relational understanding is reflected in the basic goal and strategy of spiritually-oriented psychotherapy and counseling. The basic goal is: "empowering persons to realize even greater self-transcendence in their lives. To a great degree, this means helping people to liberate themselves from the countless defense mechanisms and other distortions of personality that constitute a drag on the desire for self-transcendence" (Conn, 1998, pp. 326–327).

The strategy of therapy is to "deal with those limitations in order to increase the probability of self-transcendence in individual lives" (Conn, 1998, p. 327). In short, the goal of is to facilitate the development of self-transcendence.

☐ The Object Relations Perspective

Object relations theory is a relatively recent development in psychoanalytic thinking. It has made a major contribution to the understanding of an important component of the spiritual dimension: the formation of God representations (Rizzuto, 1979). It has been observed that negative God representations can and do block progress on the spiritual journey. The "spiritual journey may be blocked if we carry negative attitudes toward God from early childhood. If we are afraid of God or see God as an angry father-figure, a suspicious policeman, or a harsh judge, it will be hard to develop enthusiasm, or even an interest, in the journey" (Keating, 1994, p. 22). Thus, it is important for those practicing spiritually-oriented therapy and counseling to assess and to endeavor to modify negative God representations.

Object relations theory takes its name from 'object relations' or 'object representations.' Object relations signifies the child's internalization of early significant individuals and the relational dynamics with such individuals, and the continuing psychic influence of these internalized object relations. It describes three phases of early childhood development: symbiosis, separation–individuation, and object constancy (Mahler, Pine, & Bergman, 1975). The basic development of one's God representation occurs during these phases, and specifically involves transitional objects.

Symbiosis

This is the stage of development wherein a child develops a sense of himself in relation to other persons. The child needs caretakers, usually the parents who from birth will provide a self-regulating or 'holding environment' for him. A holding environment is created by the parents' capacity to communicate to the child the message: 'I'm strong enough to take care of you and protect you. I'm going to hold you. I'll take care of you. I'll comfort you. I'll soothe you." Things are perfect in the beginning, as the child's sense of self is merged with that of mother. The child most likely believes he is in control of everything, and is as long as mom is at his beck and call.

Separation–Individuation

A major change in the child's developmental needs are noted around 10–14 months of age, just as life begins to let the child know that he is expected to gradually assume the holding and self-regulating function himself. However, the child is not ready to directly assume this responsibility so he essentially 'tricks' himself. It is as if he says to himself, "Let me take that holding function that's not under my control, but transfer it to an object that is going to be much more clearly under my control." His blanket or teddy bear not only will be under his total control but it soothes his anxiety of growing and becoming a separate person. There is a distortion of external reality, because the child treats the object as though it embodies the properties that previously were the properties of the parent, the one who really had the soothing capacity. This 'transitional object' allows the child to progressively exercise this holding/soothing function by proxy. Transitional objects help one in exploring one's environment and learning how to master it. Their use represents an intermediate step in the process of internalizing this self-regulating capacity. By age three or four the child has developed enough capacity to understand and master the environment around him that he is now able reduce his distortion of reality.

A transitional object is an intermediate experience between self and object which serves to soothe separation anxiety and facilitate individuality, the sense of one's own unique identity. A related term is 'transitional phenomena' which includes both transitional objects and 'transitional modes.' Transitional modes refer to later life experiences in normal persons. A transitional mode is a resting place or temporary suspension of higher ego functions, such as logical thinking, which can free the person to deeply experience other modes of reality, such as music, the performing arts, or creative expression. In essence, the transitional mode has a soothing function, but for the purpose of further self-integration and self-transformation.

When speaking of God, the term transitional object is not used. This is because God is not an object, but rather a special type of object representation "created" by the child in that unique psychic space where transitional objects (whether toys, blankets or mental representations) are provided with their powerfully real illusory lives. He is a transitional phenomena because he does not follow the usual course of other transitional objects. Generally, over the course of life, the transitional object loses its meaning and value as the individual becomes his own self-regulating person. On the other hand, instead of losing meaning, God becomes more meaningful over the years. Although transitional objects can be repressed or even forgotten, God cannot be fully repressed. God is always potentially available for further love, acceptance, anger, or even rejection. God is psychically useful to us. He remains a transitional phenomenon at the service of gaining leverage with oneself, with others, and with life itself. According to Rizzuto (1979, 1991), God, like the teddy bear, has obtained half of his stuffing or holding function from the child's parents, and the other half of God's stuffing comes from the child's capacity to 'create' a God according to his own needs (1979, p. 179). This process of creating and finding God—this transitional phenomenon—never ceases in the course of life. It is further shaped and reinforced by culture. God has a special place in our culture such as in the dedication of our Constitution, our money system ("In God We Trust" on coins and bills), mainstream holidays such as Easter and Christmas, church and synagogue buildings, tax credits, and the like.

Object Constancy

Assuming the child more or less successfully navigates through the first three to four years through to object constancy—the child's capacity to enter into stable and loving relationships with people perceived as fully separate and independent from himself—the child's image of God becomes less concrete and more conceptual. This cognitive development is facilitated, in large part, through fantasy. The earliest stage of fantasy is the imaginary companion (Rizzuto, 1979). The imaginary friend or companion helps to solve daily problems in relating to others. The child's newly developing imagination serves as a buffer in the harsh world the child begins to experience. The imaginary companion plays a specific positive role in child development and once that role is fulfilled it tends to disappear. Specifically, it can serve as a scapegoat for badness or negative impulses, a playmate when no one else is available, a confirmer of the child's sense of omnipotent control, etc. The nature and structure of fantasy elaborates as the child grows and develops. For the male child, the sequence from three years onward is: monster → devil → hero → super hero (Rizzuto, 1979).

Imaginary companions and monsters help the child to tolerate his badness, rageful impulses, deceptions, and frustrations. They also represent the child's grandiose sense of power. It's been said that monsters help the child know, master, and forget the monster the child feels or fears himself to be. At the age of two the child learns that God is taken seriously by adults, that God will punish him, bless him, or love him. Though the child can't see God, he comes to sense that God is powerful, everywhere, and rules everything. Of necessity, the child's God image utilizes the representation of the most significant parent available at the moment.

At two and one-half years of age the child discovers that things are made by people and then he questions how things like clouds or oceans are made and hears from another that God made them; the child needs to imagine that God is formidable enough to make big things, like clouds. This kind of questioning and wonder continues through age five.

At age six the child grasps the concept of God as creator of the world, of animals, and beautiful things. And he begins to develop a feeling relationship with God. Prayer becomes important and he believes that prayer will be the answer. In Christianity, God's counterpart at this stage is the Devil. It probably reflects the child's hostile, sadistic, parental representation. Later as the child begins to experience disillusionment with his parents, he is likely to have elaborate fantasies about having a set of ideal, imaginary parents, and fantasies of having a twin or a guardian angel to play with and guide him. Actually, it may be that bible stories and pictures of heaven and a better life serve the same function as some of these fantasies.

Thus, by about the age of six a formal God representation is formed. Rizzuto (1979) notes that finally together with this colorful crowd of characters and amidst fantasies, wishes, fears, and sexual preoccupation, God formally arrives. God acquires a special and superior status because of multiple sociocultural religious, ritualistic, and family factors. This representation continues to be modified and reinforced throughout latency and adolescence particularly with images of heroes and super heroes: rock stars, sports figures, movie stars, and even politicians.

To summarize then, object relations theory suggests this developmental sequence of the God representation: As the child grows, he develops a transitional reality, an intermediate space in which he can momentarily shift from being centered and dependent on his mother to being a part of the larger outside world. When he is between the ages of approximately two-and-a-half to five years old, he experiences this transitional reality as one which is "alive" with imagined people and monsters. These images provoke intense feelings of fright and vulnerability that heretofore had been buffered by mother's deeply reassuring words and very presence. Often in this period God arrives on the scene of the youngster's consciousness. Because of what he has been taught by others, God becomes supreme, God is the ultimate male. He is the strongest, the biggest, the best. As a result, monsters now lose their terrifying power and grip over the child's imagination. By the age of five or six, the young boy has internalized a simple cognitive notion of God which becomes part of how the child sees himself in the world. As the boy grows and begins the process of separating from his mother, he now can join the larger, male-oriented world of his particular culture. This process is facilitated because he has both his own father and a male God with whom to relate. It appears forming a God representation is somewhat different for a young girl (Heller, 1986).

If the developmental process proceeds normally, the child learns to differentiate the earthly father from the Heavenly Father who is all-knowing, all-powerful, and all-protective. In this process of differentiation the earthly parent becomes less divine and more a fallible human being. In this critical time, the God image can become confused and distorted if differentiation is poorly accomplished. Distortions can also occur if the quality and consistency of his bonding to mother is compromised. The parent's own image of God also influences the formation of the young male's image of God. To the extent that the parental God image is relatively mature and that parent–adolescent relations are relatively harmonious, the adolescent is likely to have a realistic, balanced and healthy God image. But to the extent that the parental God representation is distorted and parent adolescent relations are ambivalent and convicted, the young man is likely to develop a distorted representation and style of relating to God (Heinrichs, 1982). The quality of the relationship between parents cannot be overemphasized.

Clinical Implications

What is the clinical value of God representations? Rizzuto (1991) describes the potential therapeutic value of clinicans' understanding their clients' God representation: "Careful exploration of the subjective description of an individual's God may reveal precious information about the type of psychic and interpersonal events that led to the particular characteristics attributed to God. . . . An understanding of an individual's God representation may provide, in turn, information about his or her psychic history and the types of obstacles that interfere with potential belief, or with the updating of the God representation. I am referring now to [intrapsychic] processes . . . that may obstruct the transformation of the God representation and of religious behavior to a level more compatible with the individual's developmental moment" (pp. 56–57).

☐ Conversion Theory Perspective

Conversion is a central focus of spiritually-oriented psychotherapy as well as spiritual guidance (Gratton, 1992, p. 122). Conversion can have several meanings and definitions (Rambo, 1993) from a change in religious affiliation to significant life transformation. The definition used here was first articulated by Bernard Lonergan (1972) and amplified and extended by Donald Gelpi (1998). Gelpi defines conversion as the decision to repudiate irresponsible behavior and to take responsibility for the subsequent development of some aspect of one's own experience. Two forms of conversions are distinguished, initial and ongoing. Initial conversion involves moving from irresponsible to responsible behaviors in some dimension of experience, such as affective, intellectual or the religious dimension. Ongoing conversion is the interaction between various dimensions of conversions and the continuous process of change throughout life. Gelpi presumes that ongoing conversion will be integral, meaning that there is a commitment to living out these fundamental changes in all areas of life: affective, moral, intellectual, religious, and sociopolitical. A somatic dimension of conversion has recently be added (Sperry, 1999b). These six dimensions are described below.

1. **Affective Conversion:** Affective conversion involves taking responsibility for one's emotional life and requires the willingness to acknowledge and forgive past hurts. Growing in emotional maturity is incompatible with racism, sexism, militarism, and other forms of social bigotry. Affective conversion requires moving from a self-oriented focus to that of a love of others. It presumes some measure of repentance, particularly the renouncement of the rage, fear, and guilt that separate the individual from God. As these negative affects are brought to healing in faith, individuals need to learn to own and express their positive affects, including love, friendship, compassion, sensitivity, and enthusiasm. Ongoing affective conversion may require "sound spiritual direction and psychotherapy when necessary or helpful" (Gelpi, 1993, p. 197). Ongoing affective conversion demands a willingness to face one's own unconscious capacity for violence and destructive behaviors. Forgiveness is essential in this type of ongoing conversion as it

inaugurates a new level of conscious integration. The measure of growth in this area of conversion is the increasing capacity to see God in all things, to respond with enthusiasm to the vision of the Kingdom, to translate that enthusiasm by working to bring about God's will on Earth, and to share one's possessions and life with those in greatest need.

2. **Moral Conversion:** Moral conversions challenges the person to move from simple gratification of immediate personal needs to living by consistent principles of ethics and justice. It assumes a formed conscience (i.e., that individuals can distinguish right from wrong), and the capacity to deal with moral dilemmas and challenges faced in everyday life. It leads one to treat other persons as persons made in the image of God, and to foster the common good. Ongoing moral conversion challenges and eliminates the likelihood and impulse to selfishness, acts of deceit, violation of laws and statutes, sins of omission, spitefulness, and destructive behavior. It requires that the individual grasp the practical consequences of dedication to the common good. It also requires an increasing capacity to criticize false value systems that corrupt one's conscience.

3. **Intellectual Conversion:** Intellectual conversion requires an individual to be able to understand and express his or her relationship to God in personally meaningful terms. It is not simply the capacity to recite passages from scripture or doctrinal statements, but rather it is a willingness to pursue the truth and confront any form of false ideology and personal prejudices that rationalize immoral conduct. Ongoing intellectual conversion requires that individuals develop a balanced philosophy of life. In the process of ongoing intellectual conversion, they should have moved beyond mere knowledge of religious beliefs and tenets, and have come to a personal appropriation of these beliefs. In terms of Fowler's stages of faith development, Gelpi contends that initial conversion requires at least at the synthetic-conventional level of faith, while ongoing conversion requires movement to or beyond the individuative-reflective level of faith (Gelpi, 1993). Accordingly, individuals would be able to sufficiently understand theological issues and controversies surrounding their faith tradition to formulate their own position or response to these issues.

4. **Religious Conversion:** This form of conversion challenges individuals to live for the true God rather than idols. While the dynamics of religious conversion are the same for all of the great religious traditions, Gelpi emphasizes Christian conversion where the goal is a commitment to unconditionally finding God's will revealed in the person

of Jesus, and his vision of the Kingdom of God. True religious conversion transcends the concerns of narrow, denominational sectarianism, since religiously converted individuals are committed to reaching out in compassion to anyone in need regardless of race, creed, or class. Repentance sensitizes the convert to natural beauty and Divine beauty. Strategies for ongoing religious conversion include regular prayer and meditation, fasting, spiritual reading, and almsgiving. Finally, religious conversion mediates between affective and moral conversion.

5. **Sociopolitical Conversion:** While affective, intellectual, moral, and religious conversion are personally focused, sociopolitical conversion is socially focused, meaning it involves engaging social systems, such as corporations and government to be accountable and responsible for their actions. Beyond personal moral principles, sociopolitical conversion generates its own moral principles. These include the right of all persons to share in the good things of life, and the principles of legal, distributive, and commutative justice. It challenges individuals to resist the social pressure to think and act with 'political correctness.' Ongoing sociopolitical conversion involves a commitment to a reexamination of one's biases and prejudices against certain groups and subcultures, and challenges a lifestyle of convenience and personal luxury that fosters insensitivity to the needs of the poor.

6. **Somatic Conversion:** Somatic refers to the human body, to body structure, and to bodily sensations, and feelings—including sexual feelings, and memories. It involves the physical expression or manifestations of an individual's soul and spirit. Subsequently, when the body is injured, as in a motor vehicle accident or by a stroke, this somatic expression becomes distorted and limited, and the individual may experience a reduced capacity in the expression of his or her full personhood. Likewise, if the individual's soul and spirit is pained, such as in mourning the loss of a loved one, a predictable somatic expression would be symptoms of grief and depression.

Somatic conversion is primarily about wellness. Wellness is similar but not synonymous with health, because wellness can coexist with chronic illness, disease, and even terminal illness. Individuals with a high level of somatic conversion can be expected to experience a high level of wellness irrespective of their health status. To experience a high level of wellness, individuals need ongoing conversion in the somatic dimension. Preventive measures such as proper diet, exercise, and sleep can contribute effectively to one's degree of vitality, somatic wholeness, and somatic conversion. However, preventive measures do not guarantee wellness, since wellness is not dependent on health

TABLE 2.2. The key insights of stage models for incorporating the spiritual dimension

Stage Model	Insights for incorporating the spiritual dimension in psychotherapy
Psychosocial development	Development is relational; and there is a developmental sequence to the acquisition of virtues.
Moral development	Moral reasoning does not necessarily produce moral actions; women's moral reasoning can differ from men's moral reasoning.
Faith Development	Belief is a process of growth in the transforming of religious meanings rather than the clinging to a particular formulation of the content of a belief or doctrine.
Self development	Spiritual maturity = freely surrendering oneself and risking a genuinely mutual relationship with others and God.
Spiritual development	Spiritual development = process of developing integrity, wholeness, self-responsibility, and self-transcendence.
Spiritual growth	Depending on the definition of spirituality, spiritual growth may occur before, alongside, or after psychological development, but always requires spiritual disciplines.
Stages of the spiritual journey	Dismantling the false self and recovering the true self is the road map of the spiritual journey; spiritual growth requires meditation/contemplation and spiritual practices.

status. Finally, individuals with a high level of somatic conversion are likely to have life-affirming attitudes toward their bodies—including sexuality—and will have integrated these attitudes into their philosophy of life.

☐ Concluding Note

Chapter 2 has described six perspectives on the spiritual dimension as they related to the process of spiritual development. Presumably each of these perspectives can contribute something to one's understanding and appreciation of the process of spiritual development. What potential clinical value do these various perspectives offer for the practice of spiritually-oriented psychotherapy and counseling? Table 2.2 indicates some key insights that are applicable in incorporating the spiritual dimension in a clinical setting.

☐ References

Allport, G. (1937). *Personality: A psychological interpretation*. New York: Holt.

Cloninger, R., Svrakic, D., & Przybeck, T. (1993). A psychobiological model of temperament and character. *Archives of General Psychiatry, 50,* 975–990.

Cohen, E., & Cohen, G. (1999). *The virtuous therapist: Ethical practice of counseling and psychotherapy.* Belmont, CA: Brooks/Cole.

Conn, W. (1997). Understanding the self in self-transcendence. *Pastoral Psychology, 46*(1), 3–17.

Conn, W. (1998). Self-transcendence, the true self, and self-love. *Pastoral Psychology, 46*(5), 323–332.

Cortright, B. (1997). *Psychotherapy and spirit: Theory and practice in transpersonal psychotherapy.* Albany, NY: State University of New York Press.

Cushman, P. (1990). Why the self is empty. *American Psychologist, 45,* 599–611.

Cushman, P. (1995). *Constructing the self, constructing America: A cultural history of psychotherapy.* Reading, MA: Addison-Wesley.

Engel, G. (1977). The need for a new medical model: A challenge to biomedical science. *Science, 196,* 129–136.

Frank, J. (1978). *Psychotherapy and the human predicament.* New York: Shocken.

Gelpi, G. (1993). *Committed worship: A sacramental theology of converting Christians.* New York: Michael Glazier.

Gelpi, G. (1998). *The conversion experience.* New York: Paulist Press.

Gratton, C. (1992). *The art of spiritual guidance: A contemporary approach to growing in the spirit.* New York: Crossroad.

Heinrichs, D. (1982). Our father which art in heaven: Parataxic distortions in the image of God. *Journal of Psychology and Theology, 10,* 120–129.

Heller, (1986). *The children's God.* Chicago: University of Chicago Press.

Hillman, J., & Ventura, M. (1992) . *We've had a hundred years of psychotherapy and the world's getting worse.* San Francisco: Harper.

Keating, T. (1994). *Intimacy with God.* New York: Crossroad.

Keating, T. (1998). *Invitation to love: The way of Christian contemplation.* New York: Continuum.

Koenig, H. (1999). *The healing power of faith: Science explores medicine's last great frontier.* New York: Simon & Schuster.

Levin, J. (1994). Religion and health: Is there an association, is it valid, and is it casual? *Social Science and Medicine, 38,* 1475-1484.

Levin, J., & Chatters, L. (1998). Research on religion and mental health: An overview and empirical findings and theoretical issues. In H. Koenig. (Ed.). *Handbook of religion and mental health* (pp. 34–50). San Diego: Academic Press.

Lonergan, B. (1972). *Method in theology.* New York: Herder & Herder.

MacIntyre, A. (1982). *After virtue: A study in moral theory.* Notre Dame, IN: University of Notre Dame Press.

Mahler, M., Pine, F., & Bergman, A. (1975). *The psychological birth of the human infant.* New York: International Universities Press.

Merton, T. (1974). *New seeds of contemplation* (Rev. ed.). New York: Norton.

Rambo, L. (1993). *Understanding religious conversion.* New Haven, CT: Yale University Press.

Richardson, F., Fowers, B., & Guignon, C. (1999). *Re-envisioning psychology: Moral dimensions of theory and practice.* San Francisco: Jossey-Bass.

Rieff, P. (1959). *Freud: The mind of a moralist.* Chicago: University of Chicago Press.

Rieff, P. (1966). *The triumph of the therapeutic.* New York: HarperCollins.

Rizzuto, A. (1979). *The birth of the living God. A psychoanalytic study.* Chicago: University of Chicago Press.

Rizzuto, A. (1991). Religious development: A psychoanalytic point of view. In Oser, F. & Scarlett, W. (Eds.). Religious development in childhood and adolescence. [special issue]. *New Directions for Child Development, 52,* 47–60.

Sperry, L. (1999a). *Cognitive behavior therapy of DSM-IV personality disorder.* New York: Brunner/ Mazel.

Sperry, L. (1999b, Fall/Winter). The somatic dimension in healing prayer and the conversion process. *Journal of Christian Healing, 21*(3 & 4), 47–62.

Svrakic, D., Whitehead, C., Przybeck, T., & Cloninger, R. (1993). Differential diagnosis of personality disorders by the seven-factor model of temperament and character. *Archives of General Psychiatry, 50,* 991–999.

Taylor, C. (1995). *Philosophical arguments.* Cambridge, MA: Harvard University Press.

Wilber, K. (1977). *The spectrum of consciousness.* Wheaton, IL: Quest.

Wilber, K. (1995). *Sex, ecology, spirituality: The spirit of evolution.* Boston: Shambala.

Wilber, K. (1999). *Integral psychology: Consciousness, spirit, psychology, therapy (A synthesis of Premodern, modern and postmodern approaches).* Boston: Shambala.

Wilber, K., Engler, J., & Brown, D. (1986). *Transformation of consciousness: Conventional and contemplative perspectives on development.* Boston: Shambala.

Winnicott, D. (1960). *The maturational processes and the facilitatory environment.* London: Hogarth Press.

Worthington, E., Kurusu, T., McCullough, M., & Sandage, S. (1996). Empirical research on religion and psychotherapeutic processes and outcomes: A 10 year review and research prospectus. *Psychological Bulletin, 119,* 448–487.

Developmental Models
of the Spiritual Dimension

Chapter 2 introduced the five dimensions of human experience as well as six perspectives or frames of reference for understanding the spiritual dimension and the process of spiritual development. This chapter describes seven additional perspectives. Unlike the perspective in Chapter 2, these perspectives represent stage models of human development that directly or indirectly address the spiritual dimension and the process of spiritual development. The next section provides a general introduction to these stage models, including an overview of historical and contemporary models and critiques of stage theories in general. Subsequent sections then describe each of the these seven new perspectives.

☐ Stage Models and Human Development

Foundational to theory and practice in spiritually-oriented psychotherapy and counseling are developmental theories rooted in four traditions: 1) psychodynamic theory—Freud, Erikson, and Jung; 2) structural-developmental theory—Piaget, Kohlberg, Fowler, Kegan, and Helminiak; 3) transpersonal theory—Wilber; and 4) spiritual traditions—Keating.

This chapter describes representative theories or stage models in all four traditions. Among the psychodynamic theories, Erikson's stage model (1959) has some relevance for spiritually-oriented psychotherapists and counselors in that it is a relational model of the development of virtues. For Erikson, an individual's ego develops through eight stages during the human life cycle. At each stage the ego must integrate somatic, psychological, social, moral, and cultural factors in order to achieve a stable sense of self. In Erikson's model, a developmental crisis which precedes the next stage, and resolution of this crisis, requires the individual to synthesize both positive and negative elements (e.g., generativity vs. stagnation).

In contrast, rather than being based on the life-cycle, the structural-developmental theories are based on formal structures which develop according to predictable, universal, sequential, and hierarchal patterns. Each stage represents increasingly complex and differentiated ways of cognitively structuring one's experience of reality. Piaget (1929/1965) was the first of the structural-developmentalists and established a developmental paradigm for identifying stages of cognitive or intellectual development in children and adolescents. Kohlberg (1984), Fowler (1981), Kegan (1983), and Helminiak (1987) have elaborated stage models of moral, faith, self, or religious development based on a Piaget's paradigm. Not surprisingly, three of these stage models—those developed by Kohlberg, Fowler, and Kegan—have had particular appeal for professionals involved in Christian spiritual formation.

It should be noted that Kohlberg's and Fowler's stage models have generated considerable research, both have also generated considerable criticism and controversy. It is beyond the scope of this chapter to systematically review this research or the criticism and controversy. Rather, since the purpose of presenting these stage models is to suggest their clinical utility in understanding the spiritual dimension and spiritual development, critiques specifically related to clinical utility in will be briefly noted.

Because of such criticisms and the increasing appeal of Eastern religions and the recovery of the Christian contemplative tradition, there is mounting interest in the writings of Ken Wilbur, from the transpersonal tradition, and Thomas Keating, from the Christian spiritual tradition. As will become evident, both of these spiritual theorists and writers have complimentary models of the spiritual dimension and spiritual development.

☐ Historical and Contemporary Models Relating to Spiritual Development

Historical Models

From the beginning, spiritual writers have attempted to describe the process of spiritual development. The spiritual life was viewed as an 'ascent' to God and the metaphors 'ladder' and 'stages' were often used to describe the process of spiritual growth. For instance, John Climacus, a seventh-century monk, described the spiritual life as consisting of thirty steps in his classic book the *Ladder of Divine Ascent*. On the other hand, Origen of Alexandria viewed the spiritual life as passing through three stages beginning with purification from sin, which led to illumination by the grace of God, which finally led to union with God (Cunningham & Egan, 1996). In the Christian spiritual tradition this three-stage approach to spiritual development—Purgative, Illuminative, and Unitive—came to be known as the Three Ways, and designated spiritual aspirants as beginners, proficients, and the perfect (O'Keefe, 1995). Table 3.1 contains a capsule summary of the stages in the Three Ways.

It is noteworthy that the ways of purgation and illumination reflect the moral dimension in that they "presuppose that any growth in prayer and holiness requires a moral conversion and vice versa. For the person to grow in holiness he or she must grow as a person of virtue. To become holy, one must become truly good" (O'Keefe, 1995, p. 49). O'Keefe contends that the Three Ways require both religious and moral conversion. Gelpi (1998) would add that intellectual, affective, and sociopolitical conversion are also required for full ongoing conversion or transformation. .

Contemporary Models

In order to understand the process of spiritual development over the life span is it is useful to recognize how major domains of human development such as cognitive, psychosocial, and moral, undergird and find expression in specifically spiritual experience and content. For example, Erikson's stages of psychosocial development provide a useful perspective for recognizing how religious content is woven into major life processes

---

TABLE 3.1. A summary of the 'three ways' of spiritual growth

Purgative: The beginner undergoes a progressive purgation or purification of all attachments which hinder total surrender to God. Prayer is largely discursive and spiritual practices include fasting and almsgiving. The outcome is elimination of vice.

Illuminative: The proficient moves from discursive to affective prayer, namely, more heart centered. Growth in virtue movement away from the darkness of sin leads to 'illumination.' The outcome is growth in virtue.

Unitive: The virtues and prayers of the illuminative way have created a heart open and docile to the promptings and actions of the Spirit. A state of union or 'spiritual marriage' between the self and God occurs. The outcome is increased spiritual gifts.

such as identity formation and interpersonal intimacy, as well as growth in virtue and religious sentiment. Furthermore, Piaget's theory of cognitive development forms a heuristic basis for understanding how object permanence, symbolic representation, logical thinking, and formal operational thought are involved in increasingly advanced cognitive abilities for representing the presence of an unseen God. Also accented in his theory are how concepts of moral development may be affected by the religious context in which they arise, as well as in symbolizing objects of faith, thinking about religious questions, and conceptualizing the complex interactions between faith and life experiences, as it has been articulated in both Kohlberg's theory of moral development and Fowler's theory of faith development.

Although the spiritual and religious dimension interact with development processes differentially for individuals and groups, it is clear that spirituality and religion play a significant part, in casual and consequential ways, in the lives of many individuals. While this resultant interaction usually has developmentally beneficial repercussions, sometimes they are negative or mixed.

☐ Stage Models Addressing the Spiritual Dimension

The following sections briefly describe seven stage theories of development that have direct or indirect bearing on spiritual development. We begin with Erikson's stages of psychosocial development (1984), then describe Kohlberg's model of moral development (1984), which is followed by Fowler's model of faith development (1981) and Kegan's theory of self development (1983). Table 3.2 lists these seven models.

TABLE 3.2. Stage models addressing the spiritual dimension

1. Stages of psychosocial development

2. Stages of moral development

3. Stages of faith development

4. Stages of self-development

5. Stages of spiritual development

6. Stages of spiritual growth

7. Stages of the spiritual journey

Stages of Psychosocial Development

As noted above, Erikson's stages of psychosocial development (1959) provide a useful perspective for recognizing how religious and spiritual content is woven into major life processes such as identity formation and interpersonal intimacy. It is interesting to note that Erikson recognizes the domain of character in his system. He does this by specifying the specific virtue associated with each stage. Surprisingly, theorists in the fields of moral psychology and moral philosophy do not appear to have recognized the importance of Erikson's insight regarding the process of the development of virtue.

The eight stages of psychosocial development with their associated virtues are:

1. **Trust versus mistrust.** At birth, infants are dominated by biological needs and drives. The quality of their relationship with caregivers will influence the extent to which trust (or mistrust) in others and the world in general is sensed. The virtue of *hope* is associated with this stage.
2. **Autonomy versus doubt and shame.** Social demands in early childhood for self-control and bodily regulation (i.e., toilet training) influence feelings of self-efficacy versus self-doubt. The quality or virtue of *will*, the will to do what is expected and expectable, emerges at stage two.
3. **Initiative versus guilt.** During the preschool period children begin actively to explore and intrude upon their environment. The virtue of *purpose*—the courage to pursue personally valued goals in spite of risks and possible failure—now ascends.
4. **Industry versus inferiority.** The social context in which the first three crises are negotiated is predominantly the home and immediate family. In stage four, however, children begin school or formal instruction of some sort. Mastery of the tasks and skills valued by one's teachers and the larger society is now the focal concern. The quality or virtue of *competence* is said to develop.
5. **Identity versus diffusion.** Adolescence is the pivotal time when adolescents actively attempt to synthesize their experiences in order to formulate a stable sense of personal identity. While this process is psychosocial in nature—a social fit or "solidarity with group ideals" must occur—Erikson emphasizes the role of accurate self-knowledge and reality testing. Individuals come to view themselves as products of their previous experiences; a continuity of experience is sensed. Positive resolutions of prior crises—being trusting, autonomous, willful, and industrious—facilitate identity formation, whereas previous fail-

ures may lead to identity diffusion. The virtue of *fidelity*, namely, the ability to maintain commitments in spite of contradictory value systems, emerges during adolescence.

6. **Intimacy versus isolation.** In young adulthood one must be willing and able to unite one's own identity with another's. Since authentic disclosure and mutuality leave one vulnerable, a firm sense of identity is prerequisite. The quality or virtue of *love* ascends during this stage.

7. **Generativity versus stagnation.** This stage associated with middle adulthood is the time in the life span when one strives to actualize the identity that has been formed and shared with selected others. The generation or production of offspring, artifacts, ideas, products, and so forth is involved. The virtue of *care* now emerges: Generative adults care for others through parenting, teaching, supervising, and so forth, whereas stagnating adults are absorbed in their own personal needs.

8. **Integrity versus despair.** The final stage focuses on the perceived completion or fulfillment of one's life cycle. The last virtue to emerge is *wisdom*. The wise person understands the relativistic nature of knowledge and accepts that one's life had to be the way it was.

Stages of Moral Development

As noted in the introduction, Kohlberg (1984) proposed a stage model of moral reasoning based on the structural-developmental paradigm established by Piaget. Kohlberg's intent was to describe the developmental process of moral reasoning rather than moral action. He recognizes that the theoretical link between moral reasoning and action is elusive, such that individuals can exhibit the same action for different reasons. Kohlberg proposed three levels of moral reasoning: pre-conventional, conventional, and post-conventional, and predicted that the relationship between moral reasoning and action would be strongest at the post-conventional level where actions are theorized to be mediated by rational principles. Unfortunately, data does not consistently support this prediction. So why bother to describe this stage model? First, these stages of moral development serve as benchmarks for comparing other stage theories and even some perspectives, such as the stage theories of faith, self, and religious development and the conversion theory perspective. Second, character development is being rediscovered today. Training programs, some of which are based on this stage model, are being utilized in public education, in community development circles, and in some spiritual formation programs. And, third, the moral dimension, which involves the character and ethics perspectives (i.e., becoming a virtuous therapist) is emphasized in this text.

Kohlberg's model describes three levels, each with two stages. They are:

1. **Pre-Conventional Levels:** In these stages morality is externally based, and there is a decided emphasis on external control.
   a) **Punishment and obedience orientation.** Right and wrong are decided upon based on whether one obeys authority or whether one gets punished for one's actions.
   b) **Instrumental relativist orientation.** Right and wrong are decided upon based on whether one gets a reward, whether by others, society, or God, for what one does.
2. **Conventional Level:** In these stages the emphasis is on pleasing others or maintaining standards.
   a) **Interpersonal concordance.** Also called "good boy"/"nice girl" orientation. Right and wrong are based on what a "good" person would do under the circumstances; motives and intentions are taken into account in efforts to please others.
   b) **Social system maintenance.** Also called the law-and-order orientation. Right and wrong are based on maintaining the social system and living within reasonable, established rules; showing respect for higher authority and doing one's duty is important.
3. **Post-Conventional Level:** In these stages moral reasoning is based on an understanding of abstract moral principles upon which more concrete rules and laws are based. There is an acknowledgment that conflict and internal choice among alternatives exists.
   a) **Social contract orientation.** Right and wrong are decided upon based on agreed upon social contracts. Concern about the common good make contractual laws obligatory and binding. At this stage an individual's moral judgement reflects and values the implicit or explicit will of the majority.
   b) **Universal ethical principles orientation.** Right and wrong are decided upon based on internalized standards regardless of conformity or nonconformity with social mores. Personal commitment rather than social consensus informs one's choice among moral principles, and conduct is dictated by a self-selected ideal irrespective of the reaction of others.

Critique of Moral Development Theory and Research

It is interesting to note that much of the research and writing on moral development for the past 30 years has been based on the work of Kohlberg and Gilligan (1982, 1988) with little or no awareness of the significant limitations of their theories. Unfortunately, much of this work appears to be based on flawed empirical responses from Kohlberg's stages 3 and 4. Even by his own measure, almost no one attains the highest stage of moral development, and on the newer scoring system the highest stage has not been empirically confirmed (Flanagan, 1991).

Criticism of this moral development theory has intensified (Shweder & Haidt, 1993). Recently, Flanagan (1996) remarked that Kohlberg's theory was "a dismal failure, an utterly degenerate research program despite many true believers" (p. 138). Even staunch advocates of Kohlberg's approach now concede that moral sensitivity, motivation, and character must be studied as well as moral judgment (Rest, Edwards, & Toma, 1997). Finally, neither Kohlberg nor his followers have successfully demonstrated that moral thinking produces morally correct action. In fact, research conducted on the cognitive processes of morally exemplary individuals indicated that they scored primarily at the level of conventional morality, a finding that seriously challenges the value of the testing and moral education programs inspired by Kohlberg (Colby & Damon, 1992).

Carol Gilligan's work on moral development also appears to suffer significant limitations. In *In a Different Voice*, Gilligan (1982) challenged Kohlberg's model of moral development and proposed two key ideas. The first was that there are two basic moral perspectives, one based on justice and the other on caring. The second was that men mostly prefer the justice perspective while women mostly prefer the care perspective. These ideas resulted in a vigorous debate about the adequacy of the care/justice hypothesis and the widespread impression that Gilligan had demonstrated distinct gender differences in moral thinking. Despite her caveats, her book was read not as a hypothesis about a different voice but rather as proof of her discovery of a different voice. In the subsequent debate, empirical evidence was advanced that men and women do *not* in fact score differently on moral reasoning, and that whether an individual utilizes a care or justice perspective may relate more to the nature of the problem presented than with gender. The data also indicated that men and women switch readily from one perspective to another, with only very small numbers of either gender using one perspective exclusively (Kerber, 1986; Walker, 1991).

Gilligan's original position and subsequent hypotheses rest on theories of childhood development which have been criticized by a number of female researchers (Flanagan & Jackson, 1987; Friedman, 1993; Larrabee, 1993; Tanner, 1996). Nevertheless, the popularity of Gilligan's model has neither been diminished by its many critics, nor dimmed by her inability to verify a distinct moral developmental pattern for females, a project she posited was essential before any further comparisons between the moral experience of men and women could be made (Gilligan, 1988).

Stages of Faith Development

For James Fowler (1981), faith is directed toward a person's object(s) of ultimate concern, irrespective of the specific content of faith. Fowler (1981) conceptualizes faith structurally, rather than in terms of specific beliefs, but recognizes that lived faith expressed presses itself in specific belief. In this sense, faith represents how individuals develop cognitively and spiritually in dealing with ultimate, transcendental reality and meaning. Understood in this way, faith is clearly relevant to the spiritual dimension in psychotherapy and counseling since it represents the inner orientation to questions of meaning and value, that is, to questions that for many people are associated predominantly with spirituality and religion. Fowler (1981) describes faith development in six stages, with a pre-faith stage representing an emergent stage in which a fund of trust and mutuality is built up during the first years of life. Fowler's six stages are:

1. **Intuitive-projective faith.** This stage (ages 3–7) is a fantasy-filled, imitative stage in which the child can be powerfully and permanently influenced by the visible faith of primally related adults. Imagination predominates in this stage. For example, a child may imagine a world of kind angels and feel trusting toward reality, or a child may imagine a punitive God and develop guilt and fear.
2. **Mythic-literal faith.** This stage, which ranges from age 7 to puberty, is one in which individuals begin to take on for themselves the stories, beliefs, and observances that symbolize belonging to their community. Beliefs and symbols are understood literally, and anthropomorphic stories are the major way of understanding faith content.
3. **Synthetic-conventional faith.** From adolescence to early adulthood, faith is presumably structured in interpersonal but mostly conformist terms, with authority as important. Beliefs and values (ideology of clustering values) are felt deeply but are largely unexamined. Fowler maintains that this stage is typical of adolescents and normative for adults.
4. **Individuative-reflective faith.** The fourth stage of faith is one in which the self and one's beliefs begin to take on a personalized system of explicit meanings to which one is personally committed. Symbols are translated into concepts for self-examination and critical reflection, although there is still much unconscious material.
5. **Conjunctive faith.** Stage five involves the integration into the self of much that was suppressed or unrecognized in the interest of stage four's self-certainty and conscious adaptation to reality. Sensitive to paradox and ready for closeness to that which is different, one strives

to establish syntheses of opposites and sees the possibility of an inclusive community of being. People in this stage are ready to exert themselves energetically for their beliefs.

6. **Universalizing faith.** This final stage involves looking beyond the constraining paradoxes and the specific content of one's particular faith to seek a future order of relating justly and lovingly to others. People at stage six exhibit qualities that shake our usual criteria of normalcy: heedless to self-preservation; vivid attention to transcendent moral and religious actuality; devotion to universalizing compassion; and an enlarged vision of universal community. The rare person in stage six resembles in many respects such individuals as Mohandas Ghandi and Mother Teresa, for whom the final challenge of integrity was a lifelong journey.

Critique of Faith Development Theory and Research

Given that Fowler's model is based on Kohlberg's research, it should not be surprising that the Faith Development model would be subject to criticism. Ford-Grabowsky's critique of Fowler's model of faith development is trenchant. Ford-Grabowsky (1987) argued that masculine and cultural biases resulted in Fowler's focus on cognition to the neglect of religious sentiments and to focus on the positive aspects of development to the neglect of deception and sin as stumbling blocks to the development of faith. Johnson (1989) has leveled a more basic criticism of stage theories. She contends that because stage theories do not address the matter of character and virtue—and focus rather on ego development—they have limited value in understanding the process of spiritual growth and development, at least from a Christian perspective. Finally, others have criticized the basic structural-developmental premise that these stages are universal and invariant.

Implications of the Faith Development Model for Clinical Practice

Fowler's developmental scheme has several implications for the spiritual dimension in counseling. By outlining cognitive, affective, and behavioral elements of religious development at different life stages, Fowler provides the counselor with a way of understanding typical and problematic spiritual development. Spiritual belief is a process of growth in the multiple dimensions of faith, of transforming religious meaning, not clinging to a particular symbolization or formulation of content. Thus, faced with issues involving the spiritual dimension, the developmentally aware counselor may help a client examine and transform literal and symbolic formulations of religious meanings and at the same time retain the essential reality of religious meaning behind the words and symbols. In this way, the counselor helps the client personalize and individualize faith meanings without breaking from the authentic core of one's religious roots. For clients who are concerned about remaining faithful to their religious tradition and overcoming the restraints and problems associated with specific symbols or formulations of earlier stages of believing, the counselor who understands the developmental dynamics of faith may be able to help the client to consider alternative perspectives that are still essentially congruent with the client's core spirituality/religiousness. For example, for a client whose disturbance involves a connection between the power of God and the symbol of a stern father, the counselor may help the client rethink and feel God's power as a supporting, transforming care linked to people who symbolize human care irrespective of gender.

Stages of Self Development

Although much has been written about the development and dynamics of self, namely, Object Relations Theory and Self Psychology, there have been relatively few efforts to articulate a stage model of self-development. Even though Jane Loevinger (1976) has extensively researched ego development and devised a theoretically-derived and data-based theory of the stages of ego development, it was Robert Kegan (1983) who proposed a stage theory of self-development that is highly regarded by spiritual directors and spiritually-oriented psychotherapists. The appeal of Kegan's model for contemporary spirituality is that it addresses the two basic human desires expressed in all spiritual literature: the desire for attachment or relationship as well as for separation or autonomy. Furthermore, this theory is particularly attractive to therapists and spiritual directors since Kegan addresses the functions of attachment in women as well as in men (Conn, 1989; Liebert, 1992) .

In the book, *The Evolving Self*, Kegan (1983) describes a constructive-developmental approach to human development in which the basic dynamic is meaning-making activity. Meaning-making unifies and generates thought and feeling as well as self (subject) and other (object). For Kegan, emotion is the experience of defending, surrendering, and reconstructing a center of meaning. Human activity involves creating the other (i.e., differentiation), as well as relating to it (i.e., integration). Self–other relations emerge from the ongoing process of development which involve a succession of increasing differentiations of the self from the world. The result of this process is a more complex object of relation.

Basic to every stage of development, including infancy, is meaning-making evolution. Fusion, differentiation, and belonging are activities that recur in new forms at each phase of development as a person makes the meaning of 'self' and 'other' again and again. Each stage of development can surrender its controlling independence for freely chosen interdependence involves balancing the universal longing for both autonomy and attachment. Unlike other stage theories, Kegan describes the necessity for development beyond the stage of autonomous self-direction wherein control is favored over mutuality which inhibits intimacy. For Kegan, the most mature stage is one in which the self surrenders its controlling independence for freely chosen interdependence and relates to others with mutuality and equality. From this perspective, spiritual maturity becomes a matter of freely surrendering oneself and risking a genuinely mutual relationship with others and with God.

Kegan's theory of the evolving self specifies five stages of development. They are:

1. **The Impulsive Stage.** This self evolves from the 'Incorporative' which is undifferentiated and controlled by reflexes; Kegan labels it Stage '0.' The impulsive self is embedded in and subjected to impulses and perceptions which are unorganized and constantly changing. The result is that the impulsive self can rapidly alternate between extremes of emotion. It cannot tolerate ambivalence.

2. **The Imperial Stage.** With the emergence of concrete operational thinking the child creates an interior world and objectifies impulses and perceptions. The results is that the self no longer controlled by impulses and perceptions and can actively and purposively explore its environment.

3. **The Interpersonal Stage.** This self is able to relate to others by coordinating its needs with the needs of others and by exhibiting some measure of empathy. Nevertheless, this is a pre-identity stage which means relationships are characterized by clinging fusion, i.e., this self is unable to separate itself from its relationships. Although feelings of mutuality are all important to this self, it fears the loss its own self and the experience of nothingness.

4. **The Institutional Stage.** A coherent sense of identity is achieved which means this self is able to separate itself from its relationships and can experience a sense of self ownership. Nevertheless, control and independent strength constitute its main agenda or organization, and these outweigh the pull of attachment and intimacy. Furthermore, this self is unable to fully and critically reflect on this organization.

5. **The Interindividual Stage.** This self is no longer constrained by its organization, but is free to relate to others fully as a 'universal' person with others. At this stage the self becomes capable of surrendering its

controlling autonomy and independence for freely chosen interdependence, and can thereby relate to others with mutuality and equality. This self is capable of genuine intimacy with self and others and can tolerate inner emotional conflict. Accordingly, this self is capable of and disposed to the transforming union of divine love.

Stages of Spiritual Development

Extending the tradition of the structural theories of human development, Helminiak (1987) has described what he calls the stages of spiritual development in his book *Spiritual Development: An Interdisciplinary Study*. His basic assumption is that spiritual development is not a separate line of development alongside physical, emotional, intellectual, moral, ego, or faith development. Rather, spiritual development embraces all these dimensions of human development. Spiritual development is best conceptualized as *human* development when it is characterized by four factors: 1) integrity or wholeness, 2) openness, 3) self-responsibility, and 4) authentic self-transcendence. It is the ongoing integration of the human spiritual principle into the very structures of the personality until the personality becomes the adequate expression of the fully authentic person. Helminiak describes five distinct developmental stages in this process of integration.

1. **Conformist Stage.** This is the beginning point of spiritual development. It is characterized by a deeply-felt and extensively rationalized worldview, accepted on the basis of external authority and supported by approval of our significant others.
2. **The Conscientious Conformist Stage.** This stage is characterized by beginning to assume responsibility for our awareness that because of unthinking adherence to an inherited worldview, we have actually abdicated responsibility for our life. At this stage we begin to learn that our lives are what *we* decide to make of them.
3. **The Conscientious Stage.** This stage is the first stage of true spiritual development. It is characterized by the achievement of significantly structuring of our lives according to our own understanding of things, by optimistically regarding our newly accepted sense of responsibility for ourselves and our world, and by commitment to our own principles.
4. **The Compassionate Stage.** At this stage we learn to surrender some of the world we have so painstakingly constructed for ourselves. Our commitments are no less intense, but they are more realistic, more nuanced, and more supported by deeply felt and complex emotion. We become more gentle with ourselves and with others.

5. **The Cosmic Stage.** As this final stage unfolds, our habitual patterns of perception, cognition, interrelation, and all others become more fully authentic. We become more fully open to all that is, ever willing to change and adjust as circumstances demand, alive and responsive to the present moment, in touch with the depths of our own selves, aware of the furthest implications of our spiritual nature, in harmony with ourselves and with all else—and all this, not as a momentary, passing experience but as an enduring way of being, permeating the very structure of our concrete selves. There is a profound merging, insofar as it is possible, between spirit and self. It is that state of full integration when the personality is the adequate instrument of the authentic person. It becomes a way of life that has been variously described by the great spiritual traditions as mysticism, samadhi, satori, kensho, moksha, cosmic consciousness, or enlightenment.

Stages of Spiritual Growth

Ken Wilber (1999) has proposed a stage theory of spiritual development from a much different perspective than the one articulated by Helminiak. It is an integrative theory of consciousness that Wilbur contends embraces the essential truths of Eastern and Western thinking, from ancient wisdom traditions to modern science. He calls this theory the Full Spectrum Model of the stages of human growth and development. Over the past two decades this generic model has undergone changes and modifications. Three renderings of it follow.

The Evolutionary Spectrum Model

The first is the evolutionary model of consciousness. Wilber describes the evolving structures of consciousness which make up what he calls the spectrum or the Great Chain of Being. There are six major, increasingly differentiated levels of consciousness from lowest to highest (Wilber, 1983/1996b). These six levels are:

1. **Reptilian consciousness** is the most primitive level of consciousness. It is characterized by immersion in nature, immediate fulfillment of instinctual needs, and the absence of any consciousness of self.
2. **Typhonic consciousness** is the level of consciousness involving the development of a body-self distinct from other objects. It is characterized by the inability to distinguish the part from the whole, and images in the imagination from external reality.
3. **Mythic membership consciousness** is the level of consciousness

characterized socially by the stratification of society into hierarchical forms. It is characterized by an unquestioned assimilation of the values and ideas of one's social group, and involves the phenomena of over-identification and conformity to the group's value systems. In short, one's identity and self-worth is drawn from one's family, ethnic, or religious community.

4. **Mental egoic consciousness** involves the development of full reflective self-consciousness, beginning with the capacity for logical reasoning at about eight years of age and arriving at abstract thinking around 12 or 13. This level of consciousness is characterized by the sense of personal responsibility and guilt feelings regarding one's attitudes and behavior.

5. **Intuitive consciousness** is the level of consciousness that is beyond rational thinking. It is characterized by harmony, cooperation, forgiveness, negotiation to resolve differences, and mutuality rather than competitiveness. It involves having a sense of oneness with others and of belonging to the universe.

6. **Unitive consciousness** is that level of consciousness involving the experience of transforming union together with the process of infusing the experience of divine love into all one's faculties and relationships.

The Developmental Spectrum Model

This developmental model is a subset of the evolutionary model of consciousness. Each stage consists of developmental tasks which require new abilities and levels of adaptation. As these tasks are met, the individual psychic organization becomes more differentiated. Failure to meet such tasks results in fixation or interferes with full consolidation of the next stage. Wilber indicates the correspondence of his seven-stage model to various other models and constructs (Wilber, 1983/1996b, pp. 246–248). The seven stages are:

1. **Archaic:** This stage includes the material body, sensations, perceptions, and emotions. It is equivalent to Piaget's stage of sensorimotor intelligence, Maslow's physiological needs, and Loevinger's autistic and symbiotic stages.

2. **Magic:** This stage includes simple images, symbols, and the first rudimentary concepts, or the first and lowest mental productions. They are 'magical' in the sense that they display condensation, displacement, and 'omnipotence of thought.' It is equivalent to Freud's primary process, Piaget's preoperational stage of thinking, and is correlated with Kohlberg's preconventional morality, Loevinger's impulsive and self-protective stages, and Maslow's safety needs.

3. **Mythic:** This person at this stage is more advanced than magic, but not yet capable of clear rationality or hypothetico-deductive reasoning. The stage is equivalent to Piaget's stage of concrete operational thinking, Loevinger's conformist and conscientious-conformist stages, Maslow's belongingness needs, and Kohlberg's stages of conventional morality.

4. **Rational:** This stage is equivalent to Piaget's stage of formal operational thinking and is correlated with Loevinger's conscientious and individualistic stages, Kohlberg's post-conventional morality, and Maslow's self-esteem needs.

5. **Psychic:** 'Psychic' does not necessarily refer to 'paranormal,' but rather to 'psyche' as a higher level of development than the mind per se. Its cognitive structure has been called 'vision logic' or integrative logic, and is correlated with Loevinger's integrated and autonomous stages, and Maslow's self-actualization needs.

6. **Subtle:** This stage involves archetypal meaning and the 'illumined mind.' It is essentially the transpersonal structure of life, where intuition predominates. It is the beginning of Maslow's self-transcendence needs.

7. **Causal:** This level is the endpoint of all growth and development. It is 'Spirit' in the highest sense, and Tillich's 'Ground of Being' or Spinoza's 'Eternal Substance.'

The Transpersonal Spectrum Model

Wilber contends that the seven stages of the Developmental Spectrum Model can be further reduced to three general realms: the pre-personal (i.e., pre-conventional), the personal (i.e., conventional), and the transpersonal (i.e., post-conventional). Here it will be referred to as the Transpersonal Spectrum Model. Recall that Kohlberg also uses the designations pre-conventional, conventional, and post-conventional.

There is widespread agreement among transpersonal philosophers and psychologists that these three stages or realms are the most basic and useful way of differentiating reality (Cortright, 1997; Walsh, 1999). Wilber has linked his spectrum model of consciousness to spectra of psychopathology and psychotherapy in addition to development. Movement through these three basic stages is from lesser to greater consciousness and from fragmentation to wholeness. This third rendering of the spectrum model can be summarized as:

1. **The Pre-Personal Level:** This is a primitive level of development and so developmental failures involve more primitive psychopathology such as psychoses, severe personality disorders like narcissistic and borderline disorders, and neuroses. Standard psychotherapeutic

methods include those such as dynamic psychotherapy and what Wilber calls 'structure-building therapy.'

2. **The Personal Level:** While the individual at this level may lead a conventional daily life, he or she is far from being happy and enlightened. Anxiety and worry about the meaning of life, the future, relationships, and matters of conscience are common concerns. Wilber describes typical psychopathology at this stage to include 'cognitive script pathology,' 'identity neurosis,' and 'existential pathology,' for which he recommends transactional analysis, cognitive therapy, introspection, and philosophical analysis.

3. **The Transpersonal Level:** At this level the self has developed full self-consciousness, has gone beyond any psychic wounds and defenses, and has actualized or is actualizing much of its finite potential. The spiritual traditions refer to psychopathology here as the ' perils of the path' (Cortright, 1997, p. 69). Predictable perils include 'spiritual emergencies,' 'dark nights of the soul,' 'psuedo-nirvana,' and 'failure to integrate.' Treatment or interventions at this level include structure-building therapy, meditation and other spiritual practices, and spiritual direction (Wilber, 1983, 1996b).

☐ Stages of the Spiritual Journey

As described by Thomas Keating (1998), a Trappist monk and noted authority on contemplative prayer, self-transformation is a spiritual journey. A spiritual journey is basically a journey of self-discovery since the encounter with God is also an encounter with one's true self. Like Wilber, Keating (1995) has attempted to integrate basic insights from ancient spiritual traditions with the insights of contemporary psychology. While Keating recognizes the wisdom of the Eastern Religious and spiritual traditions, he has developed a model that is primarily based within the Christian contemplative tradition. Like Wilber, the domain of consciousness is a core consideration for Keating. Not surprisingly, there is some correspondence between the stages of evolutionary consciousness and the traditional stages of Christian spiritual journey. Table 3.3 illustrates this comparison.

These six stages refer to different levels of relating to God (Keating, 1992, p. 142). Even though Keating has not provided a systematic account of these stages, they are well known in the Christian tradition. The following is an attempt to succinctly and systematically describe these stages.

1. **Initial contemplation.** This stage corresponds to Wilber's mental egoic stage of consciousness in which an individual is capable of fully reflec-

TABLE 3.3. A comparison of the stages of consciousness and
the spiritual journey

Stages of Consciousness	Stages of the Spiritual Journey
Unity Consciousness	Unity
Unitive consciousness	Transforming union Dark night of the spirit
Intuitive consciousness	Intermediate contemplation Dark night of the senses/soul
Mental egoic consciousness	Initial contemplation
Mythic membership consciousness Typhonic consciousness Reptilian consciousness	

Based on Material from Wilbert (1983/1996b) and Keating (1998)

tive self-consciousness. For this stage Keating indicates a number of prayer forms and spiritual practices called *lectio divina*. These include contemplative prayer which is praying or communing beyond words, thoughts, and feelings. Contemplative prayer is a "process moving from the simplified activity of waiting upon God to the ever-increasing predominance of the gifts of the Spirit as the source of one's prayer" (Keating, 1998, p. 145). Centering prayer, a passive form of contemplative prayer, is commonly practiced at this stage.

2. **Dark night of the senses.** This dark 'night' refers to a stage or period of spiritual dryness and desolation in which the individual feels abandoned by God and is unable to pray and receive spiritual consolations as before. The goal of this stage is the purification of one's motivation, a time of passive purification. In the spiritual literature this is also called the Dark Night of the Soul.

3. **Intermediate contemplation.** This stage corresponds to Wilber's intuitive stage of consciousness in which an individual can experience a sense of oneness with others and of belonging to the universe. Keating designates this stage as 'stages of prayer' and indicates representative prayer forms that foster and maintain a sense of oneness and belonging: the prayer of full union, the prayer of union, the prayer of quiet and infused recollection.

4. **Dark night of the spirit.** Stage four refers to the purification of the

unconscious beyond the dark night of the senses, and aims to eliminate the remaining remnants of the false self, particularly spiritual pride. "The final purgation of spiritual pride is traditionally as the dark night of the spirit" (Keating, 1995, p. 98).

5. **Transforming union.** In this fifth stage is the full and ongoing sharing of God's life and loving presence sharing in all five dimensions of human experience. Unlike previous, occasional experiences of unity and God's presence, daily life is experienced with "the invincible conviction of continuous union with God" (Keating, 1998, p. 101). This stage involves a restructuring of consciousness in which the divine reality is perceived to be present in oneself and in all that is. While relatively few achieve this stage, Keating indicates that it should be regarded as the normal Christian life.

6. **Unity.** In this stage the individual is nearing the completion of the spiritual journey. It is also called the stage of perfect wisdom, the kind of wisdom in which one finds happiness in persecution for the sake of the Kingdom of God. Individuals have "moved beyond self-interest to such a degree that they no longer have a possessive attitude toward themselves. . . . they become sources of divine life and peace for others' (Keating, 1998, p. 112).

The Stages of Consent on the Spiritual Journey

The stages of the spiritual journey correspond to the passage of human life from birth to death. The spiritual journey requires a series of consents about life that most spiritual seekers were unable to make in childhood, adolescence, and early adulthood for various reasons, including unhealed emotional damage. Keating describes four such stages of consent (Keating, 1998). The four stages are:

1. **First Consent.** Associated with childhood, this is the consent to accept the basic goodness of one's being as a gift from God and to be grateful for it.

2. **Second Consent.** Associated with early adolescence, this the consent to accept the full development of one's being by activating one's talents and creative energies, and to assume responsibility for oneself and one's relationships.

3. **Third Consent.** Associated with early adulthood, this is the consent to accept the fact of our non-being and the diminutions of self that occur through illness, old age, and death.

4. **Fourth Consent.** This is the consent to be transformed. The transforming union requires consent to the death of the false self. Many,

even those advanced on the spiritual journey, are more afraid of the death of the false self than of physical death.

The Dynamics of the Spiritual Journey

Briefly stated, Keating's perspective on the spiritual dimension is that one's inmost center is the divine ground of one's being from which the true self unfolds. Because of the human condition, Keating believes, living out of the power of the true self is greatly compromised. In response to the traumas and pain associated with birth and infancy, individuals develop a false self which represses the true self and hides its potential. The false self remains operative when individuals are emotionally dominated by external events or unconscious defenses instead of acting with freedom. Through spiritual practices and Centering prayer individuals are able to break through these unconscious barriers and recover their true selves. In other words, the spiritual journey involves the dismantling of the false self and the recovery of the true self. The remainder of this section elaborates Keating's view of the dynamics of the spiritual journey as interpreted from the psychological and spiritual perspectives.

Keating's formulation of the early life development of the false self and the reclamation of the true self as the basis for personal transformation on the spiritual journey is both original and compelling. He develops an integrative formulation of spiritual growth which incorporates insights from developmental psychology, depth psychology, family systems theory, transpersonal psychology, anthropology, the neurosciences, as well as from the contemplative tradition and Christian mysticism (Keating, 1995).

The ability to truly love oneself and others requires a considerable degree of self-sacrifice and self-denial. Such love is easier spoken about than put into practice. This is because of a flaw in human nature inclining one to selfishness. Christianity refers to this flaw as original sin, and Keating (1999) calls it the 'human condition.' Because of the human condition, one's best actions are marred by selfish motives, though these tend to be unrecognized. The writings of St. John of the Cross describe the spiritual journey which begins when the individual responds to the call to move away from self-love toward a truly disinterested love, that is, a love which seeks the best for the other and neither clings nor manipulates. Everyone begins the spiritual journey distorted and in need of healing. The journey is about accepting a transforming love that deactivates one's limited and imperfect human ways of thinking, loving, and acting, and changes them into divine ways.

Human ways of thinking, loving, and acting are limited and imperfect because they are subject to the distortions of the *false self*. This false self must be transformed in the *true self*. The false self is described by Keating (1999) as the self we think we are as compared to the true self, which is the self we actually are. The false self seeks fame, power, prestige and wealth. It emerges from what could be called the human condition. All individuals are born into life and into a particular culture with three basic instinctual needs: 1) the need for love and affection; 2) the need to survive; and 3) the need for power and control.

The need for affection affects how individuals believe they are perceived by others, and how individuals desire to belong and to feel valued, needed, and loved by others. The basic instinct to survive affects how individuals perceive the trustworthiness of reality, as well as their sense of security or threat in a given environment. The need to exercise power in one's life affects how individuals treat others, and the extent to which they attempt to control other people's lives. These instinctual needs are natural, good, and essential. Yet, when they are not satisfied they become demands.

Happiness is equated with the prompt and constant fulfillment of these needs, clustered by a complex of emotions for achieving one's needs and wants. This complex of emotions can be likened to a computer program in which a single action can trigger a whole series of responses which are designed to achieve happiness through the satisfaction of our demands. Keating (1999) calls this phenomenon 'emotional programs.' Eventually these emotional programs for happiness become exaggerated into centers of motivation that function below the level of conscious awareness. Thus, what may be intended as a completely selfless action is actually driven by an unconscious selfish motive.

The false self is formed by compensatory behavior, through which individuals seek to protect themselves from real or imagined deprivations in regard to the needs for affection, survival, or control. The false self seeks happiness in overcompensating these needs. When one's instinctual needs are not being fulfilled we try to make sure they will be through our behavior. This then becomes an ingrained pattern of behavior which severely limits one's freedom. Certain emotions which Keating calls "afflictive emotions" are created by one's emotional program (Keating, 1995). Afflictive emotions include anger, fear, and discouragement—emotions which are spontaneous reactions to the failure to acquire things perceived to be good and difficult to attain, or to the failure to avoid things perceived to be evil and difficult to avoid.

Basically, the false self is a constellation of energies involving frustration of the basic needs for affection, survival, and control. To the extent to which individuals feel deprived of something believed necessary for their happiness, they are likely to feel upset and disconcerted. Until the false self is addressed, individuals are essentially victims of their beliefs and emotions.

Unless and until these needs are met, individuals experience themselves as out of balance, and their emotional programs for seeking happiness attempt to compensate. Emotional programs cause problems only when they surreptitiously influence one's behavior to overcompensate. In such circumstances, even when one's intention is to help another, the other is subtly manipulated to satisfy one's own needs.

Another determinant of the false self is what Keating (1999) calls 'cultural conditioning.' Culture refers to any social group to which one belongs or has belonged in the family and community. Cultural conditioning begins very early in life and involves the processes of identification and overidentification with the groups that provide for our needs for security, affection, and control. Conformity with group norms insures both acceptance and socialization. Accordingly, individuals acquire their preconceived ideas, values, biases, and prejudices. The result is that emotional programs are established by early childhood and tend to be relatively resistant to modification by logic or reason. They are largely nonrational and because they remain at a preconscious level, individuals are unaware of their operative functioning. They are addictive because whenever the perceived needs are met, needs for bigger and better things arise. They are insatiable since no symbol can ever fully satisfy our thirst for happiness.

"The combination of these two forces—the drive for happiness in the form of security . . . affection . . . power and control, and over-identification with the particular group to which we belong—greatly complicates our emotional program for happiness. In our younger days, this development is normal. As adults, activity arising from such motivation is childish" (Keating, 1999a, p. 15). In short, the false self is programmed for human misery.

As noted earlier, emotional programming is like a computer software program with unlimited memory. These programs store every emotional experience from the womb to the present moment, irrespective of our ability to remember or recall such experiences. While an event may be forgotten, the emotional responses to it are not. They can very easily be retrieved in a situation similar to the one that triggered the emotional response in the first place. Thus, when any event resembling those once felt to be harmful, dangerous, or rejecting occurs, the same feelings surface, usually disproportionate to the situation. Even though one may not have experienced serious trauma, nearly everyone has experienced early childhood losses and conflicts, which typically result in the emotional wounding and sense of unfulfillment carried into adulthood. Predictably, individuals compulsively enact a pattern of seeking approval, security, and a sense of well-being from others or from situations, even though these are never fully satisfying.

When individuals decide to seriously commit themselves to the spiritual journey, they do not begin with a clean slate or new tape. Much reprogramming is required. Initially, this involves ascertaining the content of that tape by listening to it, and then attempting to remove any aspects that are obstacles on the spiritual journey. We are dealing with subtle forces that are very powerful. To dismantle the false self system requires more than good resolutions. Spiritual practices and disciplines are necessary to help in facing the shadow side of personality. As these obstacles are gradually brought into the light, individuals begin, or continue, the process of deep healing and transformation. Such healing is not merely superficial nor external but is the beginning of a transformation of the entire personality.

Unless the entire array of one's preconceived values and ideas are directly examined and squarely confronted, the prospect of genuine spiritual growth is compromised. Until these hidden motivations are faced, individuals cannot act out of the true self, but will continue filtering reality through their needs and wants, which is, of course, the false self.

It is absolutely essential to realize that the false self can operate in a very subtle manner. As soon as it thinks it may come under attack, it camouflages itself and hides its true nature. The naked false self is totally self-centered and can array itself in religious and spiritual guises that are eminently acceptable and difficult to discern. Individuals can appear to be leading exemplary lives observing the externals of etiquette and religiosity. The false self will utilize spiritual disciplines and religious vestiges to subtly feed its needs for acceptance, security, and power.

Coming to grips with the false self requires a conscious plan and deliberate effort. Psychotherapy alone may not be sufficient. Nevertheless, the first step is to accept the reality of the false self and begin to recognize its operational patterns. Failure to do so obviates one's good intentions and efforts involving spiritual practices. That is because the false self acts like an electronic air cleaner, filtering out what it does not want to see and hear. It sees and hears what suits it, and dismisses whatever challenges it with anger and immediate rationalizations.

Curiously, a major deterrent to recognizing the operation of the false self is the subtle manner in which it adapts itself to the spiritual life. It will still seek happiness through the emotional programs of esteem, power, and security; and it will seek to remain in control of the relationship with God. Furthermore, it will seek esteem in spiritual ways, but will react in anger when one's talents or personal holiness is not recognized. Service to others will be about power over them rather than about self-sacrifice or self-giving. It is only by examining one's reactions to others' lack of gratitude or lack of notice that one begins to glimpse one's true motivation. In short, the false self is extraordinarily subtle, and unless it is faced head on it will continue to influence one's thoughts and actions.

What can be done to reverse the effects of the false self? Centering prayer is the method Keating advocates for dismantling the false self. He notes that this form of prayer can heal the emotional wounds and can open the individual to greater interior freedom and union with God. As a result of the deep rest of body, mind, and spirit experienced in the regular practice of centering prayer, the individual's defense mechanisms loosen and the undigested material of early life emerges from the unconscious in the form of primitive feelings or a barrage of images or commentaries. Another effect of this process of dismantling of the false self is an increase in self-consciousness. Furthermore, one's "idea [representation] of God becomes more expanded and profound" (Keating, 1995, p. 102).

"Our awareness during prayer becomes a channel of evacuation similar to the evacuation channels of the physical body. . . . Early emotional traumas were never fully digested, integrated or evacuated because as infants and children we could not articulate our pain. . . . They can only be dissipated by acknowledging or articulating them" (Keating, 1995, pp 78-79). Keating calls this process 'unloading the unconscious' and indicates that it can occur both during the time of contemplative prayer and outside the time of prayer. As noted earlier, he calls this process Divine Therapy. By

---

TABLE 3.4. The process and dynamics of self-transformation

1. The true self, which is centered in God, is the basic core of one's goodness. While God and the true self are intimately related, the true self is not God.

2. The human condition, also called original sin, is the universal experience of achieving reflective self-consciousness without certitude of personal union with God. This gives rise to a sense of incompletion, alienation, and guilt; includes all of one's emotional damage from early life experiences and self-serving habits woven into one's personality; is culturally conditioned; and its constellation is one's emotional program, called the false self. The false self motivates all one's basic drives for security and survival, affection and esteem, and power and control. It blocks awareness of the true self.

3. Dismantling the false self requires spiritual practices and purification—called unloading the unconscious, the process of surfacing previously unconscious emotional programming from early life in the forms of primitive feelings or images. This unloading begins when one regularly practices forms of meditation like Centering prayer. This self-directed process is called Divine Therapy. It can be facilitated by spiritual guidance and/or psychotherapy, particularly if the individual gets "stuck" or is overwhelmed by the process.

4. An increasing awareness of one's true self, along with a deep sense of spiritual peace and joy accompanying this process, balances the psychic pain of the disintegrating and dying of the false self. This is self-transformation.

such means the roots of self-centeredness are healed and the emotional programming of the past is erased and replaced. "The *practice of virtue* is the traditional term for erasing the old programs and writing new programs" (Keating, 1992, p. 16).

In contrasting Divine Therapy with traditional psychotherapy, Keating notes that in Divine Therapy it is "not a question or analyzing or discovering what the original difficulty was that might have caused the emotional damage. It is simply a process of unloading the emotional garbage of a lifetime . . . normally, if we can put up with the purging process, it heals our deepest wounds and uncovers the Divine presence that was present within us all along" (Keating, 1999b, p. 25). He suggests that spiritually-oriented psychotherapy or counseling may be indicated if the individual becomes 'stuck' in or becomes too distraught or otherwise cannot tolerate the purging process.

In short, Keating offers a compelling restatement of the ancient description of the spiritual journey in contemporary psychological language. Not surprisingly, practicing clinicians and spiritual guides have found Keating's formulation clinically useful in conceptualizing their practice of spiritually-oriented counseling and psychotherapy. Table 3.4 summarizes Keating's conceptualization of the process and dynamics of spiritual transformation.

TABLE 3.5. Comparison of single multidimensional models and perspectives

Dimensions of human experience	Single dimensional models and perspectives	Dimensions of conversion	Spectrum model of development
Spiritual	Self-transformation perspective Spiritual development model Transpersonal perspective Self-transcendence perspective	Religious	Spiritual
Psychological	Faith development model Self development model Object relations perspective	Intellectual	Cognitive
		Affective	Affective
Social	Psychosocial development model	Socio-political	Interpersonal
Moral	Moral development model Ethical perspective character perspective	Moral	Moral
Somatic		Somatic	

☐ Concluding Note

This chapter has described seven developmental stage models that directly or indirectly address the spiritual dimension. By and large, those models were single dimensional models in that these models focused a single dimension or aspect of one dimension, such as, Kohlberg's stage of Moral Development and the moral dimension. A notable exception was Wilber's Spectrum Model which is more multidimensional in scope. Chapter 2 has described other perspectives (i.e., non-stage theories and models) of the process of spiritual development. While most of these have focused on a single dimension, or dual dimensions, one, namely conver-

TABLE 3.6. Key insights for incorporating various perspectives in the spiritual dimension

Perspectives	Insights for incorporating the spiritual dimension
Object relations	Object relations are internalized relationships, and God representations (images) reflect early parental object relations. Negative God images negatively impact the spiritual journey, and can be modified in therapy.
Self-transcendence	Spiritual hunger reflects one's basic drive for self-transcendence. Spiritual development means increasing self-transcendence which requires balancing autonomy and relationship. The goal of spiritual counseling and therapy is to the facilitate the process of self-transcendence.
Transpersonal	Consciousness is the central concept. The spiritual and psychological dimensions differ but overlap; and the spiritual dimension is central to all of human experience. Spiritual emergencies differ from psychopathology. Self-transcendence is a function of increased consciousness.
Character	Personality consists of character and temperament. Self-responsibility, cooperation and self-transcendence are the basic components of character. Low levels of these components are associated with personality disorders.
Ethical	A virtuous therapist is a professional person of good moral character whose actions reflect both the practice of virtue and the ability to incorporate professional ethical standards in daily practice.
Conversion	Conversion means self-transformation. Self-transformation requires moving from irresponsible to responsible behavior in each of the dimensions of human experience; a continuous process of change.

sion theory, is multidimensional. Table 3.5 compares the various models and perspectives described in both Chapters 2 and 3.

Presumably each of these stage models can contribute something to one's understanding and appreciation of the process of spiritual development. What potential clinical value do these various stage models offer for the practice of spiritually-oriented psychotherapy and counseling? Table 3.6 indicates some key insights from these stage models that are applicable in incorporating the spiritual dimension in a clinical setting.

☐ References

Colby, A., & Damon, W. (1992). *Some do care: Contemporary lives of moral commitment.* New York: Free Press.

Conn, J. (1989). *Spirituality and personal maturity.* New York: Paulist Press.

Cortright, R. (1977). *Psychotherapy and spirit.* Albany, NY: State University of New York Press.

Cunningham, L., & Egan, K. (1996). *Christian spirituality: Themes from the tradition.* New York: Paulist Press.

Erikson, E. (1959). *Identity and the life cycle.* New York: International Universities Press.

Flanagan, O. (1991). *Varieties of moral personality: Ethics and psychological realism.* Cambridge, MA: Harvard University Press.

Flanagan, O. (1996). *Self expression: Mind, morals and the meaning of life.* New York: Oxford University Press.

Flanagan, O., & Jackson, K. (1987). Justice, care and gender: The Kohlberg—Gilligan debate revisited. *Ethics, 97,* 622–637.

Ford-Grabowsky, M. (1987), Flaws in faith-development theory. *Religious Education, 82(1),* 81–83.

Fowler, J. (1981). *Stages of faith: The psychology of human development and the quest for meaning.* San Francisco: Harper & Row.

Friedman, M. (1993). *What are friends for?: Feminists perspectives on personal relationships and moral theory.* Ithaca, NY: Cornell University Press.

Gelpi, D. (1989). Conversion: Beyond the Impasses of Individualism. In D. Gelpi (Ed.), *Beyond Individualism,* (pp. 1-30). South Bend: Notre Dame University Press.

Gelpi, D. (1998). *The conversion experience: A reflective guide for RCIA participants and others.* New York: Paulist Press.

Gilligan, C. (1982). *In a different voice: Psychological theory and women's development.* Cambridge, MA: Harvard University Press.

Gilligan, C. (1988). Remapping the moral domain: New images in self and relationship. In C. Gilligan, J. Ward, & J. Taylor (Eds.), *Mapping the moral domain: A contribution of women's thinking to psychological theory and education* (pp. 3–19). Cambridge, MA: Harvard University Press.

Gratton, C. (1992). *The art of spiritual guidance: A contemporary approach to growing in the spirit.* New York: Crossroad.

Helminiak, D. (1987). *Spiritual development: An interdisciplinary study.* Chicago: Loyola University Press.

Johnson, S. (1989). *Christian spiritual formation in the church and classroom.* Nashville, TN: Abingdon Press.

Keating, T. (1992). *Open mind, open heart.* New York: Continuum.

Keating, T. (1995). *Intimacy with God.* New York: Crossroads.

Keating, T. (1998). *Invitation to love: The way of Christian contemplation* New York: Continuum.

Keating, T. (1999a). *The human condition: Contemplation and transformation*. New York: Paulist Press.

Keating, T. (1999b). Practicing centering prayer. In G. Reininger (Ed.), *The diversity of centering prayer* (pp. 16–26). New York: Continuum.

Kegan, R. (1983). *The evolving self: Problem and process in human development*. Cambridge, MA: Harvard University Press.

Kerber, L. (1986). On In A Different Voice: An interdisciplinary forum. *Signs*, 304–333.

Kohlberg, L. (1984). *Essays on moral development*. New York: HarperCollins.

Larrabee, M. (Ed.). (1993). *An ethics of care: Feminists and interdisciplinary perspectives*. New York: Routledge.

Liebert, E. (1992). *Changing life patterns: Adult development in spiritual direction*. New York: Paulist Press.

Loevinger, J. (1976). *Ego development: Conceptions and theories*. San Francisco: Jossey-Bass.

Lonergan, B. (1972). *Method in theology* (pp. 235–244). New York: Herder & Herder.

O'Keefe, M. (1995). *Becoming good, becoming holy: On the relationship of Christian ethics and spirituality*. New York: Paulist Press.

Piaget, J. (1929/1965). *The moral judgment of the child*. New York: Free Press.

Rambo, L. (1993). *Understanding religious conversion*. New Haven, CT: Yale University Press.

Rest, J., Edwards, L., & Toma, S. (1997). Designing and validating a measure of moral judgement: Stage preference and stage consistency approaches. *Journal of Educational Psychology, 89,* 5–28.

Shweder, R., & Haidt, J (1993). The future of moral psychology: Truth, intuition, and the pluralist way. *Psychological Science, 4*(6), 360–374.

Tanner, K. (1996). The care that does justice: Recent writings in feminist ethics and theology. *Journal of Religious Ethics, 24,* 171–191.

Walker, L. (1991). Sex differences in moral reasoning. In W. Kurtines & J. Gewirtz (Eds.), *Handbook of moral behavior and development* (pp. 333–364). Hillsdale, NJ: Lawrence Erlbaum.

Walsh, R. (1999). *Essential spirituality*. New York: John Wiley & Sons.

Wilber, K. (1983/1996a). *Eye to eye: The quest for the new paradigm*. Boston: Shambala.

Wilber, K. (1983/1996b). *Up from Eden: A transpersonal view of human evolution*. Wheaton, IL: Quest Books

Wilber, K. (1999). *Integral psychology: Consciousness, spirit, psychology, therapy (A synthesis of premodern, modern and postmodern approaches)*. Boston: Shambala.

CHAPTER

Spiritual Dynamics, Crises, and Emergencies in Psychotherapy

Most people believe the spiritual life and journey to be a stress protector and a health-enhancer, as witnessed by the many recent books and articles heralding the heath advantages of participation in religious activities and spiritual practices. In other words, the spiritual journey is considered a safe path. Actually, the spiritual journey involves a number of dangers and risks. One of these is a sense of exaggerated self-importance or ego-inflation, particularly the belief that one is holier and better than others. But there are a number of spiritual crises and spiritual emergencies that can be experienced on the spiritual journey, and clinicians are faced with the prospects of differentiating these from major psychopathology. Furthermore, when individuals seek psychotherapy, their spiritual and religious issues predictably reflect their unique personality dynamics. This chapter describes the DSM-IV diagnostic category relevant to religious and spiritual problems, as well as details the most common spiritual crises and spiritual emergencies noted in psychotherapy clients. It then describes the importance of differential diagnosis and provides useful criteria for differentiating spiritual crises and emergencies from severe psychopathology. Finally, it discusses the unique religious and spiritual dynamics and issues operative in individuals seeking psychotherapy and counseling.

☐ DSM-IV

The American Psychiatric Association's (1994) *Diagnostic and Statistical Manual of Mental Disorders*, Fourth Edition (DSM-IV) contains one diagnostic designation regarding religious and spiritual matters. It is the V code: 'Religious or Spiritual Problem' (V 62.89). This diagnostic code and category focuses more on 'spiritual crises' as brief reactive responses to specific religious and spiritual experiences. "This category can be used when the focus of clinical attention is a religious or spiritual problem. Examples include distressing experiences that involve the loss or questioning of faith, problems associated with conversion to a new faith, or questioning of spiritual values than may not necessarily be related to an organized church or religious institution" (American Psychiatric Association, 1994, p. 685). Although this category may seem rather brief and sketchy and is designated as a 'V code,' meaning it is not recognized as a reimbursable code by third-party payors, it should be noted that no such category existed in previous editions of the *Diagnostic and Statistical Manual of Mental Disorders*. Parenthetically, it should also be noted that the conditions described in the subsequent sections on 'Spiritual Crisis' and 'Spiritual Emergency' would appropriately be given the same V code.

☐ Spiritual Crisis

Webster's dictionary defines *crisis* as an emotionally significant event or radical change of status in a person's life; an unstable or crucial time or state of affairs in which a decisive change is pending. During a crisis an individual's sense of coherence and faith in the continuity of life is shaken, or even shattered, by the stress of a life event. Furthermore, the core elements of an individual's being and connectedness to others are often stretched to the breaking point in a crisis situation. Crises can be of varying degrees of severity, with some being of relatively brief duration while others are longstanding or intermittent. If one assumes that the spiritual dimension is central to all other dimensions of human experience, then it follows that all or most crises are essentially spiritual crises. There are critical transition points in the spiritual life and individuals are greatly influenced by various life events which must be integrated into one's "belief structures or they become split off from one's very being resulting in unhealthy rebellion, denial or apathy. Many honest seekers have turned away from the church and formal religion or, at least, have been puzzled by how their spiritual lives have not fit into the neat pattern so often presented of the faith journey" (McBride, 1998, p. 4).

TABLE 4.1. Common spiritual crises

- Trauma
- Relationships and family problems
- Disillusionment with the Church
- Belief transition
- Denominational identity
- Losses
- Physical illness
- Extremes of thinking or living
- Psychological disturbance
- Religious burnout
- Ethic conflicts
- Personal identity
- The crisis of working with people in crisis

McBride (1998) describes, in considerable detail, the issues and dynamics associated with several life crises that involve the spiritual dimension. Table 4.1 provides a list of such crises. McBride's book-length description of these various crises is important for a number of theoretical and clinical reasons. A significant theoretical reason is that McBride demonstrates the breadth and depth of scientific literature related to this new DSM-IV category.

☐ Spiritual Emergencies

Spiritual emergency is a term for describing "how the self becomes disorganized and overwhelmed by an infusion of spiritual energies or new realms of experience which it is not yet able to integrate" (Cortright, 1997, p. 156). The subtitle of the classic text in this area, *Spiritual Emergency* (Grof & Grof, 1989), is quite apt in elucidating the meaning of spiritual emergencies: "when personal transformation becomes a crisis. Crises arising when a process of growth and change becomes chaotic and overwhelming are not uncommon and have been described in the sacred literature of all ages as a result of meditative practices and as signposts of the mystical path" (Grof & Grof, 1989, p. x). Individuals experiencing such epi-

---

TABLE 4.2. Spiritual emergencies

- Peak experiences
- Near-death experiences
- Possession states
- Past-life experiences
- Experiences of UFO encounters
- Communicating with spirit guides and channeling
- The crisis of psychic openings
- Psychological renewal through return to the center
- The awakening of kundalini
- Shamanic crisis

---

sodes believe their sense of self-identity is fragmenting, that their old be-liefs and values no longer hold true, and that the ground beneath their personal reality is radically changing. New realms of spiritual experiences can appear suddenly and dramatically leading to immense confusion, anxiety and, sometimes, impaired functioning. Such individuals, who may have no obvious personal vulnerability or family history of mental ill-ness, may wonder if they are experiencing psychosis or psychotic-like symptoms.

Traditionally, psychiatry has not differentiated mysticism from psycho-sis. As a result, such transformational crises and non-ordinary states of consciousness tend to be treated with psychotropic medication and hos-pitalization. Not surprisingly then, mental health professionals are likely to misdiagnose.

Following are ten of the most common spiritual emergencies described in the Grof's classic text (1989). Six of these are quite well known to the American public since they have been highlighted in various popular movies and television series. In this book, these ten are presented in the order of their everyday familiarity to most Americans and mental health professionals. Table 4.2 lists these ten spiritual emergencies

1. **Peak experiences.** These are also called episodes of unitive con-sciousness, and sometimes are misdiagnosed as depersonalization or derealization. In this states, individuals report a sense of becoming one with other persons, nature or the entire universe. Time and space seem to be transcended and the feelings range from profound peace to ecstatic rapture.

2. **Near-death experiences.** Because these experiences have been well publicized in the past two decades they are less likely to be misdiagnosed as delusional disorders as in the past. Typically the experience involves passage through a tunnel or tube toward a source of light. During this passage the individual describes feeling unconditionally loved, forgiven, and accepted, and then returns to live according to this higher vision. This experience may either be profoundly disturbing and difficult to integrate or appreciated as a second chance to live a more spiritually balanced life.

3. **Possession states.** This phenomenon can be diagnosed as a dissociative identity disorder, such as schizophrenia, or as a conversion disorder. In it the individual has the distinct impression of being invaded and controlled by an evil entity and engages in bizarre vocalizations and behaviors including contortions and wild spasms. Accurate differential diagnosis is important here. Traditionally, psychology has formulated this phenomenon as an invasion of the ego with id impulses and energies, resulting in a diagnosis of psychosis. It may well be that in some situations this psychological explanation is accurate, while in other instances the phenomenon is entirely spiritual in origin; in still other instances there is a mixture of psychosis and possession.

4. **Past-life experiences.** Commonly misdiagnosed as hallucinations or delusions, this phenomenon occurs during an altered state of consciousness triggered by regressive therapies such as the breathwork in Rebirthing, in Primal Therapy, or in hypnotherapy. It is one of the most dramatic of the spiritual emergencies, particularly when the process occurs in an uncontrolled manner. Typically, it is associated with intense emotional catharsis and physical sensations and the convincing sense of personally remembering and reliving an event previously experienced. After the process is completed, significant improvement or resolution of present-day symptoms associated with the past-life experience is usually reported.

5. **Experiences of UFO encounters.** This phenomenon is usually diagnosed as hallucinations or delusions associated with schizophrenia or other psychoses. It is usually experienced as encounters and, sometimes, abduction by what appears to be extraterrestrial beings and spacecraft. Individuals who report these experiences believe them to have actually happened. Such 'close encounters' raise serious concerns about the relationship of consciousness to 'objective reality' as well as the personal and collective unconscious. Though it is highly unlikely that such close encounters are 'real,' some sort of inner experience has occurred which presents a challenge in differentiating

pure psychopathology from unconscious imagery and the archetypal realm of the collective unconsciousness.

6. **Communicating with spirit guides and channeling.** Most likely to be diagnosed as dissociative identity disorder or schizophrenia, this phenomenon involves contact with a suprahuman entity by a channeler or medium, either while in a trance or telepathically. Such an experience is very troublesome for some individuals in that the experience of seeing spirits and hearing voices can lead to serious philosophical confusion in someone with a conventional scientific world view.

7. **The crisis of psychic openings.** Likely to be misdiagnosed as hallucinations or delusions, or as a depersonalization or dissociative disorder, this phenomenon involves an influx of information from nonordinary sources such as telepathy, clairvoyance, indiscriminate verbalizations, out-of-body travel, or precognition. It precipitates a spiritual emergency when the individual has no conceptual framework in which to make sense of these experiences, namely, seeing subtle beings or hearing others' thoughts. As their ordinary self/other boundaries fragment, individuals may believe that their very self is also fragmenting.

8. **Psychological renewal through return to the center.** Not surprisingly, this experience has been diagnosed as psychoses, such as schizophrenia or bipolar disorder. In this spirited emergency individuals report having experienced a death followed by a regression to the beginning of their lives wherein a clash between the cosmic forces of good and evil is reenacted. A sacred marriage with a divine or mythic figure symbolizing the balancing of the masculine and feminine aspects of one's personality may occur. Then, as the experience begins to subside, there may be a vision of a transformed universe in which the individual is given the task of bringing about world renewal. Finally, as the intensity of the process recedes, the realization that the drama was an inner, psychological transformation rather than an outer reality allows the individual to return to ordinary consciousness.

9. **The awakening of kundalini.** This is the most commonly experienced and widely known form of spiritual emergency. Since it tends to be misdiagnosed as mania, an anxiety disorder, or conversion disorder, it is essential that clinicians are aware of its manifestations. Kundalini, a Sanskrit term, is a form of creative cosmic energy believed to reside in the body's energy centers or chakras. These may be activated by meditation or other spiritual practices, releasing new levels of consciousness which can have a spiritual purification func-

tion. This is called Kundalini awakening. The energy flow may be gentle or overwhelmingly intense, resulting in visions, widening of consciousness, clairvoyant perception, or frightening involuntary spasms, jerking, or repetitive movements.

10. **Shamanic crisis.** This crisis tends to be misdiagnosed as schizophrenia or depression. It is a dramatic episode of transition involving a level of consciousness that resembles what anthropologists have called 'shamanic illness,' the initiation experience of shamans. Americans reporting such crises indicate experiencing similar emotional and physical torture, death, rebirth and a sense of connectedness to animals, plants or the whole of nature.

☐ Differential Diagnosis

As individuals are encouraged to discuss spiritual matters, a clinician's skill in differentiating healthy from pathological religious experiences becomes important. Two common differential diagnostic considerations are: 1) differentiating psychosis from 'mystical voices and visions' and other 'spiritual emergencies'; and 2) differentiating clinical depression from the 'dark night of the soul.'

Differentiating spiritual emergency from psychosis can be quite challenging. Cortright (1997) indicates that it is essential that three sets of criteria be employed to adequately and accurately make this determination. The three sets of criteria are: 1) criteria for spiritual emergencies; 2) criteria for psychosis; and 3) criteria for spiritual experience with psychotic features.

The criteria for making the DSM-IV diagnosis of brief psychotic disorder (298.8) are rather straightforward, namely, one or more of the following: delusions, hallucinations, disorganized speech, or grossly disorganized or catatonic behavior. Three criteria for spiritual emergency have been proposed by Grof and Grof (1989). They are: 1) changes in consciousness in which there is significant transpersonal emphasis; 2) the individual's capacity to view the condition as an inner psychological process and approach it in an inner way; and 3) the capacity to form an adequate therapeutic alliance and maintain a spirit of cooperation. Finally, four criteria for spiritual experience with psychotic features, when elements of both spiritual emergency and psychosis appear to be present, have been described by Lukoff (1985). The criteria are: 1) ecstatic mood; 2) sense of newly gained knowledge; 3) if present, delusions with mythological themes; and 4) no conceptual disorganization.

Barnhouse (1986) provides specific criteria for differentiating the hallucinations of the psychotic individual from the voices and visions related to mystical experiences in the nonpsychotic. She suggests asking in detail what the individual "thinks an appropriate response to the voices and visions might be. Psychotic responses are highly idiosyncratic, usually having to do with the self, or another being involved only in a paranoid way. Normal responses are in the direction of healthier self-understanding, better relations with others or constructive action of some sort" (p. 102).

Differentiating clinical depression from the 'dark night' of the spiritual seeker can also be challenging. Both may include such features as hopelessness, helplessness, emptiness, loss of self-confidence, and decreased motivation. May (1992) offers three differentiating criteria: functioning, sense of humor, and compassion. In the dark night, impairment of work and relationships is not noted as it is in major depression. A healthy sense of humor is retained in the dark night as contrasted with anhedonia in major depression and the cynical, bitter humor of dysthymia. Finally, May notes that compassion for others in enhanced during the dark night, which contrasts with the self-absorption observed in clinical depressions.

☐ Spiritual Dynamics and Personality Styles

Personality may be thought of as the stable and enduring patterns that influence an individual's perceptions, thoughts, feelings, and actions. Such patterns define us as the unique individuals we are. Those patterns that are healthy and adaptive are designated as *personality styles*. Those patterns that are overly rigid, maladaptive, and affect others negatively are called *personality disorders*. To keep matters in perspective, the distinction between a trait and a personality disorder needs to be made. Any person can manifest one or more of the traits or features of any of the personality styles without possessing the extremely rigid, compulsive, and maladaptive or disordered pattern of that style.

The disordered pattern, originally called the character neurosis, is rigid and maladaptive and negatively impacts others. That is, others experience varying degrees of anger and suffering as a result of relating to individuals with disordered personalities. Most individuals have a mix of two or more personality patterns that makes them unique.

Where an individual resides on the continuum between personality styles and personality disorders is, in part, a function of early life experiences, but is largely a matter of day-to-day decisions. Just as virtues and vices are outcomes of a lifetime of positive or negative habits and disciplines which are related to moment-to-moment choices involving moral actions, so too is one's personality. The biblical correlate of the personality disorder would be a "hardened heart," while a healthy personality would correspond to a "heart of flesh."

The more rigid and disordered personalities are, the more they adopt rigid conceptual categories and ideologies, and "need" simple answers to complex problems and issues. Not surprisingly, they adopt rigid behavior patterns, particularly compulsive behaviors. Fortunately, psychotherapy and spiritual growth can transform these disordered patterns into healthier styles, at least in some instances.

What follows is a description of the unique religious and spiritual dynamics associated with six personality styles. When Individuals with these personality styles seek advice and counsel on spiritual matters in the course of psychotherapy or counseling, it is useful when the clinician has some understanding of how they image God or the higher power in their lives, as well as how they are likely to engage in prayer and spiritual practices, and other religious and spiritual features. Accordingly, following a concise summary of the psychological dynamics of each style (based on Sperry, 1995), there is a brief description of the image of God, prayer style, and other religious and spiritual features associated with each personality style (based on Sperry, 2000).

The Spiritual Dimension and the Narcissistic Personality

Narcissistic personalities usually exhibit tremendous potential and great things are expected of them. While some of these individuals can be extremely effective personalities, eventually, and inevitably, problems arise. For one, their unceasing need for admiration and the exploitative nature of their relationships becomes irritating. And, as time goes by, their personal presence seems less than genuine, having a gamey quality to it. In their striving for success, they easily and readily manipulate others. Typically, it is significant stressors such as the onset of physical aging, career setbacks, and the increasing experience of the emptiness in their relationships that precipitates crises, which they may interpret in spiritual and religious terms.

Narcissists believe they must rely on themselves rather than on others for the gratification of their needs. They live with the conviction that it is unsafe to depend on anyone's love or loyalty. Instead, they pretend to be self-sufficient. But, in the depths of their being they experience a sense of deprivation and emptiness. To cope with these feelings and assuage their insecurity, narcissistic individuals become preoccupied with establishing their power, appearance, status, prestige, and superiority. At the same time, they expect others to recognize their entitlement and specialness, and meet their needs. What is particularly striking is their interpersonal exploitativeness. Narcissistic individuals live under the illusion that they are entitled to be served, that their own desires take precedence over those of others, and that they deserve special consideration in life.

Religious and Spiritual Dynamics

The religious and spiritual dynamics of narcissistic personalities are rather predictable and unique and are reflected in their image of God, their prayer style, and other religious and spiritual patterns.

Image of God.   Because of their self-absorption, self-deceiving narcissists must creatively distort the precept to love God and neighbor to fit their pathological perspective. For them, God—and everyone else—exists for one purpose: to love and take care of them. Their basic spiritual deficit is a lack of awareness of grace and an incapacity for gratitude. Not surprisingly, they imagine God as an all-giving father, and they perceive faith as magical entreaty.

Prayer Style.   Consequently, they believe God will do exactly as they ask in their prayers, with no regard to the kind of claim God has on them. For them, theirs is only one kind of prayer: the prayer of petition or demand. Prayer as praise, self-examination, forgiveness, or thanksgiving has little meaning for them. Some narcissistic personalities may have intense mystical leanings that pull them in the direction of mystical experience, including the occult. This is understandable in light of their sense of specialness and grandiosity. However, they are more likely to experience a hypomanic state of self-exaltation than a true mystical state. When prayers are not answered as they expect, they become narcissistically wounded and feel deeply rejected. As a result, they may reject God, becoming an atheist for an instant or forever, because God has let them down.

Other Religious and Spiritual Features.   Spirituality provides a ready-made forum to reinforce and reconfirm their grandiose self. For the narcissistic personality, the notion of vocation as a "call" from God or as a sign of "being set apart" serves as further reinforcement and confirmation of their belief in their inherent specialness and superiority over others. The roles of minister, spiritual guide, or teacher provides a forum to exhibit that special call. Thus, the spiritual forum is first and foremost a performance where the audience or spiritual directee "mirrors" (i.e., admires and praises) this personality. Essentially, the narcissist believes that the actual purpose of spiritual activity is "worship" of themselves!

Narcissistic individuals are also likely to be insensitive to the suffering and needs of others. While they may help others in need and engage in acts of charity, they will do it only if their charitable deeds are noticed by others. If their efforts do not bring attention to them they won't make a donation, extend a helping hand, lend a listening ear, or for that matter, continue it when the attention and praise of others stops.

The Spiritual Dimension and the Obsessive-Compulsive Personality

Obsessive-compulsive individuals seem to be naturally attracted to religious and spiritual practices. This is probably because obsessive-compulsive individuals tend to be preoccupied with rules and duties. Rules provide a sense of orderliness in their lives as well as a measure of control. Although obsessive-compulsivity is not necessarily synonymous with a conservative ideology, it certainly is not inconsistent with it. Following rules and the established order is comforting to this personality, as it confirms their view that the world functions best when there is order rather than chaos, and life is gentle and predictable rather than harsh and unpredictable.

Individuals with an obsessive-compulsive personality are also those individuals who are unable to express warmth and caring except in limited situations. They tend to believe that any spontaneous expression of emotion could be dangerous, and that the extreme expression of emotion represents 'craziness.' Therefore, they keep their feelings under control. Even their cognitive processes are attenuated and rigid, lacking a sense of playfulness and flexibility. Interpersonally, they are often polite and loyal, although somewhat rigid and stuffy in their dealings with others. While they are likely to show respect and deference—even to the point of obsequiousness—to superiors, they tend to show relatively little interest in collegiality with peers and those who report to them. They seldom delegate responsibilities for fear that the task will not be done properly. Accordingly, they are firm believers in the dictum: "If you want it done right, do it yourself."

In Western culture, a certain degree of compulsivity in one's work is highly esteemed and rewarded by others. But for individuals with an obsessive-compulsive personality such cultural reinforcement becomes a burden and an invitation to workaholism. When these individuals are not working, they believe they are not being responsible and thus have no self-worth. Therefore, they must always be doing something. They must take work home with them, and even when they are on vacation, at the very least, they must stay in touch with their office by phone, fax, or e-mail. Since many obsessive-compulsives have also internalized the theologically-ridiculous dictum: "idleness is the devil's workshop," they also feel morally obliged to work compulsively.

They are inclined to be overconscientious and excessively moralistic and inflexible about matters of ethics, law, or values. Although they may generally seem to be mild mannered individuals they can become quite self-righteous and unpleasant when a pet idea or ideology of theirs is attacked. They may find it difficult to be generous in donating money, time, or gifts to others when little or no personal gain will result. And, they find it difficult to relinquish worn-out and worthless objects even when these objects have no actual or sentimental value to them. Generosity is not a high priority for them: They believe in conserving everything they can. They may have large collections of books or records or whatever. They seem to have literally internalized the belief that it's better to save things for a rainy day than to be unprepared and unprotected.

Not surprisingly, these individuals experience excessive guilt feelings because of their internalized sense that they must assume tremendous amounts of responsibility for life. As a result, they are chronically anxious and tense, and seldom are able to look and feel relaxed. They are seldom spontaneous and almost never euphoric, and they cannot live in the present because of their fear of what the future may hold for them. So, they are always prepared—like good Boy Scouts and Girl Scouts—for the expected and unexpected. Since they secretly doubt their ability to deal with the enormity of life, they reduce life to its smallest pieces. They believe that by managing these small pieces, they will eventually control the whole. Of course, it won't happen this way, because life cannot be controlled. But, they religiously cling to this fiction. Thus, their lives tend to be characterized by a quiet sort of desperation, drabness, and worry.

Religious and Spiritual Dynamics

The religious and spiritual dynamics of obsessive-compulsive personalities are rather predictable and unique and are reflected in their image of God, their prayer style, and other religious and spiritual patterns.

Image of God.   These individuals typically image God as a taskmaster, judge, or police officer. Because of their early life expectation or demand—from parents or caretakers—to be responsible and perfect, these individuals come to believe that God holds these same expectations of them. The belief is that God expects great things of them and will judge them accordingly. Certain scriptures further reinforce this expectation. For instance, "Be perfect, as your heavenly Father is perfect," and the parable of the talents, tend to be interpreted literally by these individuals.

Prayer Style.   It should not be surprising that the prayer style of obsessive-compulsive individuals tends to focus on their own faults, failings, and need for forgiveness. They will hear and say the words: "Lord, I am not worthy that you should come under my roof, but speak the words and I shall be healed," but they can only allow themselves to believe the first part: "Lord, I am not worthy," and find it almost impossible to believe that they can be healed and be worthy. Rather, they easily believe and feel that they are sinful and are not, and cannot become, lovable. The words: "You are my beloved in whom I am well pleased" seem directed at others, but could never refer to them. Parenthetically, one of the markers that pastoral psychotherapists look for as the obsessive-compulsive personality grows and matures, is their increasing acceptance of their status as God's "beloved".

Other Religious and Spiritual Features.   Spiritually-oriented obsessive-compulsive personalities are likely to believe they were meant to do something important with their lives. They often report that when they were teens or young adults they experienced a "call" to do something important spiritually or religiously with their lives. Since obsessive-complusive personalities believe that they must always do what is right and what is expected of them, they look outside themselves for a sense of direction or confirmation. This confirmation may come in a scriptural passage they read or in talking to a revered spiritual person, and they conclude that God has somehow clarified the direction.

In spiritual circles, these individuals are more likely to be viewed by others as spiritual or religious overachievers rather than as friendly and caring persons. They tend to be somewhat emotionally immature and are seldom satisfied with their lives. Although they may extol the virtue of living in the moment, they seldom, if ever, take the time to smell the roses. Their interpersonal relationships tend to be predictably remote and lacking in all but superficial intimacy. Yet, they have some capacity for deeper intimate sharing and risk-taking if they can let down their intellectual defenses.

Under moderate levels of stress, these individuals can become overly obsessive regarding religious matters. This may be manifested by guilt feelings, complaining, or scrupulosity. They may find themselves overwhelmed with anxiety or depressive feelings. Then a recurrent thought or scriptural passage convinces them that they are spiritually lost because they "sinned" and cannot be forgiven. As a result they become agitated and depressed and refuse all measure of reassurance and comfort. They may even become irrational, clinically depressed, and preoccupied with suicidal thoughts.

The Spiritual Dimension and
the Passive-Aggressive Personality

The predominant feature that characterizes the passive-aggressive personality is resistance to demands for performance both in their work and their relationships, as well as in their spiritual beliefs and behaviors. Passive-aggressive personalities follow a strategy of negativism, defiance, and provocation, and are unable to make up their minds as to whether to adhere to the demands of others or to resist their demands. Consequently, their behavior is characterized by both passivity and aggressiveness. They appear to be ambivalent about nearly everything and cannot decide whether to be independent or dependent, or whether to respond to situations actively or passively. They constantly struggle with the dilemma of whether to be submissive or assertive. They resolve this dilemma with a compromise: They express their anger and resistance indirectly through procrastination, dawdling, stubbornness, inefficiency, and forgetfulness. The passive aggressive's resistance often reflects hostilities that he or she is afraid to show openly, but instead has displaced on others. An aura of agreeableness and cordially usually masks their negativistic resistance. They may smile when they 'agree' to do something but under their breath they express their true thoughts and feelings.

These individuals were likely to have experienced being cut off and displaced from their parents' affection at the time of the birth of a younger sibling which contributed toward their ambivalence of feelings and behavior. Often, these individuals were 'chosen' to play a peacemaking role in conflicted families. Therefore, they became fearful of commitments, unsure of their own desires, competencies, the reactions of others, and afraid to express feelings directly. Indecisiveness, contradictory behavior, and fluctuating attitudes were practiced and reinforced. As children, and then as adults, they developed a pattern of shifting rapidly and erratically from one type of behavior to the next, while refusing to acknowledge their own responsibility for their difficulties.

Their basic stance toward life is one of noncooperation. Because they firmly believe that life has not and cannot be fair, and that other persons have failed to cooperate with them, they feel justified in not only being uncooperative, but in making everyone else's life miserable. Because of their ambivalent self-image, they feel misunderstood, cheated, and unappreciated by life. Subsequently, they easily adopt the role of martyr or 'injustice collector' to prove their distress and disaffiliation with others. Furthermore, they are convinced that nothing has ever or will ever work out for them. Needless to say, their selective memory screens out all the past successes they have experienced. Yet, they are resentful and envious of others. If things are going too well for themselves or others, they will make sure that they spoil it. By 'snatching defeat out of the jaws of victory' they recreate their expected disillusionment. Consequently, these individuals learned to appear agreeable and show good intentions, but not necessarily enact them. Over time, they established a characteristic personality pattern marked by irresponsibility, uncooperativeness, and lack of commitment.

Religious and Spiritual Dynamics

The religious and spiritual dynamics of passive-aggressive personalities are intimately related to their pattern of ambivalence and negativity. This pattern is reflected in their image of God, prayer life, and other religious and spiritual features.

Image of God.   They tend to hold harsh and unloving images of God, and their pessimistic spiritual outlook mirrors the rest of their rather unhappy, unproductive lives. Not surprisingly, obedience is not their strong suit, as they basically distrust and resent authority. Unfortunately, there is one 'obedience' to which they are faithful: that is, not to appear angry or show negative affect. They are exasperating to other members of the community as well as to leaders, particularly because they are never at a loss to 'excuse' their own shortcomings in their ministry or blame these shortcoming or failures on others.

Prayer Style.   Among the various personality types, the prayer life of passive-aggressive personalities is quite unique. While other personality types may storm heaven with all kinds of petitions or demands of God in their prayers, the passive-aggressive personality's prayer life is remarkable in that hardly exists. While in public liturgical settings they may go through the motions of rituals of praying and may fool peers or superiors, but in private they may not even bother. After all, they find it very difficult to trust God to meet their needs, so they don't even try.

Other Religious and Spiritual Features.   Consistent with their overall pessimism, procrastination, and disorganization in their lives, these personalities tend to be so devoid of faith that their lives aren't in any way meaningful in the present, and so devoid of hopefulness about anything working out for them in the future, that they seldom make efforts to grow spiritually. If they have begun spiritual direction, they are likely to be early drop-outs. If they start reading a religious inspirational book, they are unlikely to finish it. One might surmise that they would surely become atheists, but that requires more courage and resoluteness than they believe they are capable. So, instead of leaving the faith community they stay, and make their lives and the lives of those around them miserable. Over time, these individuals have a reputation of being "spiritual sourpusses." In short, they often lead lives of quiet desperation; more specifically, lives of quiet spiritual desperation.

The Spiritual Dimension and the Borderline Personality

The borderline personality is easily recognized by a pattern of emotional instability and relational extremes. Impulsive, unpredictable, and intense verbal outbursts and threats, as well as physical displays of temper or self-damaging acts, including suicide attempts and self-mutilation, are characteristic of this personality. Surprisingly, this emotional lability tends to be short-lived. After that the person calms down, and tends to behave as if nothing unusual had happened. Characteristically unstable in relationships, the borderline individual sometimes overidealizes another person, viewing that individual as incapable of any wrong—yet when frustrated with that person, he or she devalues that individual in the next instant. Because of their personality dynamics these individuals tend to be perpetual 'spiritual seekers.' They are highly attracted to religious organizations and spiritual practices in hopes of obtaining healing and 'salvation.' Not surprisingly, they are also attracted to psychotherapy, and are particularly fascinated with depth psychologies, such as Jungian analysis, which they imagine can make them whole and complete persons.

Experienced religious and spiritual leaders are likely to have considerable experience with this personality. It would not be unusual for a church community or large meditation group to have one borderline personality. Religious organizations with an emphasis on love and acceptance can expect to attract individuals who struggle with feelings of emptiness and isolation. Initially, the borderline personality may appear guarded in such a setting. As the organization persists in extending love and acceptance, however, the borderline personality will form intense attachments. These individuals may give glowing testimony to the group's concern and hospitality, and they will predictably respond by giving even more of themselves. As the demands of the borderline personality increase, the organization begins to feel controlled, manipulated, or trapped and predictably withdraws from these individuals. In response to what they perceive as a rejection and the possible loss of the relationship, they may offer to do anything, or accept nearly any humiliation or abuse to save the relationships and avoid the dread and pain of rejection. In anticipation of the threat of rejection, borderlines utilize a variety of psychological defensive maneuvers, particularly the primitive defense of "splitting." Since they have difficulty tolerating both negative and positive feelings simultaneously for the same person, they tend to view others as either 'all good' or 'all bad.' Not surprisingly, those deemed 'bad' become targets for the borderline's emotional outbursts.

Overwhelming personal charm is another defense they utilize. To win and maintain the emotional support of others, they may lavish these individuals with gifts, time, or praise. Similarly, borderline females may use flattery or seductiveness to secure the attention of male leaders or those who are otherwise influential in the religious organization or spiritual group. When others do not respond as they expect, borderlines will experience feelings of abandonment and worthlessness.

Religious and Spiritual Dynamics

In terms of religious beliefs and spiritual behavior, borderline personalities are considerably ambivalent in their beliefs, feelings, relationships, and behaviors. This theme is reflected in their image of God, prayer life, and other religious and spiritual features.

Image of God.   Predictably, borderline personalities tend to be as confused about the nature and presence of God as they are about their own identity and purpose in life. Not surprisingly, borderline personalities have difficulty maintaining constancy in their spiritual lives. As in other relationships, they are likely to view God as 'all good' and themselves as 'all bad.' As such, they have difficulty dealing with their feelings toward God. Not surprisingly, their image of God can be as variable as their moods. When they are elated, God is imaged as kindly and beneficent, but when they are angry and depressed, God is imaged as a tyrant and source of all their problems. Because of their propensity to project blame outside themselves, they will harbor rageful thoughts and feelings against God and their religious organization even though they are extremely hesitant about admitting they harbor such thoughts and feelings.

Prayer Style.   Borderline personalities tend to use spiritual discipline in a self-centered fashion. Prayer becomes a tool for getting God's attention. Their prayers tend to be exclusively prayers of petition: "Oh, God, get me that pastorate, so I can really love you," or "God, make the pastor care as much about me as I do about him." In a childlike fashion, they may make all kinds of promises if their prayers are answered. When their prayers go unanswered, they are crushed and conclude that will never be acceptable and lovable in God's eyes. God hates them, they contend, because unanswered prayers means that God has rejected them.

Other Religious and Spiritual Features.   Normally mild-mannered, higher-functioning borderline personalities are occasionally observed to engage in vengeful behaviors, such as vitriolic character assassinations and impulsive acts such as summarily firing a parish council member over what others would consider a trivial matter. What accounts for such unChristian-like actions? James Masterson, M.D., has studied the moral thinking process and behaviors of borderline individuals and indicates that they utilize the 'talionic principle' in guiding their moral behavior. The talionic principle or 'lex talionis' is the principle of retributive justice based on the Mosaic law of 'eye for an eye, tooth for a tooth.' This revengeful, retribution-based moral code, which is more primitive than the Christian moral code of forgiveness, is consistent with the primitive splitting defense so characteristic of this personality disorder. In the movie *Fatal Attraction*, the borderline personality-disordered character played by Glenn Close 'gets even' with the character played by Michael Douglas by pouring acid on his car, disclosing their affair to Douglas' wife, and then cooking his daughter's pet rabbit on the family's stove. These vengeful behaviors are in retribution for Douglas' rejecting her. Needless to say, borderline personalities have difficulty with the concept of forgiveness. There are some profound implications of this avenging belief with regard to the borderline personality's participation in both psychotherapy and spiritual direction, which are discussed in the treatment section.

Furthermore, their spiritual perception is greatly dependent on relational experiences with others. To the extent to which they regularly experience rejection, they find it difficult, if not impossible, to tolerate a relationship with God. Predictably, they will idealize a minister or spiritual leader as a kindly, loving substitute father figure. However, whenever this idealized individual fails to live up to their private expectations or because of some minor shortcoming, the idealized individual becomes the target of the borderline personality's rage and is immediately devalued. Since they have not learned to integrate opposite perceptions and feelings, such as love and hate, they are perpetually in turmoil, the kind of turmoil that affects most others around them.

This is why relatively healthy religious groups and organizations have the potential for being the instrument of deep healing for the borderline personality: Only in such a context of a sustained and consistent atmosphere—a holding environment—of love and concern can borderline personalities ever be able to experience God's love in a sustained way. The challenge, of course, is for such religious organizations to set realistic limits for such personalities and maintain these limits in the face of the borderline's instability. Unfortunately, there are relatively few religious and spiritual communities that can consistently provide the kind of 'holding environment' that borderline personalities need. Unless these individuals are fortunate enough to have this sustained experience, it is unlikely that they will achieve a sufficient degree of healing and wholeness to function adequately.

It is for this reason that borderline individuals, even highly functioning ones, are such a poor risk as ministers or spiritual guides. They are very likely to fail at all but the least stressful of ministries, which are those that have minimal work expectations and deadlines and even fewer interpersonal demands. Since the majority of ministry positions today are high stress, high demand positions that require considerable interpersonal skills, borderline personalities are a poor fit for most religious organizations today. Nevertheless, borderline individuals are very attracted to the spiritual life in hopes that it can make up for the early trauma and deprivations they experienced.

The Spiritual Dimension and the Depressive Personality

The DSM-IV includes an investigational diagnosis called Depressive Personality Disorder that has considerable face validity and clinical utility in understanding and treating a growing number of personalities today. Basic to this disorder of personality is a persistent and pervasive feeling of dejection, gloominess, joylessness, and unhappiness. Individuals with this disorder lack a sense of humor, are overly serious, and seem to be incapable of relaxation and enjoyment. They view both the present and the future negatively. They judge others as harshly as they view themselves and tend to focus on others' failings rather than their positive attributes. They may exhibit a wry sense of humor or they may be openly cynical. In short, pervasive pessimism is a guiding factor in their lives.

Individuals with this personality style also tend to be quiet, passive, and introverted. They tend to be followers rather than leaders and will often allow others to make a wide range of decisions for them. To the extent to which they have histories of early abusiveness, they tend to be ambivalent about authority figures. Though they may appear friendly and gregarious, they also fear isolation and being alone. They may experience periods of clinical depression and anxiety. Such episodes of depression are usually precipitated by a real loss or abandonment, such as divorce or the death of a spouse. The depressive personality shares some common features with Dysthymic Disorder and Major Depressive Disorder. Dysthymic Disorder is characterized as a chronic form of depression that lasts two years or longer, and that has less severe depressive symptoms than Major Depressive Disorders. While Depressive Personality Disorder is a chronic disorder (actually, it is a life-long condition), it emphasizes cognitive (e.g., self-criticalness, negativism, and pessimism), intrapersonal (e.g., unhappiness, brooding, inadequacy, and worthless-ness), and interpersonal (e.g., judgmentalness and criticalness of others, and blaming) dimensions which Dysthymic Disorder does not.

The depressive personality, according to Weiser (1996), is relatively common in spiritual circles. Weiser notes that individuals with depressive personalities, especially those with compulsive features, are increasingly attracted to religious and spiritual training programs, and are prime can-didates for acceptance to these programs. To the extent that such pro-grams encourage and support dependence and compliance rather than independence, these programs can expect to attract certain personality types. Such individuals are likely to be dutiful, obedient, and loyal and can be expected to ascribe to traditional beliefs and values and orthodox practice. They may have a history of volunteer activity, and tend to be cooperative rather than competitive. Interestingly, they are likely to be viewed as psychologically healthy individuals simply because they are not a threat to others. They are unlikely to be creative, visionary, or pro-pose new ideas or new programs.

Religious and Spiritual Dynamics

In terms of religious and spiritual dynamics, these individuals appear to be orthodox in their beliefs and are loyal followers, despite their ambiva-lence. This theme is reflected in their image of God, prayer life, and other religious and spiritual features.

Image of God.   Depressive personalities tend to view God as all powerful as well as merciless at times, and themselves as insignificant and not likely to experience His mercy. So, God is imaged as a blend of Rescuer and Punisher. When prayers are not 'answered' or they are not otherwise 'rescued,' they are likely to fear that God has abandoned them.

Prayer Style.   Just as they depend on others to take care of them, they depend on God to take care of their needs. Not surprisingly, petitionary prayer predominates with these individuals: 'God help me . . . protect me . . . take care of me . . . comfort me. . . . ' When their prayers are not answered as they would like, they easily loose faith and fear they have been abandoned by God. At such times they turn to others for consola-tion and comfort.

Other Religious and Spiritual Features.   Because of their sense of inadequacy and limited experience in taking responsibility for themselves, they tend to seek out religious counselors repeatedly. They may shift their dependency to spiritual directors or counselors and make numerous telephone calls to them for reassurance between interviews. If the counselor is away on a vacation, they may feel devastated by their sense of abandonment. Not surprisingly, they may have two or more counselors at once without telling them about each other. Interviews and telephone calls are ways of reducing anxiety about the fear of separation.

The Spiritual Dimension and the Hypomanic Personality

The hypomanic personality has been a part of the psychiatric and psychoanalytic literature for nearly a century. Recently, interest in this personality style has been revived due to the clinical and research focus on both the personality disorders and the so-called bipolar-spectrum disorders. Unlike hypomania, which is an episode of an elevated mood that must last at least four days, hypomanic personality refers to a style of personality—both character and temperament—that is stable, fixed and enduring rather than episodic. Currently, Hypomanic Personality Disorder is not included as a distinct and separate diagnostic entity in the DSM-IV, but it is included in the International Classification of Diseases (ICD-9).

The hypomanic personality is consistently described in the literature as being characterized by: high energy, needing little sleep, being success-oriented, work addiction, playfulness, and talkativeness, but also by empathic deficits, impulsivity, disregard of limits, meddlesomeness, and a corruptible conscience. Aktar (1986) has succinctly described the clinical features of the hypomanic personality. He notes that their self-concept is grandiose and overconfident. There is a sense of specialness that they share with narcissistic personalities. Moreover, they tend to be cheerful and optimistic most of the time, and they have little doubt about their capacity to make things happen. Nevertheless, they are given to self-doubt and find being alone difficult. Their cognitive style is characterized as glib, articulate, and knowledgeable. They have a penchant for recalling trivia and enjoy punning and the playful use of language. Thus, although they may have a breadth of knowledge they may often lack depth in most areas. In terms of interpersonal relationships, they quickly and easily develop a broad network of friends and acquaintances, yet they exhibit empathic deficits. They also have a tendency to overidealize others, which can easily switch to contempt. Typically, they foster one or two extremely dependent relationships with individuals who serve and care for them. With regard to love and sexuality they tend to be seductive and flirtatious and are fond of gossip and sexual innuendo. Hypomanic personalities may be sexually precocious and promiscuous. Sustaining a commitment to a intimate partner may be difficult, and they find equality in such relationships disquieting, preferring to be the dominant individual instead.

In terms of social adaptation, they tend to be successful in their endeavors because of their energetic, workaholic style, and because of their capacity to be decisive and daring. In the process they may display questionable judgment in social and financial matters. Not surprisingly, they gravitate toward leadership positions. Unfortunately, they become inordinately dependent upon praise and acclaim.

Religious and Spiritual Dynamics

The religious beliefs and spiritual dynamics of the hypomanic personality are unique. These individuals embody a unique image of God, manifest a particular style of prayer, and manifest predictable religious behaviors. These religious and spiritual dynamics reflect their basic spiritual deficit which is a lack of awareness of grace and an incapacity for gratitude.

Image of God.   Hypomanic personalities tend to image God as an all-giving father whose only purpose is to love and care for them. As an all-giving father, God looks down on them with great favor. He will make all their grand plans materialize. And, He is there to admire their many accomplishments. Because God is all giving, they assume that God will answer all their prayers. In short, God's purpose is to serve them. They are on earth not to serve God or others, but are instead privileged to be recipients of others' service. Not surprisingly, they understand faith as their response to an all-giving God, namely, that faith is the assurance that their needs and wants will be met, that their various projects will be blessed and flourish.

Prayer Style.   Like narcissists, hypomanic personalities believe God will respond exactly as they request in their prayer, irrespective of the claim God has on them. For them, there is only one type of prayer: petititionary prayer. Prayer of praise and thanksgiving may be for other people, but not for them. In the prayers of hypomanic personalities, bad things may happen to good people, but certainly not to special people like them.

Other Religious and Spiritual Features.   Because of their self-preoccupation and the belief that God's purpose is to serve them, they are likely to be insensitive to the suffering and needs of others. While they can and do engage in acts of charity, it is for one of two reasons. First, the act is related to the accomplishment of one of their grand plans; that is what is important, not the disadvantaged little people that may receive some benefit from it. Second, charitable acts are performed because they will be noticed by others. However, if their charitable efforts fail to bring attention to themselves, they are less likely to make the donation, lend a listening ear or a helping hand. And, when the attention and praise of others stops, so will their charitable behavior.

With regard to ethics and moral standards, these individuals tend to be enthusiastic about ethical and moral matters, but can cut ethical corners and can be corrupted. In their enthusiasm, they tend to set high standards for themselves and others, though they may fall considerably short of them. Because of their fascination with all aspects of life, they can become particularly enamored of new trends in psychology, philosophy, and theology.

☐ References

American Psychiatric Association. (1994). *Diagnostic and statistical manual of mental disorders* (4th ed.). Washington, DC: Author.

Aktar, S. (1986). Hypomanic personality disorder. *Integration Psychiatry, 6*(1), 37–52.

Barnhouse, R. (1986). How to evaluate patients' religious ideation. In L. Robinson (Ed.), *Psychiatry and religion: Overlapping concerns* (pp. 89–106). Washington, DC: American Psychiatric Press.

Cortright, B. (1997). *Psychotherapy and spirit: Theory and practice in transpersonal psychotherapy.* Albany, NY: State University of New York Press.

Gersten, D. (1998). *Are you getting enlightened or losing your mind? How to master everyday and extraordinary spiritual experiences.* New York: Random House/Three Rivers Press.

Grof, S., & Grof, C. (Eds.). (1989). *Spiritual emergency: When personal transformation becomes a crisis.* New York: Tarcher/Putnam.

Lukoff, D. (1985). The diagnosis of mystical experiences with psychotic features. *Journal of Transpersonal Psychology, 17*(2), 155–181.

May, G. (1992). *Care of mind, care of spirit: A psychiatrist explores spiritual direction.* New York: HarperSanFrancisco.

McBride, J. (1998). *Spiritual crisis: Surviving trauma to the soul.* New York: Haworth.

Sperry, L. (1995). *Handbook of diagnosis and treatment of DSM-IV personality disorders.* New York: Brunner/Mazel.

Sperry, L. (2000). *Ministry and community: Recognizing, healing and preventing ministry impairment.* Collegeville, MN: The Liturgical Press.

Weiser, C. (1996). *Healers: Harmed and harmful.* Minneapolis, MN: Fortress Press.

STRATEGIES FOR INCORPORATING THE SPIRITUAL DIMENSION

The greater the degree and level of incorporation of the spiritual dimensions into clinical practice, the broader the range of implications and applications. Part III of the book describes and illustrates these implications and applications.

The process of eliciting religious and spiritual concerns and developing an appropriate diagnostic and treatment formulation requires specific knowledge and skills. Eliciting a client's spiritual and religious history is part of what is currently being called spiritual assessment. Chapter 5, Engagement and Assessment Strategies, suggests a variety of interview formats and paper and pencil inventories for eliciting a religious/spiritual history and other information relevant to the process of spiritual assessment. It also describes indications and guidelines for the use of spiritual interventions and discusses the issue of engagement in the treatment process, including common countertransferences associated with spiritual dimension.

Strategies for incorporating psychotherapeutic and spiritual interventions, including spiritual practices, in spiritually-attuned psychotherapy and counseling are addressed in Chapters 6 and 7.

Chapter 6, Spiritually-Oriented Interventions with Individuals and Couples, describes and illustrates four different approaches to incorporating the spiritual dimensions with individuals and couples. These include psychodynamic strategies, cognitive behavioral strategies, focusing strategies and systemic strategies. Case studies illustrates each of these strategies.

Chapter 7, Incorporating Spiritual Disciplines, describes and illustrates several spiritual disciplines, practices and techniques that are appropriate for use in the context of psychotherapy. Spiritual practices are focused activities which foster spiritual qualities which can result in a balanced and disciplined lifestyle. These include prayer, meditation and contemplation, fasting, reading sacred writings, forgiveness and repentance, worship and ritual, fellowship, service, seeking spiritual direction, and moral instruction.

CHAPTER 5

Engagement and Assessment Strategies

Three phases of Spiritual Counseling were briefly described in Chapter 1. These phases are common across most psychotherapy systems, irrespective of orientation. Accordingly, they should have some value for any approach to psychotherapy and counseling that is spiritually attuned. The first phase focuses on engaging the client into the therapeutic process; the second phase involves performing a comprehensive assessment; while the third phase involves planning and implementing a strategy of healing, growth, and development. This chapter focuses on the first two phases, while Chapter 6 describes and illustrates the third phase.

☐ Engagement Strategies and Issues

In the first phase, the clinician focuses on establishing a therapeutic alliance and engaging the client in the treatment process. This alliance is most likely to develop in an atmosphere of caring, trust, faith, and hope. Of course, because a client attends sessions does not mean that growth and change will occur. The client's motivation and readiness for change must be assessed and dealt with if it is insufficient. Finally, the client's expectations for the process and outcomes for psychotherapy need to be articulated and clarified. It is usually quite early in the course of treatment that the client's need for and/or desire to focus on psychospiritual issues becomes evident.

Transference and countertransference phenomena can interfere with engagement. Facilitating the engagement process requires that clinicians recognize and deal forthrightly with countertransference issues. Issues surrounding prayer may or may not be countertransference issues, but they can potentially impact the engagement process. Accordingly, countertransference and the place of prayer in the process are discussed in the following sections.

Transference and Countertransference Issues

Transference and countertransference issues can arise in the course of incorporating the spiritual dimension in therapy. Countertransference can be manifested in several ways. These range from the therapist actively arguing with clients about spiritual doctrine and regarding it as destructive, to passively avoiding discussion of spiritual topics or labeling them as 'resistance' (Lovinger, 1984). Spero (1981) describes several other types of countertransference problems that can arise when religious or spiritual issues are involved. When the client and clinician share the same religious beliefs, there can be idiosyncratic or conflicting differences based on differing needs for religion in the client and clinician. For instance, the client might have expectations and fantasies of magical cure by the clinician or might even view the clinician as punitive, demanding, and judgmental as was a religious figure or parent in their past. The clinician, on the other hand, might experience countertransference reactions to the client that range from rescue fantasies to neurotic projections resulting in contemptuous feelings for the client. The clinician's own spiritual beliefs may result in rejecting or harshly judging clients who engage in an adulterous affair, persist in abusing substances, or refuse to alter lifestyles that are incompatible with their own spiritual principles.

Spero (1981) provides clinicians with seven strategies for managing countertransference issues that arise in these situations:

1. Develop an understanding of the client's neurotic and non-neurotic needs for religion and spirituality.
2. Identify neurotic forms of religious belief (e.g., the ways religion is used as a defense mechanism for aggressive drives) that reflect underlying psychological conflict and separate these immature forms of belief from mature forms that are adaptive.
3. Perform a self-examination in order to identify one's own neurotic needs for religion and spirituality, and for immature beliefs that arise from those needs. Then, recognizing how these are similar to or differ-

ent from the client's needs and beliefs will help the clinician to avoid or at least be conscious of countertransference reactions during therapy.

4. When experiencing negative feelings toward the client, attempt to recognize if overconcern or overidentification with the client is the cause for such feelings.

5. Avoid special treatment for clients with similar spiritual backgrounds. This should assist in maintaining therapeutic neutrality and objectivity.

6. Recognize the limits placed on therapeutic goals when religious commitments are similar since this may restrict one's ability to see how such commitments are used as unhealthy defenses by the client.

7. Avoid providing the client with one's own spiritual insights into the client's problems, as this can limit one's recognition of how the client's religious beliefs are involved in his or her neurotic conflict.

The Place of Prayer in the Treatment Context

Prayer is the most distinctive and characteristically spiritual of all activities associated with the spiritual dimension. It can have a significant impact, positively or negatively, on the engagement process. There are at least four different ways prayer can become a part of the treatment process: 1) the clinician may pray *for* the client's healing and well-being outside treatment sessions; 2) the clinician may pray silently *for guidance* about diagnostic and treatment issues as they come up in a session; 3) the clinician may allow or encourage the client to pray silently or aloud in the session; or, 4) the clinician may pray *with* the client during the treatment session.

Spiritually-attuned clients may expect that clinicians will pray *with* them in treatment sessions. Some clinicians believe that it is appropriate and useful to respond to such requests or even offer to pray with clients. Praying with clients in the context of psychotherapy and counseling is a controversial intervention, particularly for clients with severe emotional issues (Koenig & Pritchett, 1998). Incorporating this form of the spiritual dimension may have unpredictable consequences for the therapeutic relationship. Some clinicians may recoil at any mention of prayer in psychotherapy and view it as a clear violation of clinician–client boundaries. Unfortunately, at this time there are no research studies nor professional standards, nor a consensus among experts on guidelines to guide clinical practice. Prayer remains a delicate issue with psychotherapy clients because of the matter of boundary issues. Praying with clients can produce an intimacy that is threatening to both patient and therapist. Some experts express deep reservations about clinicians praying with clients in treatment sessions (Richards & Bergin, 1997).

In specific circumstances, a clinician may choose to pray with certain clients. But what are the benefits and risks of praying with clients? There are at least four benefits: 1) prayer can effect comfort and hope that can extend beyond the treatment session; 2) it can convey a sense of the clinician's caring and commitment for the client; 3) it can combat the client's sense of isolation and loneliness; and (4) it can enhance trust in the client-clinician relationship.

At least four risks are possible in praying with clients during a treatment session: 1) prayer could be dangerous in some circumstances, namely, for fragile clients with poor ego boundaries and a history of intimacy issues that prayer could activate; 2) it could threaten the therapeutic alliance; 3) it could adversely affect the client's psychological stability; and 4) It could disrupt the clinician's neutrality and objectivity, such as in some psychoanalytically-oriented psychotherapies (Koenig & Pritchett, 1998). In short, routinely praying with all clients is probably unwise and counterindicated. If the client insists on it and the clinician feels uncomfortable with the request, referral to a religious professional is a reasonable option.

Indications for Praying with Clients

Koenig and Pritchett (1998) list five *general indications* for determining the advisability of utilizing prayer as a treatment intervention. The five are: 1) the client clearly indicates that religion is an important way of coping with his or her problems; 2) the client and clinician are from the same religious background; 3) the client either asks for prayer or shows no hesitation when the clinician asks for permission to pray; 4) the client has sufficient ego strength, stability, and disturbance of boundaries is not an issue; and most important, 5) the situation indicates that prayer would help advance the goals of treatment.

What are appropriate *specific indications* for praying with client? These include 1) acute situational stressors such as the death or serious injury of a loved one; 2) deep personal disappointment such as marital separation or job loss; and 3) life-threatening medical illness such as a diagnosis of cancer or need for major surgery.

Prayer can also be helpful to clients struggling with chronic behavioral problems that seem impossible to overcome such as chronic substance use or compulsive gambling. It might also be helpful in counteracting the feeling of hopelessness that might otherwise paralyze further efforts to overcome the problem.

Protocol for Praying with Clients

Koenig and Pritchett (1998) offer the a protocol that they suggest is non-intrusive, non-offensive and minimizes risks of adverse consequences. The protocol is:

1. Assess whether prayer is congruent with the client's worldview. If so, the clinician might say: "Some clients find comfort in prayer while others do not. Would my praying with you over this situation be helpful to you, or do you feel that it would not be particularly helpful?" The client must be given clear and explicit permission to reject the offer for prayer without feeling uncomfortable or that he or she has they have disappointed the clinician. Even if the clinician has prayed with the client before, the same cautious approach should be taken each time a new occasion for prayer arises.
2. If the patient agrees and shows sincere interest in proceeding, then prayer might be conducted in the following manner. The prayer should be brief, lasting less than one minute, particularly if the clinician does the praying. It is preferable for client to do the praying, in which case the clinician can listen attentively and answer 'Amen' at the end of the prayer. By carefully listening to the client's prayer, the clinician might learn things about the client's motivation and priorities that may otherwise not be revealed.
3. If the client asks the clinician to pray, then the prayer should be general, supportive, affirming, and hopeful.
4. Finally, during a subsequent session, explore the client's reaction to the prayer, encouraging both negative and positive experiences.

☐ Assessment Strategies and Issues

The process of eliciting religious and spiritual concerns and developing an appropriate diagnostic and treatment requires specific knowledge and skills. A model curriculum in religion and spirituality has been adopted by the psychiatric profession for its residency training programs. It specifies the basic knowledge, skills, and attitudes as well as guidelines for completing a spiritual assessment (Larsen, Lu, & Swyers, 1996). Currently, no such curriculum or set of guidelines has been adopted for psychologists, social workers, or counselors. Nevertheless, until such guidelines are available, clinicians will continue to perform spiritual assessments based on whatever training or access to assessment methods and strategies is available to them. This section offers a number of methods and strategies for completing such an assessment.

The **assessment phase** of spiritually-attuned psychotherapy and counseling involves conducting a comprehensive assessment. Since transformation and self-transcendence are holistic processes, it is essential to assess the individual from a holistic perspective. This includes obtaining pertinent information on biological and somatic factors, psychological factors including affective and intellectual dimensions, social factors including family, cultural, and sociopolitical dimensions, as well as the moral and religious dimensions. Usually within the first session or two it is possible for a clinician to gather sufficient information to formulate a strategy for enhancing the process of psychospiritual growth. Data about the biological or somatic domain involves the present and past health status, treated and untreated medical conditions and response to such treatment. In the psychological realm, it is useful to elicit the individual's self-description and self-image, and information about the presence of persistent negative affects such as anger, fear, guilt, sadness, and defensiveness, as well as psychic conflicts and traumas. In the sociocultural domain it is useful to elicit information about the client's family of origin and nuclear family. Constructing a genogram or family tree can prove useful in tracing generational patterns of physical, psychological, and spiritual health and pathology. A brief review of functioning in school and in the workplace is useful, as well as an inquiry into social friendships and intimacies. Also, eliciting the presence or absence of childhood 'best friends' is useful in estimating past and current level of social and relational functioning. The clinician should clarify the client's attitudes and beliefs about religion and the spiritual dimension of life. In the spiritual domain it is useful to elicit data on the individual's religious and spiritual formation from early childhood to the present, including information on denominational affiliation(s); current spiritual disciplines and practices; image(s) of God; spiritual mentors along their journey; and an estimation of their level of faith development and conscience development should be elicited.

If they have had previous traditional psychotherapy, combined psychotherapy and medication management, pastoral counseling, or spiritual direction it is essential to review the outcomes of these efforts. The purpose of this assessment is twofold: first to assess their overall level of bio-psycho-socio-spiritual functioning and level of well-being, and second, to plan a strategy for healing and enhancing psychospiritual growth.

Assessing the Spiritual Dimension by Interviewing

It is presumed that an unbiased, systematic spiritual assessment of clients' spiritual life requires that clinicians be sufficiently aware of their own spiritual belief orientations. Furthermore, it is helpful, if not essential, to know something of the basic tenets of a given client's religious tradition. For example, in some clients it may be difficult to differentiate between delusions and compulsions and the basic beliefs and rituals of different spiritual traditions. If a clinician is unaware of these basic beliefs and rituals, it may be necessary for him or her to request that clients briefly describe their interpretation of these beliefs or rituals.

Reasons for Performing a Spiritual Assessment

There are several reasons for performing such an assessment (Richards & Bergin, 1997, pp. 172–175). Here are five key reasons: 1) understanding clients' spiritual orientations and communicating to clients that their entire life experience is of interest and value to the clinician; 2) determining the degree of health of clients' spiritual orientations and its impact on presenting problems and disturbances; 3) determining whether clients' spiritual beliefs and communities can be used as healing and coping resources; 4) determining whether clients' spiritual needs and concerns should be addressed in treatment; and 5) determining which spiritual interventions may be useful and effective.

Performing a Brief Spiritual Assessment

It is a basic contention of this book that a brief spiritual assessment should be performed on all clients. An increasing number of researchers and clinicians insist that, at a minimum, a brief spiritual assessment should be performed on all clients because of demonstrated health consequences of religiosity and spirituality (Gorsuch & Miller, 1999; Matthews, 1998). Routine screening questions about religion and spirituality can easily be incorporated into the initial evaluation and assessment process.

Matthews (1998) describes a very brief spiritual assessment he performs in all initial encounters with patients or clients. The three questions are:

1. Is religion or spirituality important to you?
2. Do your religious or spiritual beliefs influence the way you look at your problems and the way you think about your health?
3. Would you like me to address your religious or spiritual beliefs and practices with you? (p. 274)

If clients answer 'no' to the first question the clinician would ask if religion or spirituality were *ever* important to them. Matthews reasons that since research indicates that rejection of religion is associated with higher rates of substance-related disorders and a decline in self-satisfaction and happiness, this information may be a useful prognostic indicator. A positive answer to the third question is followed up to ascertain the client's preferences and expectations. Matthews has also added another question: "Are you part of a religious or spiritual community? "(Koenig & Pritchett, 1998, p. 327). This question is added between the second and third previously noted questions. Usually such a screening assessment can be completed in three minutes or less.

Performing a Full Spiritual Assessment

Indications for a Full Spiritual Assessment

A full spiritual assessment is indicated when: 1) the client declares that religious/spiritual issues are important in his or her life; 2) a spiritual issue or concern is evident in the presenting complaint; 3) the clinical issue involves morality and guilt; or 4) persistent concern regarding meaning or purpose in life are noted.

Elements of the Full Spiritual Assessment

The content of what should be included in a spiritual assessment has been variously described (Bullis, 1996; Gorsuch & Miller, 1999; Josephson, Larson & Juthani, 2000; Richards & Bergin, 1997). At a minimum, the following information should be included in a full or comprehensive assessment: 1) a detailed spiritual history including developmental factors relevant to religious and spiritual development; 2) involvement in a spiritual and religious community and the extent of social and spiritual support; 3) the client's God representation; 4) the role of prayer and meditation in the client's life; 5) the place of other spiritual practices and rituals in the client's life; and 6) specific values and beliefs held by the client.

Spiritual History.   A detailed spiritual history is the foundational element of the spiritual assessment. In most cases, the spiritual history follows from a review of the presenting complaint. In others, the clinician will need to initiate more specific inquiry. The detailed spiritual history is an assessment tool designed to collect relevant information about the influences and determinants of the client's spiritual life and well-being. Since there are significant differences among members of the same religion or denomination, knowing a client's religious affiliations is of limited value. More useful information is gleaned by examining how the client is spiritual, rather than the religious label attached to that spiritual system. Additional information can be gleaned when clients can describe how their spirituality affects their lives today; what ideas, book, persons, etc., have influenced their current spiritual attitudes; how they have changed from their spiritual orientations as children or young adults; and what spiritual conflicts they now address (Bullis, 1996).

The following are some basic questions useful in conducting a full spiritual history (cf. Bullis, 1996, for a more detailed description on taking a spiritual history) The clinician may choose to ask some or all of them early in the course of an initial interview.

- What was the spiritual tradition of your parents?
- Were they strict or lenient in their beliefs?
- And what effect does it have on you today?
- What were their most important spiritual beliefs?
- Did they pass these on to you? How?
- What is their main religious or spiritual identity?
- In which spiritual tradition were they raised?
- Have they remained with this orientation? Why or why not?
- What religious or spiritual issues, if any, have caused problems in your relationship?
- If resolved, how did you resolve them?
- If not resolved, how do they affect your relationship?
- If you have children, do you and your significant other agree or disagree on the spiritual orientation with which they are being raised?

Involvement in a Spiritual Community.   Once clients have identified themselves with a spiritual tradition, the clinician should inquire about any involvement in a religious or spiritual community. If they are involved in such a community, relevant questioning examines the level of support received from the community and whether there have been changes in their relationship to the community.

God Representation.   Since both research and clinical practice reveal the significance of one's God representation for health and well-being, it should be elicited. Begin with the question: "What is your image of God?" For most clients, especially spiritual seekers, this line of inquiry provides invaluable information. Clients are encouraged to describe this image (i.e., 'judge,' 'a force,' 'friend,' 'policeman,' etc.) and how they define their relationship to this entity. The *God Image Inventory* (Lawrence, 1997) is a psychometric instrument for assessing God representations in clinical and pastoral contexts based on Rizzuto's theory (1979).

The Role of Prayer.   An assessment of the role of prayer, or attempts to communicate with the transcendent, can be included in this line of questioning. For the spiritual seeker, more extensive review of theologic matters may be indicated, if it is clear elaboration of such concepts will further elucidate the clinical problems under consideration.

Other Spiritual Practices.   Inquire about other spiritual practices beyond prayer. Which ones do they practice? How often and for how long? What impact or effect have these practices had?

Basic Values and Beliefs.   Finally, ask about the client's basic values and beliefs. Such traditions have views on the meaning of illness and suffering, the moral and virtuous life, the healthy family and sources of spiritual authority (e.g., scriptures, religious teachings, and tenets) which may all be relevant to assess. Such core beliefs can powerfully determine an individual's behavior, and if the clinician does not inquire about them, an entire treatment process may be undermined.

Here are some questions for eliciting such values and beliefs:

- What are the basic spiritual values that you both wish to impart to your children?
- In what religious or spiritual tradition were you raised?
- Was your instruction strict or lenient?
- What values and ideas have stayed with you?
- How has your spiritual orientation changed since your upbringing?
- Why has it changed?
- What events or experiences helped to change you?
- What is your current religious or spiritual affiliation?
- What are its major beliefs and values?

Josephson et al. (2000) provide a description and rationale for questions about an individual's spiritual history or developmental antecedents, concept of God, the role of prayer or meditation, and the importance of religious/spiritual beliefs and practices. Table 5.1 lists a number of questions useful in performing an extended spiritual assessment.

Case Formulation

Developing a case formulation is the final stage of the spiritual assessment. Similar to other conditions which are the focus of clinical attention, a religious or spiritual issue or concern can be considered in one of three ways: 1) the spiritual issue or concern is a focus of treatment and the client has no psychiatric disorder; 2) the client has a psychiatric disorder but it is unrelated to the spiritual issue or concern, or 3) the client has a psychiatric disorder which is related to the spiritual issue or concern but

---

TABLE 5.1. Spiritual assessment questions

Screening questions

Is religion or spirituality an important part of your life?
    If 'yes' → How?
    If 'no' → Was it ever? → How?

Do religious or spiritual beliefs influence your life? (i.e., the way you look at your problems and the way you think about your self and health)
    If 'yes' → How?
    If 'no' → Why not?

Are you part of a religious or spiritual community?
    If 'yes' → How are you involved?
    If 'no' → Why not?

Are there spiritual needs you'd like me to address?
    If 'yes' → Which ones? → [follow up on preferences and expectations]
    If 'no' → Why is that?

Extended assessment questions

When you were growing up how did you learn about spiritual/ religious matters? → [follow up]

What's your concept of God or a higher power? → [follow up]

What's the role of prayer or meditation in your life? → [follow up]

What religious/spiritual beliefs and values are important to you? → [follow up]

What religious rituals or spiritual practices are important to you? → [follow up]

Based on material from Josephson, Larson, & Juthani, 2000; Koening & Pritchard, 1998; and Matthews, 1998.

that issue or concern is sufficiently severe to warrant independent consideration. The relationship of the spiritual or religious issue or concern to psychiatric disorders may become more, or less, relevant in the course of disorder and planned therapeutic interventions (Josephson et al., 2000).

Spiritual Genograms and Maps

A spiritual genogram is a diagram of the important spiritual persons and influences, while a spiritual map includes much of the same information as a genogram but depicts it in terms of the spiritual journey the client has traveled. Both describe what Bullis (1996) calls a client's 'spiritual biopsychosocial geography.'

Spiritual genograms are the spiritual equivalent of family genograms which depict the emotional and psychological attachments and stresses within the family system. Similarly, spiritual genograms chart a spiritual family tree and include spiritual mentors or teachers, significant ideas or passages from sacred writings or other sources, and key events such as conversion or other peak experiences that have shaped the client's spiritual orientation. It is most useful if this genogram indicates how these key persons, ideas, and events have changed, modified, or negated earlier spiritual positions.

Similarly, spiritual maps depict the contours of the spiritual journey. They accomplish in geographic analogy what spiritual genograms accomplish in genetic analogy, and can be as varied as those depicting their journeys. Most maps will include a time line or a space line of their spiritual journey showing important events and places of the journey, such as the client's first communion, confirmation, or bar mitzvah; the 'born again' experience; or some other intense and significant spiritual awakening. Usually, the journey will begin at an early age or with a crucial spiritual event. The map might include photographs of significant events and people, and may include mementos, tokens, or remembrances of the spiritual journey.

Assessing the Spiritual Dimension with Inventories

A number of instruments have been designed to measure various aspects of the religious and spiritual dimension. However, only a few of these appear to have clinical utility for spiritual assessment. These instruments are not meant to replace the spiritual assessment interview, but rather to supplement it. Six of these instruments will be briefly reviewed in this section.

Spiritual Well-Being Scale

Spiritual well-being is conceptualized as a personal experience related to spiritual health and spiritual maturity. That is, spiritual health and spiritual maturity appear to be enduring underlying states that are expressed in the experience(s) of spiritual well-being. The *Spiritual Well-Being Scale* (Ellison, 1994) is a 20-item instrument which can be quickly completed and scored. Its three subscales—overall spiritual well-being, existential well-being, and religious well-being—can be used as a starting point for exploring the client's spiritual dimension. The instrument's nonsectarian content makes it appropriate for clients with diverse spiritual beliefs. Individual test items (e.g., "I don't find much satisfaction in private prayer with God") can be used to explore spiritual attitudes pertinent to the client's presenting and emerging spiritual issues and concerns.

Spiritual Health Inventory

The *Spiritual Health Inventory* was developed by Veach and Chappel (1992). This 18-item instrument purportedly measures four domains—personal spiritual experience, spiritual well-being, sense of harmony, and personal helplessness. Items include: "It is my experience that developing and maintaining spiritual health requires work and effort" and "I have had a spiritual experience or a sense of spiritual awakening." While only preliminary psychometric data has been reported on this instrument, it may have some value in the spiritual assessment process.

Index of Core Spiritual Experience

The *Index of Core Spiritual Experience*, also called INSPIRIT, was developed by Kass, Friedman, Leserman, Zuttermeister, and Benson (1991). It purports to assess two core elements of spirituality: a personal conviction of the existence of God, and one's perception of an internalized relationship with God. It consists of seven items including an item about involvement with spiritual practices. Although more limited in scope than the *Spiritual Well-Being Scale*, initial results with the *Index of Core Spiritual Experience* suggest that it may provide a quick and helpful method for assessing the spiritual dimension, particularly as a take-off point for discussing clients' experience of God.

God Image Inventory

The *God Image Inventory* is an 8-scale, 156-item instrument that measures image of God, developed by Lawrence (1997) for clinical and pastoral use with individuals. A 6-scale, 72-item version and a 3-scale, 36-item version called the *God Image Scales* are briefer research versions of the *God Image Inventory*. The *God Image Inventory* and *God Image Scales* are based on Rizzuto's (1979) distinction between the God concept and the God image. Both instruments assess belonging (Presence and Challenge scales), goodness (Acceptance and Benevolence scales) and control (Influence and Providence scales). The scales of the *God Image Inventory* have demonstrated adequate internal reliability and validity. Standards have been developed on a sample of 1,580 U.S. adults, but appear to be applicable only for Christians. A computerized version is reportedly available.

The Spiritual Transcendence Scale

Spiritual Transcendence is defined as the capacity to stand outside one's immediate sense of time and place and view life from a large, more objective perspective. It involves a synchronicity to life, a sense of the interconnectedness, commitment, and shared responsibility with others. The *Spiritual Transcendence Scale* was developed by Piedmont (1999) and consists of three subscales: Universality, Prayer Fulfillment, and Connectedness. Items such as "I find inner strength and/or peace from my prayers or meditations," "I believe that there is a larger meaning to life," and "It is important for me to give something back to my community" are representative of these subscales. It is a 24-item scale which has been shown to be independent of the qualities contained in the Five-Factor Model of Personality (FFM; i.e., as measured by instruments such as the NEO PI-R, Costa & McCrae, 1990). It is noteworthy that consensual validation was obtained for this scale by means of observer ratings suggesting that aspects of spirituality are not merely private phenomena. The reliability and validity data reported reflects the robustness of this instrument, and gives credence to Piedmont's contention that spirituality is distinct from personality, at least as defined by the FFM.

The Spiritual Experience Index

The *Spiritual Experience Index* (SEI) consists of 38 questions and is answered on six-point likert scales. The SEI was developed to assess spiritual maturity from an object relations, developmental perspective. The SEI intended to correlate with a five-stage model of spiritual maturity or faith. The stages are: 1) Egocentric faith, dominated by splitting; 2) Dogmatic faith, characterized by rules of fairness and clearly defined obligations, defensive and utilitarian use of doctrine; 3) Transitional faith, religious searching and doubting; 4) Reconstructed internalized faith, characterized as a more internal, differentiated and personally integrating religious system; and 5) Transcendent faith for which Genia (1991) lists ten criteria. Both of these instruments are helpful to begin to conceptualize the functional, interactive nature of the God-family relationship.

☐ Concluding Note

Engagement and assessment were described as the first two phases of the treatment process. Since countertransference and the place of prayer in the context of treatment can significantly impact the engagement process, they were discussed in some detail. Hopefully, the guidelines for dealing with countertransference and the indications and protocol for praying with clients will prove useful to clinicians attempting to incorporate the spiritual dimension in their work. Similarly, several suggestions for performing a spiritual assessment were detailed and should be useful to clinicians who have little or no experience incorporating the spiritual dimension.

The next two chapters focus on the third phase of the treatment process—intervention. Chapter 6 describes and illustrates different ways of incorporating spiritual interventions within sessions, while Chapter 7 describes and discusses a number of spiritual practices and techniques that can be useful adjuncts in the practice of spiritually-attuned psychotherapy and counseling.

☐ References

Bullis, R. (1996). *Spirituality in social work practice*. Washington, DC: Taylor & Francis.

Costa, P., & McCrae, R. (1990). Personality disorders and the five-factor model of personality. *Journal of Personality Disorders, 4*, 362–371.

Ellison, C. (1994). *Spiritual well-being scale*. Nyack, NY: Life Advance.

Genia, V. (1990). Religious development: A synthesis and reformulation. *Journal of Religion and Health, 29*, 85–99.

Genia, V. (1991). The Spiritual Experience Index: A measure of spiritual maturity. *Journal of Religion and Health, 30*, 337–347.

Gorsuch, R., & Miller, W. (1999). Assessing spirituality. In W. Miller (Ed.), *Integrating spirituality into treatment. Resources for practitioners* (pp. 47–64). Washington, DC: American Psychological Association.

Josephson, A., Larson, D., & Juthani, N. (2000). What's happening in psychiatry regarding spirituality? *Psychiatric Annals, 5*.

Kass, J., Friedman, R., Leserman, J., Zuttermeister, P., & Benson, H. (1991). Health outcomes and a new index of spiritual experience. *Journal for the Scientific Study of Religion, 30*, 203–211.

Koenig, H., & Pritchett, J. (1998). Religion and psychotherapy. In H. Koenig (Ed.), *Handbook of religion and mental health* (pp. 323–336). San Diego: Academic Press.

Larsen, D., Lu, F., & Swyers, J. (1996). *Model curriculum for psychiatric residency training programs: Religion and spirituality in clinical practice: A course outline*. Rockville, MD: National Institute for Healthcare Research.

Lawrence, R. T. (1997). Measuring the image of God: The God image inventory and the God image scales. *Journal of Psychology & Theology, 25*(2), 214–226.

Lovinger, R. (1984). *Working with religious issues in therapy*. New York: Jason Aronson.

Matthews, D. (1998). *The faith factor: Proof of the healing power of prayer*. New York: Viking.

Piedmont, R. (1999). Does spirituality represent the sixth factor of personality? Spiritual transcendence and the five-factor model. *Journal of Personality, 67*(6), 985–1013.

Richards, P. S., & Bergin, A. (1997). *A spiritual strategy for counseling and psychotherapy*. Washington, DC: American Psychological Association.

Rizzuto, A. (1979). *The birth of the living God. A psychoanalytic study*. Chicago: University of Chicago Press.

Spero, H. (1981). Countertransference in religious therapists of religious patients. *American Journal of Psychotherapy, 35*, 565–575.

Veach, T., & Chappel, J. (1992). Measuring spiritual health. A preliminary study. *Substance Abuse, 13*, 139–147.

6
CHAPTER

Spiritually-Oriented Interventions with Individuals and Couples

This chapter surveys four different approaches and sets of intervention strategies for incorporating the spiritual dimensions when working with individuals and couples. These include variants of cognitive-behavioral therapy and psychoanalytic psychotherapy as well as the focused-experiential approach and a couples or relationship dynamics approach. These represent four different ways of conceptualizing and incorporating the spiritual dimension in psychotherapy. Before turning to these approaches, the indications and contraindications for the use of such interventions is briefly discussed.

☐ Indications and Contraindications

Indications

The use of spiritually-oriented interventions are more likely to be effective in some situations and circumstances rather than in others. Spiritually-oriented interventions refers to both psychotherapeutic strategies, methods and techniques utilized within sessions and also spiritual practices and techniques prescribed for inter-session usage. Chapter 7 details a number of spiritual practices and techniques. Spiritually-oriented interventions appear to be warranted in the following situations and circumstances:

1. the client specifically asks for or consents to discussing spiritual issues and/or incorporating spiritual interventions.
2. the client has the capacity to consent and to collaborate in the treatment involving a spiritual intervention.
3. the spiritual issue or concern is related to the client's presenting problem.

Contraindications

Clients

In the absence of empirical data but based on clinical experience, Richards and Bergin (1997) have provided clinicians with some useful guidelines for evaluating the appropriateness of including spiritually-oriented interventions in the course of treatment. Table 6.1 lists various absolute and relative contraindications. Absolute contraindications refers to situations in which the intervention is not warranted and may prove harmful, whereas relative contraindications refers to situations in which the use of an intervention would be too risky, unlikely to be effective or otherwise inadvisable.

TABLE 6.1. Absolute and relative contraindications for spiritually-focused interventions

---

Absolute contraindications
- clients' unwillingness to participate in such interventions
- clients who are psychotic (i.e., delusional)
- spiritual issues are clearly not relevant to clients' presenting problems
- underage clients without parental permission to discuss religious issues or use spiritual interventions

Relative contraindications
- young children and adolescents
- severely psychologically disturbed
- antireligious or nonreligious
- spiritual immaturity
- spirituality is irrelevant to the presenting problems
- perceive God as distant and condemning
- deferring or passive religious problem-solving style

Based on material from Richards & Bergin, 1997.

Clinicians and Treatment Settings

Richards and Bergin (1997) also speculate that "therapist-initiated, denominationally specific, religiously explicit, and in-session spiritual interventions are probably more risky than client-initiated, ecumenical, religiously implicit, and out of-session interventions" (p. 253). Furthermore, they suggest such interventions are likely to be more risky in government-supported settings than in private and religious settings; if the therapeutic alliance is weak; if there is low therapist–client religious value similarity; and if therapists lack multicultural and religious sensitivity and awareness, have limited denominational expertise, or are spiritually immature.

☐ Cognitive Behavioral Approaches

Cognitive-behavioral therapy appears to offers a treatment approach that is well suited to the assessment and modification of all forms of belief, including religious beliefs, as they affect the psychological and spiritual health and well-being of individuals (Propst, 1988, 1996). That is because the theoretical perspective of cognitive therapy is a flexible therapeutic framework which can include the spiritual dimension as an active part of the therapeutic process. Although certain intervention strategies and techniques characterize the approach, the content of the therapy can vary greatly based on client need, the creativity of the clinician and what research indicates to be efficacious for the symptom or concern in question. Propst (1988) describes four intervention strategies in what she calls religious cognitive therapy. They are: 1) understanding the influence of cognition on emotion and behavior; 2) monitoring cognitions, including thoughts, beliefs, and assumptions; 3) challenging cognitions; and 4) cognitive restructuring and behavior modification. Each will be briefly described and then illustrated with a case example.

Understanding the Influence of Cognition on Emotion and Behavior

Since a basic tenet of cognitive therapy is that clients understand and believe that their thoughts and assumptions strongly influence their emotions and psychological well-being, it follows that religious clients and spiritual seekers probably should be given a spiritual rationale for this framework as well as a spiritual rationale for assessing their thoughts and assumptions. Accordingly, Propst suggests that theological reflections could be considered a strategy or tool of cognitive therapy.

Monitoring Cognitions, Including Thoughts, Beliefs, and Assumptions

Spiritual themes are, then, useful therapeutic tools that provide a motivational language to encourage clients to actively monitoring cognitions, including their thoughts, beliefs, and assumptions. This should help to overcome any initial resistance to therapy. With such a motivating language, many of the therapeutic tools originated by Beck such as the three column technique (Beck, Rush, Shaw, & Emery, 1979) can be made effective for spiritually-oriented clients.

Challenging Cognitions

After clients accept the value of monitoring cognitions and can apply this skill, the next process in cognitive therapy is the challenging and subsequent changing of thoughts and assumptions. Themes from most spiritual belief systems can play an important role in this process. Propst (1988) contends that these religious ideas can actually become cognitive restructuring techniques. For example, it is not uncommon for clients to have a cognitive schema in which any error, mistake, or a less than perfect solution to a problem can be catastrophic. Thus, they are more likely to have perfectionistic strivings rather than a basic problem-solving orientation toward life. This attitude may be intensified in some spiritual individuals because of the assumption that God expects perfection, which results in minimal risk taking and increased levels of anxiety and depression. Problem solving, on the other hand, means adopting the general orientation toward life that problems are a natural part of life and that coping with those problems is only a natural part of living. Since assumptions of perfectionism can be rooted in an individual's religious beliefs, Propst (1988, 1996) reasons that therapeutically challenging such perfectionistic schemas can be most effective when such schemas are linked to a client's religious beliefs. She notes that influential thinkers in most spiritual traditions emphasize that life is not perfect and that life has a tragic element, and that believers will rarely be problem-free or even find a perfect solution to all their problems.

Cognitive Restructuring and Behavior Modification

The use of religious imagery is an additional cognitive restructuring technique that is helpful within a spiritual context. Propst (1996) understands images as an individual's responses rather than stimuli to which individuals respond. Furthermore, images can have a greater capacity than thoughts for intensifying traumatic memories and, thus, may allow clients to focus more fully on emotionally laden ideas. Accordingly, she has found that, with Christian clients, using images of Jesus in calling forth problematic, stressful scenes (such as those resulting from posttraumatic stress responses) has been useful for many clients (Propst, 1988). For example, Christian female clients with abuse histories are often able to more easily experience the image of the abuse when they imagined Jesus with them in the image. The meaning of the image begins to change at the point that can visualize Jesus present in that image (Propst, 1988, pp. 130–138). Such an ameliorating of the negative intensity of the image may permit the client to more fully work through the terrifying aspects of the images and their meanings. Techniques of thought stopping, cognitive rehearsal, and confrontation of dysfunctional forms of thinking complement the use of biblical and theological reflection in the examination of core beliefs and assumptions. Finally, behavior modification methods have also been found useful.

The effectiveness of cognitive-behavioral therapy appears to be enhanced if aspects of the client's religious belief system are used to provide not only a motivation for self-examination, but also a challenge to some of the client's dysfunctional schemas. Usually, clients are asked to view their religious and spiritual beliefs somewhat differently. Other times, they are asked to pay attention to aspects of their religious beliefs that have previously been ignored; for example, the notion of the triune God, the Trinity, is an appropriate model for respect and mutuality in interpersonal relationships such as marriage.

Finally, Propst (1988) indicates that the disconfirmation of clients' dysfunctional beliefs are usually supported by the religious or spiritual authorities when queried by clients. She notes this is especially the case when clinicians have been careful to stay within the clients' religious tradition. However, when clients may find themselves in a conflict between the clinician and their religious community, Propst (1988) notes that such clients find other congregations within the same faith that offer them more support. A few clients will drop out of therapy. However, this is rare if the clinician has been careful to attempt to stay within the bounds of the individual's spiritual tradition when suggesting reinterpretations.

Case Example

Propst described the application of this approach to a female Christian client presenting loneliness and crying over an extended period of time (Propst, 1993). This client's only reported social outlet was involvement in church activities. Yet, she was extremely fearful of social contacts, and devastated by even mild social criticism. She met criteria for chronic depression and avoidant personality disorder.

Since the client embodied the cognitive schema that any type of negative emotions, social criticism, or uncomfortable circumstances were unbearable, Jesus was portrayed in therapy as one who chose suffering to accomplish a purpose: he was not a passive victim, but rather a courageous person who laid down his life and experienced pain for a purpose. It was emphasized that he put himself in difficult situations with possible negative consequences. Biblical illustrations provided valuable sources of inspiration and aided in the cognitive restructuring for this client. They were not imposed on the client but, rather, were used to reflect her predominant faith orientation as a believer who viewed Jesus as the model for human perfection.

When she admitted believing that it was always easier to avoid pain, including the pain of possible rejection, she was asked whether Jesus held that belief. She responded 'No.' Propst then underscored that Jesus had made the choice to go to the cross, and that facing that pain resulted in a transformation, his Resurrection. The client responded that this was a new understanding for her since she had always believed that the Christian ideal was to avoid all pain.

Consistent with the spiritual beliefs of individuals with avoidant personality disorder, she firmly believed that negative feelings were bad and that, since she experienced such feelings, she must be unhealthy (Propst, 1992). Applying Beck's three-column technique (Beck et al., 1979), she was asked to rate her belief in the notion that Jesus was vulnerable and in pain, but still a healthy human person. She rated it as 100 percent. Then she was asked to rate the belief that if she was vulnerable and in pain, she could also be a healthy person. Initially, she rated it as only 10 percent. Soon there was a recognition response, then she smiled and said she was expecting more of herself than she did of Jesus.

By means of this strategy the client was also able to confront her highly critical, overbearing, and possessive parents. In addition, she also undertook the challenge of making social relationships. Prior to the completion of treatment she had established a romantic relationship. Although initially finding the relationship rather threatening, she began to approach it with the thought that being a Christian means risking the pain of rejection (Propst, 1993).

☐ Psychoanalytic Approaches

Rizzuto (1979, 1991, 1996) describes an object relations approach to the spiritual dimension that emphasizes the client's God representation. The reader is referred to Chapter 2 of this book for an extended discussion of the object relations perspective and God representations. A brief sketch of the formation of this representation is given followed by its therapeutic implications and application. A case example then illustrates this approach.

God representations are transitional phenomena which serve the same function in relation to God that they serve with other objects. Representations permit the mind to know existing realities. For example, without the representation of the breast or of the mother, the infant has no means to know the mother. However, neither the mother nor the breast she provides is the representation. Similarly, the God sought for by the spiritual seeker should not be confused with the representation of God. Representations belong to different layers of reality. The God representation is the psychic means the mind has to seek God and its developmental and dynamic sources are unconscious and not accessible without psychic exploration. God, however, appears to the spiritual seeker as the object of conscious belief as an existing being beyond the limits of the mind.

Spiritual practices and religious elements such as prayers, scriptures, and ritual are also part of the dialectic processes of attachment and separation from parents. Each carries deep emotions and the potential for integration or rejection. With psychotherapeutic exploration their unconscious motivational and dynamic sources can be revealed.

The affective component of spiritual experience is its main source of personal meaning and is rooted in all relational exchanges extending from the beginning of life to the moment when it occurs. Thus, "all encounters with God, as with any other person, are preceded and conditioned by the psychic structure and by the momentary psychic reality of the person who is having the experience. . . . The final shape of the experience of God is always the result of complex psychic compromises between available representations, accepted and rejected feelings and wishes, superego pressures, and the effort at self-integration aided by defensive maneuvering" (Rizzuto, 1996, p. 419).

This formulation of the formation of God representations suggests that every child who has grown up in a religious culture will come to treatment with some conscious representation of God. Even though religion may be irrelevant to the person coming for psychotherapy, the clinician must not forget that in most children the God representation has played a psychic role during development and that when it emerges it may be fruitfully explored.

Rizzuto (1996) notes that three types of clients can be encountered in therapy: (a) seekers and believers for whom their belief is not a problem, (b) nonbelievers who are at peace with their religious situation and accept the treatment without any religious considerations, and (c) seekers who are concerned about their religion and fear that therapy may change their faith or their moral commitments.

Therapeutic Strategies

How does such analytically-oriented psychotherapy proceed? It begins with a detailed spiritual assessment. Rizzuto (1996) advocates the taking of a comprehensive spiritual assessment, which she refers to as a 'religious history.' This assessment should include the religious affiliation of each parent, the family's religious practices and attitudes, as well as its degree of integration within the spiritual community. It is also important to elicit the individual's major spiritual landmarks (i.e., baptism, circumcision, bar mitzvah, confirmation, etc.) including their private and public meaning. Finally, the client's current involvement in and attitudes toward religious institutions, beliefs, and spiritual practices is elicited. In short, this type of spiritual assessment reveals the client's perceptions of the significant other and self in the spiritual development process.

The clinical significance of such a spiritual assessment is enormous. For instance, in eliciting a social-developmental history a client reports that her father was a good provider for the family, but moments later in the spiritual assessment indicates that God never answer her prayers. Noting this object discrepancy, the astute clinician might speculate that the client needs to maintain the idealization of her father, whereas God can tolerate her angry complaints.

Rizzuto (1996) contends that clinicians should not reveal their religious affiliation, beliefs, or any other personal information. Witholding such information maximizes the potential the development of a transference based on the client's psychic processes, unrestricted by factual data. Nevertheless, the clinician must show respect for the clients's spiritual experiences, spiritual concerns, doubts, moral quivering, and commitments.

Does the God representation change in the course of this type of analytic treatment? Rizzuto (1989) would say that it most likely will change since it is a process of self-transformation. It is a "transformation of the ways of receiving own's own experiences and self-representations, questioning them, examining them, attending to them, being amazed that they can be looked at from another angle. As you do that you have a new self representation" (Rizzuto, 1989, p. 3). She also speculates that the God representation is transformed even if God is not discussed in the course of treatment. She bases this on the basic assumption of object relations theory that one cannot change oneself without changing one's view of others. Even though the individual may not be consciously aware of the transformation of his or her God representation, "it may remain quietly in the background and at the moment when you may have the need for a God it may reappear. . . . a conscious transformation of the God representation" (Rizzuto, 1989, pp. 3–4).

A number of other therapeutic strategies are useful in this approach which some call the 'transitional figure method.' These include the traditional psychoanalytic method of processing: clarification, confrontation, interpretation, and working through as well as guided imagery and dream analysis.

Case Example

Jason is a 46-year-old single white male who presented for psychotherapy with insomnia and difficulty concentrating. While he did not meet criteria for a clinical depression he appeared to be experiencing a delayed grief reaction. His father had died of inoperable cancer 14 months ago, and it appeared Jason did not begin the mourning and grieving process until the first anniversary of his death some two months ago.

Jason's developmental and spiritual history was instructive. He was baptized and reared by fairly strict and devout Catholic parents who had high expectations for their only child. Their expectation was that Jason would become a priest and if not, would work for and assume leadership of the family printing business when his father retired. However, Jason's only desire was to become a high school science teacher. During elementary school, Jason found himself striving to please his teachers and became almost obsessed with the idea of 'saving his soul' through achievement and by being a good boy. He recalled that his father was emotionally unavailable and never seemed satisfied with his achievements. And, he was embarrassed to add that he was then, and now, as or more critical than his father. During these years Jason's view of God was that of taskmaster and judge.

There was considerable tension between father and son throughout Jason's teen years. While he continued to complain to his mother that he felt unloved by his father, his mother's only response was "your father does care about you." But since he didn't feel it, Jason couldn't believe his mother. When he was in college it became clear that he would not fulfill his father's dream. As a result, several years of near-silence ensued between father and son. Nevertheless, Jason became a well respected teacher at the same high school he himself had attended. He also volunteered as teacher in his church's Sunday morning religious education program. Curiously, in this capacity he wrote, illustrated, and published a small book entitled "God Loves All the Little Children." While somewhat interested in women, he never married, although was never sure why he believed he was meant to remain a bachelor.

Over the course of 34 sessions Jason was able to sufficiently work through his grief and gain a greater perspective on and appreciation of his father. The brief course of psychotherapy helped him deal with the overpowering effect of his relationship with his father. He came to understand his grief as a call to deal with the unmet needs in his early life. Rather early in therapy, Jason began to realize that his failure to get his father's love and approval did not mean that he was unloved or unlovable. He discovered that not only had his grandfather deeply cared about him but so did his father, who also bragged about him to the grandfather. He had identified with his father and judged himself as sternly as he always did. Somewhat later, he began to see that remaining a bachelor was his solution for both obeying his father, at least in part, (i.e., priests don't marry), while at the same time pursuing the career he wanted. Furthermore, he discovered that his unconscious belief that the God of his feelings was as harsh as he and impossible to please, while the God of his conscious belief was quite different. He came to believe in a God who loved him. And, in the process, a gradual change in his God representation occurred.

A transforming experience involved spending a long afternoon alone with his 87-year-old paternal grandfather. Whereas he had previously felt unwelcome by his grandfather, this day was different. During this afternoon, his grandfather brought out a family photo album and reminisced over pictures of Jason's birth and baptismal ceremony. He pointed out how proud Jason's father was of his son, and casually mentioned that it was like that all time. When Jason queried his grandfather about his statement, he learned that his father regularly told the grandfather, with pride, about his son's life and achievements, especially his many academic and teaching awards. When Jason sadly said he had no idea his father felt this way, his grandfather began to tear up and said: "Son, the men in this family never learned how to show their love and appreciation to those they really cared about." For the first time Jason came to understand that his father really cared for him but could not show it directly.

Later, as therapy focused on his criticalness, Jason recalled an incident that occurred two month's before his father died. While driving his father to a chemotherapy appointment, Jason became impatient at a slowly moving car that he could not get around. He repeatedly honked the car horn and began the kind of name-calling that he had learned from his father. Rather gently his father pointed out that there were elderly occupants in the other car and that he, the father, was in no hurry. After relaying this experience in therapy he began to cry when it was interpreted that perhaps Jason's father was growing and changing even as he was dying. As this was further clarified and interpreted, Jason came to understand and accept that the angry, critical image he had of his father was also changing. As treatment terminated, Jason's grief work was well under way and his representation of God had been transformed to that of a proud father.

☐ Experiential Focusing Approach

The Experiential Focusing Method which was developed by Eugene Gendlin (1969, 1981) is a useful psychospiritual intervention strategy for working with issues related to the spiritual dimension. Gendlin's theory of experiencing (1969) and his Experiential Focusing Method (Gendlin, 1969, 1981), hereafter called 'focusing,' have been applied to the process of spiritual growth in psychotherapy and counseling by Hinterkopf (1994, 1998).

Hinterkopf (1994, 1998) suggests a number of indications for utilizing focusing in helping clients integrate their spiritual experiences. For example, focusing can help clients who have had difficulty getting in touch with the spiritual dimension because of negative experiences with religious practices during childhood. Focusing can be used to work through such blocks and to integrate the positive aspects of their past religious experiences. It can also deepen and develop spiritual experiences that already exist. Furthermore, it can foster new spiritual experiences.

Focusing is a process of paying attention to something unclear in one's experience, and letting it unfold into new, explicit meanings. When the process has been carried forward, it involves psychospiritual growth. Although focusing is a natural, flowing process, it is frequently taught in six steps (Gendlin, 1981). This process can be guided by the clinician within the session prescribed as a spiritual technique to be practiced between sessions.

Step 1. Here, the client takes an inventory of presently felt problems or issues and notes the inner experience of each issue. As each issue is identified, the client imagines setting each problem outside to perceive it more clearly and to feel better physically in order to work on it. Then one issue is chosen as a point of focus. It is usually the problem that is felt most strongly. Within the treatment setting, clients typically begin by discussing a chosen issue, and thus, the clinician may omit Step 1 and begin with Step 2 at the appropriate time.

Step 2. Now, the client is instructed to attend to the 'felt sense' of the issue. The felt sense is multifaceted, involving emotional tones and qualities, bodily sensations, and felt meanings; it can also involve images, movements, sounds, and smells. Initially, it is unclear and vague, like the uncomfortable feeling individuals experience leaving home and realizing they forgot something but are uncertain as to what it might be.

Step 3. Here, the client finds words or images to describe the emotional qualities of the felt sense, such as, 'empty,' 'tense,' or 'expanding.'

Step 4. At this step the client determines whether the words describing the felt sense are the best words to describe the felt sense at the present time. It may be changed or other words added to more accurately describe the felt sense. At times, resonating may simply involve being with the felt sense.

Step 5. The clinician may suggest that the client ask the felt sense an open-ended question. Usually, asking such an open-ended question brings new meanings for the client, such as, "What leaves you feeling this way?" The client directs the question to the felt sense and continues to attend to it, waiting for an answer. Hinterkopf (1998) notes that an answer tends to emerge in a minute or less. When a new felt meaning arises the feeling changes resulting in a 'felt shift' which is a physiological change in the client bringing a sense of relief or a release of life energy; this can be likened to the relief experienced when remembering the forgotten item. A felt shift indicates that psychospiritual growth has occurred.

Step 6. Finally, this step involves integrating the answer that elicits the felt shift. To help the client receive an answer, the clinician affirms a client's felt shift. This can be accomplished by suggesting that the client take time to notice the felt shift and the answer that came with it, by body language such as sitting more upright or looking more interested, or by adding a note of excitement to voice tone.

As noted earlier, the focusing process can be used inside or outside the treatment setting. Outside the treatment setting, Steps 2 through 5 are usually recycled until a felt shift occurs. In the treatment setting, a selected few of the six steps can be utilized. Whatever the context, the client is taught the importance of keeping a number of attitudes while attending to feelings. A receptive attitude involves allowing feelings and symbols to enter into awareness rather than trying to control or force them to happen. Other attitudes include being friendly, kind, patient, and self-accepting. Focusing, which results in physiological release and increased life energy, is contrasted with a critical self-attitude, which results in increased tension and dullness. Furthermore, clients are taught to maintain some distance from their problems, such as by remaining close enough to achieve a felt sense but sufficiently removed to appreciate that one's life is greater than one's problems. Maintaining such a distance fosters the development of an 'observer self.'

Case Example

Hinterkoft (1998, pp. 56–57) illustrates the focusing process with a professional athlete who consulted her about his increasing levels of anxiety. He reported that he had always been healthy and successful in life. He also prided himself in maintaining tight control of his emotions during the course of his athletic career. However, six weeks before the consultation, he was diagnosed with hypertension and soon thereafter noted anxiety and worry that quickly increased. He could not really explain the source of his anxiety except that he was a little concerned about his hypertension. In answer to a query about recent stressors, he mentioned a fire in his home and the arrest of his adolescent, both occurring in the past year. But he insisted that neither incident had really fazed him. He repeatedly told himself that there was nothing to worry about, nevertheless, his anxiety and worry continued. He was agreeable to engage in the focusing process during that consultation.

In Step 1, the client was instructed to quiet his mind by becoming relaxed and to focus on his breathing. Then he was asked "What stands in the way of your feeling fine?" As he named each issue, he was asked, "How does this whole thing feel in your body now?" As he noticed how the house fire felt in his body, he realized that there was some remaining fear and sadness about the losses involved. He imagined setting aside this issue, along with the fear and sadness. As he thought about his son, he noticed his sadness and anger about the arrest. He imagined putting this issue, along with his sadness and anger, into a place where his son was staying. He then named the news from the doctor about his slightly high blood pressure. He said that it felt like a large, prickly ball with anxiety in it. As he imagined setting this issue, along with the anxiety, outside of himself, he breathed a sigh of relief. He then chose this issue for focusing.

In Step 2, he was asked to notice how the news from the doctor felt in his body. In Step 3, he reported that it still felt like the ball and that it could grow larger than himself. In Step 4, it was suggested that he stay with the thing and notice if he had just the right words to describe it. He replied that he had the right words, and that he also noticed darkness. In Step 5, he was asked "What was it about the news from your doctor that leaves you with a large, prickly, dark ball with anxiety in it?" He directed this question to the felt sense and waited a few moments. With a big sigh of relief he said, "the straw that broke the camel's back." Then, he realized he had repressed his feelings about the fire in his house and his son's arrest. He noted that his blood pressure was really not as important as the fire and his son's arrest. He reported feeling relieved and more relaxed, and no anxiety. In Step 6, it was suggested that he stay with and notice the feelings of relief and relaxation that came with the words 'the straw that broke the camels back.'

After he had experienced the felt shift and the focusing segment of the session was completed, he indicated that he was able to take his emotions more seriously. This client was able to transcend his former frame of reference and to reach out to more parts of himself; specifically, his emotional self. Later, he reported an increasing acceptance of the emotions of others in his life. This example illustrates how focusing often leads clients to experience their spirituality and, consequently, to undergo psychospiritual growth.

Focusing offers a nonjudgmental approach to the spiritual and religious dimensions in psychotherapy and counseling because it is process oriented. This means that, when using focusing, the clinician follows a client's feelings and how they unfold into new meanings, rather than focusing entirely on the contents of what the client is saying. Since words have special meanings or connotations for each person, the clinician follows the client's experiencing process rather than being concerned with the vocabulary that the client is using. After the focusing segment of the session has been completed, the clinician assists the client to examine the contents and clarify the vocabulary. In focusing, whatever is said or done is checked with the client's feelings to monitor changes in life energy associated with transcending one's former frame of reference (Hinterkopf, 1994).

☐ Relational Dynamics Approaches

The media typically depicts spiritual seekers as individuals—relationally unattached individuals—seeking enlightenment on the lonely spiritual journey. The reality is that many spiritual seekers are married or in committed relationships and have embarked on the spiritual journey together. Whether they present for individual or conjoint therapy these individuals or couples come with a system of spiritual beliefs and values that affect their relational thoughts, attitudes, and behaviors. Their spiritual orientation and religiosity influence various aspects of their lives together, from ideals about marriage to power, sexuality and intimacy, gender roles, and perhaps the raising and disciplining of children. As such, religion and spirituality can either serve as an important resource or a significant source of resistance for therapy. Accordingly, it is incumbent for psychotherapists to understand the dynamics of the spiritual beliefs and spiritual practices of the couples they treat.

Sperry and Giblin (1996) have described an eclectic approach to working with relational issues. Unlike the first three approaches described in this chapter, their approach easily accommodates spiritual practices. (Cf. Chapter 7 for a detailed description of other spiritual practices that can be incorporated in various psychotherapy and counseling approaches.) This section briefly overviews some of the spiritual beliefs impacting therapy, as well as assessment strategies and intervention strategies that have been found to be useful in working with such relationship issues. Two brief cases illustrate these strategies.

Relational Dynamics and Couples

All couples relationships can be characterized in terms of three metaconstructs that essentially combine and integrate concepts and principles of most marital and family therapy schools and approaches. These three constructs are: boundaries or inclusion, power or control, and intimacy (Fish & Fish, 1986).

Boundary issues in couples relationships are those which center around membership and structure: membership in the sense of who is involved in the couples subsystem and to what degree; structure in terms of the extent to which family members are part of but at the same time apart from the couple subsystem or family unit. Boundary issues also refer to interpersonal boundaries, specifically the degree of intrusiveness which will be accepted in the relationship. For a married couple, commitment to their relationship is a core boundary issue, as is the partners' relative commitments to jobs, extended family, friends, and other outside interests. For children, boundaries usually center around the sense of belonging to the family, while at the same time having a sense of being recognized as an individual.

Power issues include responsibility, control, discipline, decision-making, and role negotiation. Family interactions continually involve overt as well as covert attempts to influence decisions and behavior. Control or power issues are typically tied to issues of money, reward, and privileges. They also manifest themselves in more subtle ways such as escalation of conflict or one-upmanship in efforts to regulate another family member's behavior. Couple interaction also involves a struggle for control of the relationship in various ways. Essentially, the basic dynamic in marital conflict involves *who tells whom what to do* under certain circumstances. Both couple and family interactions range from positive to negative, emotionally, and from laissez faire to democratic to autocratic, politically. Thus, power becomes a meta-rule for all decisions about boundaries as well as intimacy. It determines which member or partner will pursue and which will distance, and how this is accomplished.

Intimacy issues in families are evident in areas such as self-disclosure, friendship, caring, and appreciation of individual uniqueness: Intimacy involves negotiating emotional as well as physical distance between partners or among family members. In either instance, the goal is to balance a sense of autonomy with feelings of belonging. When issues of affection in a family become a source of difficulty, they can be manifest in various ways ranging from complaints such as: "You don't understand my feelings," "I'm being taken for granted," or "The romance has gone out of the relationship."

Since these metaconstructs of boundaries, power, and intimacy are broad and inclusive they can be quite useful in assessing and formulating treatment issues with all couples and families, irrespective of religious affiliation or spiritual beliefs. The clinician may find it useful to think of the spiritual dimension in terms of these constructs..

Spiritual Beliefs and Practice Impacting Couples

Couples experiencing problems can derive significant benefits from their spiritual beliefs and practices. Clinicians can assist couples in utilizing their spiritual beliefs and practices as vehicles for growth. For instance, clinicians can encourage the development of spiritual practices that support family cohesion such as family rituals and customs associated with religious holidays. Furthermore, clinicians can encourage the replacement of religious practices that negatively impact growth and functioning with more positive religious behaviors and practices. For example, parents can be counseled to substitute limit setting and forgiveness for threats and guilt when talking to adolescents about attendance at religious services.

But which religious beliefs and practices are helpful to families and facilitate the therapeutic process, and which do not? A survey of family-life professionals' (Brigman, 1984) perceptions of religious beliefs and practices helpful to families identified the following: Beliefs such as love, faith, hope, forgiveness, grace, reconciliation, relationship to God, and divine worth of persons were reported as helpful. Similarly, these professionals identified loving, caring, sharing, giving to others, taking responsibility, and shared religious observances as lifestyles or behaviors that helped strengthen families. Furthermore, these professionals perceived that the social support and networking that religious groups and organizations provide can greatly strengthen families. Brigman (1992) believes that such affiliations not only reduce loneliness and isolation with a feeling of belonging and acceptance, but also ease the burden of guilt and contribute to a sense of hope.

Several studies have demonstrated a positive relationship between marital satisfaction and spiritual well-being and/or religious maturity. Giblin (1993) proposed that in therapeutic context the affective, cognitive, and behavioral shifts from marital conflict to marital satisfaction are potentially mediated by the couple's spiritual resources, and that there is a sense in which the dynamics accompanying marital conflict are the direct inverse of a marital spirituality.

On the other hand, some religious attitudes can be detrimental to families (Pruyser, 1977). Religious beliefs and practices that could be harmful to families were also identified by family-life professionals in Brigman's (1984) study. These included rigid doctrine that is insensitive to human need, negativity regarding issues like family planning, sexuality, divorce and remarriage, and an overemphasis on concepts such as sin, a judgement leading to guilt feelings and low self-esteem. Other harmful beliefs and practices identified were the promotion of traditional, patriarchal sex roles, a bias toward the indissolubility of marriage on any grounds, and an emphasis on the individual to the exclusion of emphasis on the family particularly by activities that separate family members (Brigman, 1984).

Just as it is important for the clinician working with couples to evaluate whether spiritual beliefs and practices contribute to integration and growth or disintegration, so too must the clinician ascertain the couple's or family's expectations and perceptions of therapy. Generally speaking, the more orthodox or conservative their religious beliefs, the more sensitized and concerned they are about clinicians attacking their beliefs or encouraging them to go against their religious beliefs or the standards of the religious group to which they belong (Brigman, 1992; Koltko, 1990). Such perceptions and expectations are less likely to be present among those with less conservative beliefs, irrespective of creed.

☐ Strategies for Assessing the Spiritual Dimension

Clinicians need to be able to accurately assess the influence of spirituality and religion in a couple or family's life. Is the valence negative with the spiritual contributing to withheld emotions (e.g., anger is not to be felt or expressed), distorted thought (e.g., crises are punishment from God), or dysfunctional behavior (e.g., the married man who is about to "give it all up" including spouse and children to "follow the Lord?") On the other hand, is the valence of the religious positive but underused? That is, might the religion be better used in the service of therapeutic change and growth?

Specific Assessment Strategies

The clinician might begin by inquiring about the place of God, religion, church/community, prayer, and time in the clients' lives. He or she may ask about the felt/thought place of God/religion/spirituality in dealing with the issues that bring the couple to therapy and to the eventual resolution of these problems. The clinician wants to understand the degree to which religion/spirituality influences feelings, thoughts, and behaviors in the system, ranging from no influence, to some influence but basically outside the system, to some influence on behavior and/or thoughts, to an encompassing influence on all three dimensions of feelings, thoughts, and behaviors (DiBlasio, 1988; Giblin, 1993).

Questions about time (alone time versus couple/family time; quality of time—free/meaningful versus meaningless/compulsive) and space (alone/private space versus enmeshment) help reveal the value and practice of centering, reflection and contemplation. This, of course, assumes that individuals need a regular amount of quiet time and space in order to nurture the spiritual.

Pruyser (1976) describes seven key categories to assess in the beginning phase of treatment: 1) Awareness of the holy—what does one hold sacred, does one revere? 2) Providence—where is trust and or hope in one's life? 3) Faith—to what does one commit him/her self? 4) Grace or gratefulness—for what is one thankful, has one been given, has one been forgiven for or been forgiving? 5) Repentance or sin—how has one dealt with mistakes, where is responsibility placed? 6) Communion—with whom does one reach out, care for and feel cared for? and 7) Sense of vocation—what sense of satisfaction and purpose does one find in life and work? A number of formal assessment tools have been developed from Pruyser's work (1976, 1977).

The clinician may also utilize a paper and pencil inventory. Analysis of responses to individual questions will reveal couples' attitudes and practices, often with greater depth and detail than surfaces in interview formats. Two such instruments are the *Spiritual Well-Being Scale* (Ellison, 1983) and The *Spiritual Experience Index* (Genia, 1990, 1991). Both of these are described in Chapter 5 of this text.

Irrespective of the assessment method, the goal is to discriminate between healthy or dysfunctional spirituality in the couple subsystem. This means being able to determine whether family members form coalitions with God in an effort to gain extra power, control, or authority; whether religious conflict serves as a "stalking horse" to present underlying family conflict; and if marital or family conflict arises out of fundamentally different religious commitments (Pattison, 1982). It also means being able to determine how spirituality/religion contributes to marital/family affect (from defensiveness to openness), thinking (from certainty and absoluteness to tentativeness), and behavior (from revenge to forgiveness) (Giblin, 1993).

Finally, the clinician needs to attend to patterns of intimacy and distance in both marital/family and God relationships. This assumes that there is a high concordance between closeness and distance among intimates and closeness and distance in relationship with God. For example, Worthington (1990) has couples graph these cycles for themselves and in relation to God. Couples generally find strong parallels between the two plots which helps demonstrate the imminent, incarnational nature of God. Likewise, change in family relationships can result in change in perceived relationship with God, and vice versa. For instance, differentiation from an idealized distant parent could result in loss of both the idealized parent and God concepts/relationship (Ranges, 1980). Clinicians need to be aware of religious transference and changes in faith experience in therapy.

☐ Intervention Strategies

Respect for and incorporation of the spiritual dimension in couples or relationship therapy does not necessitate an arsenal of specific strategies and techniques. Quite the opposite. More harm is likely to be done to clients by clinicians equipped with ready scriptural references for each presenting problem, by untimely or overused prayer, and by simplistic rendering of the mysterious and paradoxical sides of life. Instead, clinicians need a range of flexible approaches including: (a) therapeutic use of self; (b) a sense of how explicitly or implicitly the spiritual dimension can be used; and (c) consideration of the appropriateness and timing of interventions such as prayer with or for clients, sacred readings such as scripture , spiritual bibliotherapy, forgiveness, and other spiritual practices and resources.

When clients are both aware of and able to articulate their relationships with the transcendent, the clinician can more directly and explicitly incorporate the spiritual dimension in therapy. For example: "Where do you think God is in your decision making?" or "What do you think God wants for you each and for your relationship?" However, when clients lack such awareness or articulation, clinicians do well to incorporate the spiritual dimension in a more indirect fashion, never speaking directly about God, but always keeping an ear open for understanding clients' value, belief, and meaning systems.

Therapeutic use of self

More important than any other single factor is the clinician's own spiritual journey and his/her awareness of and ability to articulate that process. Couples needs to know they have found a 'spiritual friend.' Spiritual friends are familiar with the religious resources, scriptures, rituals, traditions, and spiritual reading materials that the client mentions. And, if not directly familiar with these resources, he/she will become familiar. Even more important, they have first-hand experience with clients' struggles with finding meaning, with experiences of loss—in all its psychological and spiritual dimensions, as well as with hope and resurrection. Couples also need to know their values and beliefs will be respected and that they will not be shamed, ridiculed, or evangelized.

Decision Making and Change

How do a couple's values decisions we make embody the spiritual? One's deepest desire is for self-transcendence (Conn, 1998). The pulls of denial and addiction (May, 1988), materialism, careerism, egoism (Watchell, 1983) are strongly opposed to the recognition of this desire. The more open clients are to evaluating decisions in trusted relationships the more likely they will overcome blind spots in their decision making.

What are the dynamics of change and growth? Is it a cognitive, affective, or behavioral shift that initiates and maintains lasting change? From a spiritual perspective, growth or change takes time, typically involves waiting and letting go. Hendrix (1988) notes that what one partner needs the most is what the other partner is least able to give, as well as being the precise area where that partner needs to grow.

Change and growth involve differentiation in relation to spiritual dimension as well. It is painful but all too easy to go along with the cultural and religious expectations for marital and family life while failing to listen to the deeper desires and stirring of self, partner, and family members. For example, one may believe that from a spiritual point of view anger should be repressed and that self-sacrifice is always valued over self awareness and one's own needs.

God Representation

As Rizzuto (1979) notes, God representations or images are an admixture of parental, developmental, imaginative, and familial and religious influences. How a client images God, whether as distant, demanding, and critical or warm and nurturing, can influence the process and outcome of therapy. For example, in a client whose image of God is punitive, demanding, and unforgiving it might be a therapeutic error to initially focus treatment on forgiveness. Asking such a client to begin to forgive herself and accept her behaviors when she hears criticism, judgment, and nonacceptance from her spouse and her parents, and also imagines God to be saying similar things, could present an insurmountable obstacle to therapy.

Direct versus Indirect Focus on the Spiritual Dimension

The clinician also needs to determine how directly or indirectly the spiritual dimension is to be used. Experience suggests that clinicians move slowly and indirectly toward the spiritual dimension and then only after a relationship has developed with the couple. Then, comments that are semi-direct are likely to be acceptable and useful. For instance, "I wonder how God can accept you when you find it so difficult to accept yourself?" or, "I wonder what God would think about this decision?" The goal is to plant seeds, to suggest alternative ways of looking at and experiencing relationships, to create an openness to the spiritual dimension.

Case Examples

Sperry and Giblin (1996) describe two cases to illustrate various interventions with spiritual seekers presenting with relationship issues.

Jack is a 38 year old, highly verbal, minimally insightful, married man. He has two children and added a third during therapy. He is Roman Catholic, a graduate of parochial high school and college, a weekly participant in a mens' prayer and scripture study group, and a daily churchgoer. Jack is dissatisfied with his professional work and envisions himself called to be an evangelizer, minister, or perhaps a missionary. He is about to "give it all up" to follow his "call," and he declared bankruptcy to pay off debts. He reports marital satisfaction but appears minimally committed to either marriage or parenting. In terms of spiritual assessment Jack's spirituality is fueled by perfectionist images and is self-centered. It differs markedly from a spirituality that asks "What God is doing in my life?" and is God-centered.

Jack is articulate about his Christian belief system but it appears to function in a largely defensive fashion: 1) calling him out of responsible partnering, parenting, and economic providing; 2) bolstering an otherwise weak sense of self and providing a sense of specialness and entitlement; and 3) having little to do with any altruistic sense of service. In terms of Pruyser's categories, Jack presented as follows.

1. **Awareness of the holy:** Jack strongly identified with the church and its rituals. He was an active church participant on the daily level. He spoke of a strong sense of God, a God who was primarily otherworldly.
2. **Providence:** he had little sense of trust in himself and placed entire trust in God and God's representatives, the clergy.
3. **Faith:** he struggled with an appropriate locus for his commitments. It was surprising how little impact a pregnancy and birth in the family had on him during therapy.
4. **Grace, gratefulness:** Jack had little sense of thanksgiving for his life and relationships; he had a strong sense of existential guilt for not being more successful with his life.
5. **Repentance:** he had a legal, rule-governed sense of morality and would not take work that would apparently compromise his values.

6. **Communion:** he had little sense of connectedness.
7. **Vocation:** this was a primary area of therapy, what he was called to do with his life, what would provide a sense of meaning. There was a strong sense that Jack was operating less out of his heart's desires than an external sense of shoulds.

Overall Jack presented with what seemed to be a fairly rigid belief system, a strong sense of connectedness to the institutional church, and with much less of a sense of personal spirituality.

Betty is a 47-year-old divorced woman who presented for therapy to deal with her ex-husband. She is the mother of six grown children, one of whom was diagnosed with cancer only months after Betty separated from her husband. Although she was seeking a separation rather than divorce, she was soon served with divorce papers. Her son died two years later, for which she was blamed by her ex-husband and her elderly parents. Both pointed to her separation as the catalyst for the son's illness. Betty's grief and rage were palpable, her spiritual seeking was passionate but filled with doubt and questioning. Her upbringing allowed for little anger or vulnerability, much independence, and dogmatic religious practice. Not surprisingly, Betty's image of God at the outset of treatment was punitive, demanding, and unforgiving.

Some of the interventions that were utilized in these cases are described below.

Prayer. The therapist could pray with and/or for clients. Many spiritually sensitive clinicians prepare for their work with a form of centering prayer, a desire to be open to the spiritual in both self and clients. Relatively few clinicians actually incorporate in-session prayer, and do so only having assessed client comfort levels with this intervention. For detailed examples of in-session prayer with three cases—an individual, couple, and a family—the reader is referred to Wimberly (1990).

For example, Betty had a distant, sickly mother from whom she had received no nurture. She had long ago learned to be independent, a caretaker, and to "keep a stiff upper lip." She had no positive female role models. In one session Betty and I prayed to Mary the mother of Jesus that she might become the mother Betty never had. Mary was a strong competent woman who, like Betty, also let go of her son at a very young age, and she had wept. This positive identification allowed Betty to begin to trust and express her deep grief and to begin to befriend her spiritual self.

Dreams. Dreams have been referred to as the "royal road to the unconscious" and as "God's language." Religious communication is frequently conveyed in dreams in the scriptures. In marital and family work dreams provide access into both the unconscious and religious. For example, Betty had an extraordinary dream within the first few days of her son's death. The dream took place in heaven and her completely healed son bounded across an open, sunny field to greet her. He wanted to tell her that he "was doing fine, that God was OK," and that he was with two elderly loved neighbors. The dream received an amazing confirmation in a neighbor who also lost a son and reported having "Betty's dream" the same week. This dream sequence was returned to during therapy as a means to explore and challenge Betty's otherwise negative and judgmental God image.

Sacred Writings. The clinician who is familiar with the scriptures may share associations to the degree that the therapeutic process is enhanced. If done correctly, this intervention allows the couple or family an expanded perception, may help to normalize their conflicts, and might assist in overcoming a sense of isolation. For instance, Jack narcissistically identified himself with many scriptural references of self-sacrifice. The therapeutic task was to begin to temper his religious enthusiasm with "rules of discernment" drawn from his familiar background in Ignatian spirituality, and to increase dialogue of "vocation" with his spouse and other community members. He was offered the interpretation that in the reading of scriptures and spiritual works that conversion or change of heart, behavior, and the fundamental way of living one's life were most frequently fashioned out of repeated small steps rather than the major leaps. Jack's "leaps of faith" would cut him off from as yet barely nurtured marital and family commitments. He had no external affirmation of his gifts and talents for ministry from his religious community. The clinician's task was to balance a mirroring of Jack's enthusiasm while wondering aloud about how and why he did not receive affirmation or recognition for his gifts from the faith community as do most ministers in formation.

Forgiveness. At the heart of the spiritual perspective is the sense of interconnectedness, unity, and equality. Where conflict highlights differences and punctuates interactions with clear villain and victim perceptions, the spiritual perspective focuses on similarities and shares equal responsibility for initiating change. We have found the spiritual perspective to be a strong support to cognitive and behavioral interventions aimed at interrupting reactive cycles in marriage and family. "Time-out" strategies and "self talk" might include reflection on what one's depth is saying, or asking "what is God's will for us in this interaction?" Or it might involve the therapist saying: "when you are so angry with each other and only aware of each other's negatives, try to imagine how God sees and accepts you and him/her." Looking at one's family-of-origin models for acceptance, forgiveness, caring, and thanksgiving may expose poor modeling of these "spiritual activities" and allow partners to begin to be more accepting of each other. Needless to say, therapeutic work focused on forgiveness is enhanced by the addition of the spiritual perspective.

Spiritual Bibliotherapy. Furthermore, it is important to assess the impact of literature, movies, and videos on clients and the therapeutic process. Where client readings serve to maintain rigid defensiveness, prescribed reading may economically expand perspectives, correct misinformation, challenge misperceptions, and contribute to a sense of belonging and understanding. Clinicians need to have readings that they assign, follow up on their assignments, and process client understanding and/or interpretation of the material.

☐ Concluding Note

This chapter has surveyed four different approaches and sets of intervention strategies for incorporating the spiritual dimensions when working with individuals and couples. Two of these approaches, the cognitive-behavioral and the psychoanalytic, are complete orientations to furthering psychotherapeutic change with articulated theoretical formulations about the nature of development, dysfunction, and the change process, as well as having specialized intervention methods. This is not to say that a clinician could not occasionally utilize one or more of the cognitive-behavioral strategies or techniques in another treatment orientation. The clinician could, of course. Nevertheless, these variants of the cognitive-behavioral and psychoanalytic approaches are self-contained systems.

On the other hand, the focused-experiential approach is a relatively circumscribed strategy which Hinterkopf (1994, 1998) has encouraged therapists to integrate in various other therapeutic contexts. Similarly, the relationship dynamics approach, although based in the systems or systemic orientation, is a rather eclectic approach which blends and incorporates a number of intervention strategies and spiritual practices.

Whether it is necessary, advisable, or possible to establish a formal and distinct 'spiritual psychotherapy' approach is beyond the scope of this discussion. For the present, clinicians have at their disposal at least four different ways of conceptualizing and incorporating the spiritual dimension in psychotherapy. Clinicians' creativity and ongoing experience working with spiritual seekers will likely result in other strategies and approaches for incorporating the spiritual dimension in psychotherapy and counseling.

☐ References

Beck, A., Rush, A. J., Shaw, B. F., & Emery, G. (1979). *Cognitive therapy of depression*. New York: Guilford Press.

Brigman, K. (1984). Churches helping families: A study of the effects of religion on families and how churches can help strengthen families. *Family Perspectives, 18,* 77–84.

Brigman, K. (1992). Religion and family strengths: Implications for mental health professionals. *Topics in Family Psychology and Counseling, 1*(1), 39–52.

Conn, W. (1998). *The desiring self.* New York: Paulist Press.

DiBlasio, F. (1988). Integrative strategies for family therapy with Evangelical Christians. *Journal of Psychology and Theology, 16,* 127–134.

Ellison, C. (1983). Spiritual well-being: Conceptualization and measurement. *Journal of Psychology and Theology, 11,* 330–340.

Fish, R., & Fish, L. (1986). Quid pro quo revisited: The basics of marital therapy. *American Journal of Orthopsychiatry, 56*(3), 371–384.

Gendlin, E. (1969). Focusing. *Psychotherapy: Theory, Research and Practice, 6,* 4–15.

Gendlin, E. (1981). *Focusing.* New York: Bantam.

Genia, V. (1990). Religious development: A synthesis and reformulation. *Journal of Religion and Health, 29,* 85–99.

Genia, V. (1991). The Spiritual Experience Index: A measure of spiritual maturity. *Journal of Religion and Health, 30,* 337–347.

Giblin, P. (1993). Marital conflict and marital spirituality. In R. Wicks & R. Parsons (Eds.), *Clinical handbook of pastoral counseling: Volume II.* New York: Paulist Press.

Hendrix, H. (1988). *Getting the love you want: A guide for couples.* New York: Harper & Row.

Hinterkopf, E. (1994). Integrating spiritual experiences in counseling. *Counseling and Values, 38*(3), 165–175.

Hinterkopf, E. (1998). *Integrating spirituality in counseling: A manual for using the experiential focusing method.* Alexandria, VA: American Counseling Association.

Koltko, M. E. (1990). How religious beliefs affect psychotherapy: The example of Mormonism. *Psychotherapy, 27,* 132–141.

May, G. (1988). *Addiction and grace.* San Francisco: Harper and Row.

Pattison, E. (1982). Management of religious issues in family therapy. International *Journal of Family Therapy, 4,* 140–163.

Propst, L. (1988). *Psychotherapy in a religious framework: Spirituality in the emotional healing process.* New York: Human Sciences Press.

Propst, L. (1992). Spirituality and the avoidant personality. *Theology Today, 49,* 165–172.

Propst, L. (1993). Defusing the powers with Jesus as a model of empowerment: Treating the avoidant personality. *Journal of Pastoral Care, 47,* 230–238.

Propst, L. (1996). Cognitive-behavioral therapy and the religious person. In E. Shafranske (Ed.), *Religion and the clinical practice of psychology* (pp. 391–408). Washington, DC: American Psychological Association.

Propst, L., Ostrom, R., Watkins, P., Dean, T., & Mashburn, D. (1992). Comparative efficacy of religious and non-religious cognitive-behavioral therapy for the treatment of clinical depression in religious individuals. *Journal of Consulting and Clinical Psychology, 60,* 94–103.

Pruyser, P. (1976). *The minister as diagnostician.* Philadelphia: Westminster Press.

Pruyser, P. (1977). The seamy side of current religious beliefs. *Bulletin of the Messenger Clinic, 41,* 329–340.

Ranges, C. (1980). Finding religious roots in the family tree. *The Family, 8,* 71–74.

Richards, P. S., & Bergin, A. (1997). *A spiritual strategy for counseling and psychotherapy.* Washington, DC: American Psychological Association.

Rizzuto, A. (1979). *The birth of the living God. A psychoanalytic study.* Chicago: University of Chicago Press.

Rizzuto, A. (1989). Ana-Marie Rizzuto on God representation. *Psychologists Interested in Religious Issues Newsletter, 14*(2), 1–4.

Rizzuto, A. (1991). Religious development: A psychoanalytic point of view. In F. Oser & W. Scarlett (Eds.), Religious development in childhood and adolescence [Special issue]. *New Directions for Child Development, 52,* 47–60.

Rizzuto, A. (1996). Psychoanalytic treatment and the religious person. In E. Shafranske (Ed.), *Religion and the clinical practice of psychology* (pp. 409–432). Washington, DC: American Psychological Association.

Sperry, L., & Giblin, P. (1996). Marital and family therapy with religious persons. In E. Shafranske (Ed.), *Religion and the clinical practice of psychology* (pp. 511–532). Washington, DC: American Psychological Association.

Watchell, P. (1983). *The poverty of affluence.* New York: Free Press.

Wimberly, E. (1990). *Prayer in pastoral counseling.* Louisville, KY: Westminster/John Knox Press.

Worthington, E. (1990). Marriage counseling: A Christian approach to counseling couples. *Counseling and Values, 35,* 3–15.

7
CHAPTER

Incorporating Spiritual Disciplines

This chapter describes and illustrates several spiritual disciplines, practices, and techniques that can be useful in incorporating the spiritual dimension. Whether utilized as an intervention within a treatment session or prescribed as an intersession activity, spiritual practices can be a powerful adjunctive to the treatment process. What are spiritual practices? They are focused activities which foster spiritual qualities which can result in a balanced and disciplined lifestyle. These include healing prayer, meditation, fasting, reading sacred writings, forgiveness, moral instruction, and service. This chapter begins with a discussion of a taxonomy of spiritual practices, called 'essential spiritual practices,' and then proceeds to describe several spiritual practices or techniques in detail.

☐ Essential Spiritual Practices

Roger Walsh, the distinguished transpersonal psychiatrist and philosopher, describes seven basic spiritual practices in his book *Essential Spirituality: The Seven Central Practices to Awaken Heart and Mind* (1999). He indicates that while there are many spiritual practices, these seven are common to all the great world religions and consistent with the perennial philosophy, and can therefore be called 'perennial practices' (Walsh, 1999, pp. 9–10). These seven basic practices are listed in Table 7.1.

TABLE 7.1. The essential spiritual practices
---

1. Purify motivation

2. Cultivate emotional wisdom

3. Live ethically

4. Develop a peaceful mind

5. Cultivate wisdom and spiritual intelligence

6. Recognize the sacred in all

7. Engage in the service of others

Based on Material from *Essential Spirituality: The Seven Central Practices to Awaken Heart and Mind* by R. Walsh, 1999.

In his Foreword to Walsh's book, the Dalai Lama suggests that all seven practices are essentially linked to the development and practice of the virtue of compassion. It should be pointed out that Walsh distinguishes spiritual practices from spiritual techniques and exercises. He use the term 'practice' to refer to the disciplines of developing crucial capacities of the heart and mind, while the terms 'technique' and 'exercise' indicate specific methods for achieving a spiritual practice. For instance, the techniques of meditation and centering prayer are highly effective in achieving the practice of developing a peaceful mind. Some techniques can be useful in achieving two or more spiritual practices; for example, meditation is also a useful method for cultivating wisdom and spiritual intelligence.

Interestingly, Walsh indicates that these various practices are interrelated and suggests a developmental sequence to them. For example, he indicates that developing a peaceful mind, spiritual practice four, is facilitated by cultivating the first three spiritual practices. Each of these seven spiritual practices will be briefly described and subsequent sections of this chapter will describe and illustrate some additional practices and a variety of common techniques or methods.

1. **Purifying motivation.** The purpose of this spiritual practice is to reduce one's cravings and redirect one's desires. For most individuals, this means relinquishing attachments to beliefs, feelings, possessions, and the desire for possessions or experiences or vices that impede them in their quest for true happiness. In so doing, persons become better able to transform their motivations by reducing cravings and find their soul's basic desire or higher motives, which Walsh indicates is a central goal of all spiritual practices. He notes that at the peak of higher

motives is the pull to self-transcendence which is defined as "the desire to transcend our usual false, constricted identity, to awaken to the fulness of our being, and to recognize our true nature and our true relationship with the sacred" (Walsh, 1999, p. 53).

2. **Cultivating emotional wisdom.** Since emotions tend to rule a seeker's life, transforming one's emotions is an essential spiritual practice. The great religious and spiritual traditions indicate three ways in which this occurs: 1) by mastering and reducing toxic and painful affects such as fear and anger; 2) by fostering positive attitudes such as gratitude and generosity; and 3) by cultivating such positive emotions as love and compassion. The goal is neither indulgence or repression of emotions, but rather appropriateness, balance, and equanimity, namely, the capacity to experience the inevitability of the ups and downs of life without becoming victim to mood lability. Learning how to release, transform, and appropriately use emotions is the basis of emotional wisdom.

3. **Living ethically.** Walsh contends that "ethical living is one of the most powerful yet misunderstood of all religious practices" (Walsh, 1999, p. 117). However, when it is correctly understood and practiced it is an essential means for spiritual growth, and without it progress is difficult. Unethical acts "create deep deposits of fear and guilt, paranoia and defensiveness . . . agitate and cloud our minds, making it difficult to achieve calm and clarity" (p. 121). Unethical living is destructive to both self and others, and has immediate and long-term consequence because, in reality, we become what we do and how we act. To live ethically involves practicing right speech and right action. It also involves dealing with the emotional residue remaining from past unethical behavior, such as by making restitution and dealing with guilt feelings.

4. **Developing a peaceful mind.** As individuals become less compelled by craving and compulsive need, less troubled by painful affects, and less disturbed by ethical lapses, they become better disposed to concentrate and focus their attention, resulting in a sense of calm and inner peace. "This peace is the doorway to the sacred, when the mind is focused and unperturbed, it opens effortlessly to its Source" (Walsh, 1999, p. 168). The challenge of mastering this sense of attention and inner peace is a slow process aided by such methods as meditation, contemplation, yoga, and continuous prayer. It also involves transforming the busyness of everyday life and, as much as possible, transforming daily activities into sacred rituals and moments of awareness. Needless to say, this transformation requires the regular and habitual use of various meditative and focusing methods.

5. **Recognizing the sacred in all.** Awakening sacred vision is another term for discerning or seeing the sacred in all persons, things, and situations. This is a principal focus of spiritual direction in the Christian tradition as it is in other religious systems that advocate formal spiritual direction or spiritual guidance. "What we perceive is selected by our desires, colored by our emotions, and fragmented by our wandering attention. What we see outside us reflects what is inside us. The result: we do not see ourselves or the world clearly or accurately" (Walsh, 1999, p. 175). Living mindlessly, like this, exacts a significant toll physically, emotionally, and spiritually, and unhealthy cravings, motives, and emotions are most likely to surface during these moments of mindlessness. The corrective is mindfulness. "To love mindfully is to bring greater awareness to each activity, to be more present in each moment, and to catch subtle experiences that all too often go unnoticed (p. 177). Mindfulness not only enhances our awareness of relationships and the world within and around us, it also frees us from automaticity, the sense of being locked on mental autopilot. With regular practice of mindfulness, these "initial glimpses gradually become a recurrent vision, peak experiences extend into plateau experiences, altered states of consciousness become altered traits of consciousness . . . " (Walsh, 1999, p. 206).

6. **Cultivating wisdom and spiritual intelligence.** Walsh defines wisdom as "deep understanding and practical skill in the central issues of life, especially existential and spiritual issues" (Walsh, 1999, p. 216). The crux of wisdom includes finding meaning and purpose in life, managing relationships and aloneness, living in the face of mystery, coping with illness, suffering, and death, and knowing and truly accepting oneself. The wise person is one who has developed deep insight into these issues and skills for dealing with them. Wisdom is a liberating spiritual capacity. It can dissolve one's delusions about self, just as it can reduce one's suffering and speed the awakening of one's heart and mind. Finally, by "loosening the bonds of egoism, wisdom also fosters concern and compassion for others" (p. 248).

7. **Engaging in the service of others.** Altruism or helping others is viewed by the great religions as a central human desire, and recent psychological research seem to confirm that individuals are altruistic by nature. "So esteemed are generosity and service that some traditions regard them as the essence of spiritual life, the practice upon which all other practices converge . . . the supreme goal of enlightenment is sought, not for oneself alone, but to better serve and enlighten others" (Walsh, 1999, p. 256). Thus, as spiritual seekers become increasingly enlightened it is to be expected they will become sages—sages who dedicate themselves to the welfare of others and of life.

Walsh notes that the first six spiritual practices lay the groundwork for generosity. Nevertheless, he describes several specific methods and techniques for cultivating generosity directly. This spiritual practice has the advantage of transforming all of one's daily activities into spiritual practices. "With its help we need not change what we are doing so much as how and why we are doing it. . . . With this approach, work and family, far from being distractions from spiritual life, become central to spiritual life, and each project or family activity can be transformed into a sacred act" (p. 266).

☐ Common Spiritual Practices, Techniques, and Exercises

This section will describe and discuss several spiritual practices and techniques, and related exercises. These practices and techniques are correlated with Walsh's seven categories essential spiritual practices (cf. Table 7.2). Because of the centrality of prayer for the spiritual journey, a section on prayer, emphasizing healing prayer, precedes the discussion of the eight practices, techniques, and exercises.

TABLE 7.2. Categories and examples of spiritual practices

- **Purify motivation**
  fasting
  indulge an attachment/frustrate an addiction

- **Cultivate emotional wisdom**
  forgiveness

- **Live ethically**
  moral instruction

- **Develop a peaceful mind**
  meditation and centering prayer

- **Cultivate wisdom and spiritual intelligence**
  spiritual reading

- **Recognize the sacred in all**
  mindfulness

- **Engage in the services of others**
  service

Prayer

Prayer is probably the most distinctive and characteristically spiritual of all activities associated with the spiritual dimension. It is a spiritual phenomenon that is central to most seekers' spiritual journey. Most clients pray at least occasionally and many use it frequently for coping with life's difficulties. Prayer can serve as a journey marker for clients demarcating important struggles and events in their lives. Clinicians can view their clients' prayer lives as a measure of their spiritual and psychosocial functioning. It can also be utilized as a vehicle for fostering cognitive and behavioral change. McCullough and Larson (1999) note that many clients are favorably disposed to an assessment and discussion of their prayer lives in the treatment context.

Types of Prayer

Various typologies of prayer have been proposed. Meadow and Kahoe (1984) described six types: petitionary, intercessory, thanksgiving, adoration, confession, and meditation. Paloma and Pendleton (1989) describe four types: ritualistic, petitionary, colloquial, and meditative prayer. To their list can added 'healing prayer' because of its relevance to spiritually-attuned psychotherapy and counseling. Healing prayer was once "one of the chief therapeutic tools of the nineteenth-century physician, but more recently prayer has been squeezed out of the therapeutic setting by chemicals, machines, and heroic surgical procedures" (Lipp, 1985, p. 314). Today, healing prayer has been reintroduced in the clinical context.

There are four variants of healing prayer employed by clinicians in the practice of psychotherapy and counseling. The first, and most controversial, involves the clinician praying directly with a client. The second involves praying for the healing of the client outside the treatment context. The third involves praying for guidance on diagnostic or treatment matters. Finally, the fourth involves the clinician allowing the client to pray within the session while the clinician remains silent. Prayer may be the most common spiritual practice in psychotherapy and counseling, second only to spiritual assessment.

Table 7.3 lists and gives an example of each of these five types, Paloma and Pendelton's four plus healing prayer.

Indulge an Attachment/Frustrate an Addiction

Walsh (1999) recommends two complementary exercises that are powerful in developing the spiritual practice of purifying motivation. These ex-

---

TABLE 7.3. Five types of prayer

• **ritualistic prayer** — reading from a prayer book

• **petitionary prayer** —asking God to grant a request

• **colloquial prayer** — prayer of thanksgiving

• **meditative prayer** — TM or centering prayer

• **healing prayer** — clinician praying for or with a client

---

ercises are effective in reducing cravings and attachments. Craving is usually a word associated with the abnormally strong longing or desire to ingest a specific substance such as food, drugs, liquids, smoke, or solvents (i.e., glue sniffing). Cravings involve strong physiological and psychological longings for the object of desire. Attachment refers to abnormally strong longing or desire for certain objects, activities, relationships, belongings, etc. Generally speaking, attachments involve only psychological longings. The purpose of these exercises is twofold: 1) to reduce and eliminate that compelling and uncontrollable desire and its associated craving for or attachment to things that do not bring true happiness but instead enslave individuals to difficult-to-control and habit-forming activities or even harmful addictions; and 2) set the stage to redirect one's desires for toward things which bring true happiness. Walsh notes that both of these exercises are recommended in nearly all the spiritual traditions.

Indulging an Attachment

There are three simple and straightforward instructions for this spiritual practice. First, have the client choose a specific attachment and a specific date; and throughout that entire designated day, they are to indulge and enjoy that attachment and its craving as fully as possible. For example, if a client craves candy, have him or her buy a few bags or boxes of the favorite kind and prescribe that he or she eat as many as possible. The second instruction is for client to mindfully experience while indulging that craving. As with other spiritual practices, the greater the degree of awareness, the more likely the benefit. Mindfully indulging the particular attachment or craving in this manner should clearly illuminate its limitations. Have the client compare how the tenth piece tasted compared to the first. By the law of satiation, the taste and pleasure should be considerably lessened. Third, process this experience in the next therapy session.

Frustrating an Addiction

This exercise nicely complements 'indulging an attachment.' The directions are straightforward. First, have the client choose a specific craving or attachment and a designated time frame (e.g., 24 hours) during which the individual contracts to forgo the attachment. Establishing a realistic time frame for this practice is important; for example, the decision to frustrate the addiction of cigarette smoking for one low-stress work day is more likely to lead to the positive outcome than would the global decision to stop cold turkey and forever. Second, have the client carefully attend to all sensations, thoughts, and feelings experienced during this period of frustrating the attachment. Writing down these experiences during the course of the exercise is preferred. Third, encourage the client to reflect on the experience immediately after the exercise, and again in your next session together. Many individuals expect to feel anxious and fearful about the deprivation of their attachment only to find that they were able to cope rather well (Walsh, 1999).

Fasting

Fasting means abstaining from food, or eating sparingly. There are various reasons for fasting: as a means of weight loss, detoxification of the body for medical purposes, or as a spiritual practice. Done as a spiritual practice, fasting is abstention from food for the purpose of purification of one's motivation. All the great spiritual traditions recognize its merits.

More than any of the other spiritual practices, fasting can surface and uncover not only the obvious but also the more subtle cravings and desires that control one's life. Food and other substances permit individuals to camouflage aspects of their inner life, which fasting quickly surfaces. Foster (1988) notes: "If pride controls us, it will be revealed almost immediately. Anger, bitterness, jealousy, strife, fear—if they are within us, they will surface during fasting. At first we will rationalize that our anger is due to our hunger; then we will realize that we are angry because the spirit of anger is within us" (p. 55).

There are other benefits as well. Fasting can foster balance in life. In addition to revealing cravings, it uncovers how nonessentials have taken precedence in one's life. This is important self-knowledge that might not otherwise come to awareness. Fasting also helps increase awareness of the plight of others. In commenting on the social dimension of fasting, Walsh says: "I try to use each feeling of hunger to remind me of the many hungry people around the world. That way each hunger pang not only reduces the craving but also elicits concerns and compassion for the hungry" (Walsh, 1999, p. 50).

What instructions should clinicians give clients about fasting? The first is that, as with all the spiritual practices, a steady progression and moderation should be observed. That means beginning with a partial fast with a duration of no more than 24 hours. Fasting from lunch of one day to lunch of the next is the initial recommendation. This means that two meals are skipped, i.e., dinner and breakfast. Only water and fruit juices are taken during this period of fasting. This initial fast is recommended once a week for several weeks. The client should monitor both the physical and spiritual experience during each fast. Keeping a journal or log can be valuable. Particular attention should be directed at the inner attitude of the heart. As individuals go about their regular duties during this time of fasting, they are advised to inwardly pray and to be aware of thoughts and spiritual promptings and cultivate a "gentle receptiveness to divine breathings" (Foster, 1988, p. 57). This initial form of fasting is broken with a light meal of fresh fruits and vegetables.

After two or three weeks of this form, the client may be ready for a fast in which only water is consumed. After completing several fasts with a degree of spiritual success, move on to a 36-hour fast: three meals. Fasts lasting longer than this probably should be medically supervised.

Forgiveness

Next to prayer, forgiveness may be the most commonly practiced spiritual practice. Forgiveness can be defined as "a motivational transformation that inclines people to inhibit relationship destructive responses and to behave constructively toward someone who has behaved destructively toward them" (McCullough, Worthington, & Rachal, 1997, p. 321). Forgiveness is a capacity and a skill that must be practiced. It is also more than a change in feeling; it is a change in cognition as well as in action. Like many other spiritual practices, it should not be surprising that all spiritual traditions recognize its value and offer similar instructions for its practice.

How does one receive forgiveness from another? Among the various spiritual traditions there is agreement that five steps are required. First, personal responsibility must be acknowledged. Second, sincere regret must be expressed. Third, suitable reparation must be made, if at all possible. Fourth, a promise to stop the offending behavior must be made. And, fifth, forgiveness must be requested. An apology that lacks personal, sincere, or suitable qualities, or one that is followed by repeated offenses, is considered inadequate and unacceptable (Sanderson & Linehan, 1999).

Interestingly, there has been an unprecedented interest in forgiveness among researchers and clinicians in the past five years. Besides numerous articles and research studies a national institute to promote research on forgiveness has been founded. Called "A Campaign for Forgiveness Research," it has received extensive funding from the John Templeton Foundation and the Fetzer Institute, among other philanthropic organizations.

Coming out of these research endeavors have been a number of protocols and guidelines. Enright et al. (1996) and McCullough and Worthington (1995) and Worthington (1998) have developed forgiveness protocols. A few of these are reviewed here.

Protocol for Forgiveness

Worthington (1998) describes the Pyramid Model of Forgiveness. It is more comprehensive than the empathy-based model of McCullough and Worthington (1995). The five steps of the protocol spell the word REACH: 1) R is for 'recalling the hurt' as objectively as possible; 2) E stands for 'empathize' which means attempting to feel the offenders's feeling and identifying with the pressures on the offender; 3) A is for 'altruistic gifts of forgiveness,' and refers to the induction of a state of humility in the forgiver through the experience of guilt, gratitude, and gift. Although empathy is what mediates forgiveness, it is insufficient unless forgiveness is actually given. This step facilitates that process; 4) C stands for 'commit to forgive.' Being covert, forgiveness is subject to later doubts. To reduce the likelihood of a later denial, the individual should make a public commitment of the forgiveness beyond the offender. Thus usually takes the form of telling someone else, such as a therapist or friend, and writing a letter about the forgiveness, and not necessarily sending it but saving it for later reference; 5) H stands for 'holding onto forgiveness' which refers to efforts taken toward maintaining the act of forgiveness. Worthington offers six strategies for maintenance that are similar to relapse prevention strategies.

Guidelines for Letting Go of Anger and Giving Forgiveness

1. Consider the pros and cons of forgiving the person versus not forgiving the person, including the effects of one's anger on one's psychological and physical health.
2. Use cognitive reframing to understand the offending person's behavior.
3. If the offending person is sincerely sorry, practice validation of his or her distress.

4. Act opposite to angry feelings by engaging in conciliatory behavior (Sanderson & Linehan, 1999, p. 213).

Guidelines for Requesting Forgiveness

1. Give a sincere and validating apology.
2. If possible, repair the hurt.
3. Commit to not engaging in the injurious behavior again.
4. Follow through on the commitment by changing that behavior.
5. Engage in conciliatory acts (Sanderson & Linehan, 1999, p. 210).

Reconciliation

Finally, what about reconciliation? Although related to forgiveness, reconciliation "is a restoration of a violated trust (which) is earned through mutually trustworthy behavior" (Worthington, 1998, p. 129). Whereas forgiveness occurs within an individual, reconciliation occurs within relationships. Reconciliation can and does occur without forgiveness as when the offender has died, moved, or it is not safe to reconcile (e.g., when the offender is a sexual abuser). Furthermore, forgiveness can occur without reconciliation, such as when individuals are forced to forgive or the offense is considered insignificant or even too hurtful. Nevertheless, forgiveness can facilitate reconciliation (Worthington, 1998).

Moral Instruction

Historically, psychotherapists and counselors have tended to avoid the role of moral guide and teacher "although the impossibility of them fully avoiding this role is now widely acknowledged. . . . therapists need to more fully accept that they function as moral guides or teachers and think carefully about how they can function ethically and effectively in this role without becoming missionaries or usurping clerical functions" (Richards & Bergin, 1997, p. 228). One of the major functions of all the spiritual traditions is moral instruction in which ethical and moral values are transmitted, resulting in the preservation and maintenance of both the spiritual tradition and society, as well as in the healthier psychosocial and spiritual functioning of its members. Without a set of guiding ethical and moral values, individuals have no basis for regulating their behavior in a healthy and consistent manners (Bergin, 1991). Several studies indicate that the majority of clinicians "believe that values are important for mentally healthy lifestyles and for guiding and evaluating psychotherapy" (Richards & Bergin, 1997, p. 224).

Richards and Bergin (1997) indicate that there are particular occasions in the course of treatment in which clinicians should actively point out values they believe are healthy and then explicitly own and endorse them. These occasions include: when discussing informed consent, when asking clients to complete assessment measures, when helping clients set treatment goals, and when deciding to terminate treatment, when major value conflicts arise that could threaten the therapeutic relationship (p. 225).

They go on to discuss moral instruction in terms of values clarification, correction and instruction transmits. Values clarification interventions help clients articulate and clarify their moral values. Values correction interventions are efforts to correct deficiencies or distortions in the client's moral values, while values instruction interventions teach and inform clients about their moral and ethical functioning. Character education and developing virtue are values instruction interventions.

The ancient maxim "Plant an act, reap a habit; plant a habit, reap a virtue; plant a virtue, reap a character; plant a character, reap a destiny" suggests the centrality of habits and practices for becoming an ethical and moral person. Habits or practices are regular patterns of activity that shape an individual to act in a particular way. Virtues are constellations of good habits, while vices are constellations of bad habits. Accordingly, individuals need to practice and develop virtues to overcome corresponding vices (i.e., unethical living).

So how can clients be advised to develop and cultivate moral virtue? Keenan (1996) offers a simple dictum: continuously practice acting virtuously. Four steps elaborate this dictum. First, admit the moral problem concern. Second, find the right advisor. He notes that shedding a vice and acquiring virtue requires getting appropriate advice, feedback, and support. Third, find the right practices and exercises. In this step he describes four strategies: (a) seek tension or stretch and increase the challenge of the practice; (b) acquire balance of the practices in one's life; (c) achieve integration of the practice in one's life; and (d) maintain consistency and endurance. Fourth, enjoy the exercises (Keenan, 1996, pp. 90–94).

Meditation

Meditation has been described in many ways. It has been described as a means of relaxing the body-mind, as a way of training and strengthening awareness, as a method for centering and focusing the self, as well as a means of reducing high blood pressure and other cardiovascular conditions, relieving stress, bolstering self-esteem, and reducing the symptoms of anxiety and depression (Carrington, 1998). But, it is first and foremost a spiritual practice.

Psychologically speaking, there are two general types of meditation that have been described in both the spiritual and research literatures. They are concentrative meditation and external awareness meditation. Concentrative meditation seeks to restrict awareness by focusing attention on a specific object of attention such as the breath, a candle flame, a mandala or a mantra (a repeated word or sound). Transcendental Meditation (TM) is probably the most common form of concentrative meditation practiced in the U.S. Unfortunately, TM and some other forms of Eastern meditation practice may be viewed negatively by some Christian clients (McLemore, 1982).

External awareness meditation, on the other hand, focus on developing or 'opening up' one's awareness of the external environment. This form of meditation focuses one's awareness on a sacred word, image, or feeling as they consciously occur on a moment-to-moment basis. This form of meditation is also referred to as Insight or mindfulness meditation. Centering prayer is one of the most more commonly practiced forms of mindfulness meditation and is acceptable to most Christians.

There is an extensive and evolving literature on the use of meditation as an adjunct to psychotherapy. Marlatt and Kristeller (1999) and Cortright (1997) ably review this literature and discuss the various benefits and limitations of prescribing meditation to clients or actually incorporating meditation techniques within therapy sessions. Marlatt and Kristeller (1999) offer a number of guidelines for incorporating meditation techniques in clinical practice, including indications and contraindications. The interested reader is referred to these references.

Because of its acceptability to a wide variety of clients, centering prayer will be highlighted in this remainder of this section. Clinicians looking for resources and references about other forms of meditation, including the concentrative form, might consult Lawrence LeShan's (1974/1999) classic book *How to Meditate* or Patricia Carrington's recent compendium (1998).

Centering prayer is a passive form of meditation in which a sacred word or an image is silently introduced when one becomes aware of one's thoughts. It is a method for centering or focusing on one's intention of consenting to God's presence. Since it is not a concentrative form of meditation, it is not an exercise in *attention* which cultivates the faculty of the mind. Rather, it is an exercise of *intention* which cultivates the faculty of the will. In short, it is a spiritual practice for developing habits conducive to responding to the inspirations of the Spirit.

Centering prayer has been described as an initial form of contemplative prayer. Contemplative prayer is a process of interior transformation, a relationship initiated by God and leading to divine union. One's way of perceiving reality changes in this process. A restructuring of consciousness takes place that empowers one to perceive, relate to, and respond with increasing sensitivity to the divine presence and action in, through, and beyond everything that exists.

Centering prayer is not an end in itself but a beginning. It is not done to produce spiritual consolation but rather to increase the experience and expression of charity, joy, peace, self-knowledge, compassion, inner freedom, and humility. To achieve this end, centering prayer must be done regularly, preferably for a minimum of twenty minutes twice a day. To maximize the process, additional spiritual practices are recommended throughout the day. These might include: repetition of a prayer sentence, unconditional acceptance of others, and releasing upsetting emotions as soon as they arise.

Centering prayer is a method designed to facilitate the development of other forms of mediation, particularly contemplative prayer. Centering prayer is an attempt to present the ancient teaching of this method in an updated form and to put a certain order and regularity into it. It is not meant to replace other kinds of prayer; it simply puts other kinds of prayer into a new and fuller perspective. During the time of prayer the individual consents to God's presence and action within.

How is centering prayer practiced? The following method is described and outlined by Keating (1992, 1998). It is recommended that centering prayer be practiced daily, preferably for a minimum of twenty to thirty minutes twice a day.

1. A sacred word is chosen as a symbol of one's intention to open and yield to God's presence and action within. It could be one of the names of God or a comforting word (i.e., presence, silence, peace, stillness, oneness).
2. Sit comfortably and with eyes closed, relax. Then silently introduce the sacred word as the symbol of one's consent to God's presence and action within.
3. When becoming aware of any thoughts, feelings, memories, reflections, or images, return ever so gently to the sacred word. This is the only activity one need initiate after centering prayer has begun.
4. During the prayer time, avoid analyzing the experience or harboring expectations. Also avoid attempting to achieve any specific goal, such as having no thoughts, making the mind blank, feeling peaceful or consoled, repeating the sacred word continuously, or achieving a spiritual experience.
5. At the end of the prayer time, remain in silence with eyes closed for a short time. This allows the psyche a brief space to readjust to the external senses and to transfer the atmosphere of interior silence into subsequent activities (Keating, 1992, pp. 138–143).

Spiritual Reading

Each of the major spiritual traditions in the East and the West view their sacred writings as a source of spiritual and moral wisdom. There are few who discount the importance and value of sacred writings in individuals' lives. Throughout history, including the present time, the bible remains the all time bestselling book in America. Even an atheist like Albert Ellis (1993) acknowledges that the bible has been the single most significant self-help book in human history.

The purpose for reading sacred writings can differ by tradition and individual clients' needs. Some will study their tradition's sacred writings for intellectual reasons, such as to increase their doctrinal understanding of their tradition's theology or philosophy, while others will read them to find comfort or insight about particular concerns. However, a major reason spiritual seekers read and reflect on sacred writings is to put themselves into the presence of the divine.

Sacred writings can be used for a variety of purposes in spiritually-attuned psychotherapy and counseling. These include: (a) challenging and modifying dysfunctional beliefs; (b) reframing and understanding life and problems from a spiritual perspective; (c) clarifying and enriching understanding of the religious doctrines; and (d) seeking enlightenment, comfort, and guidance (Richards & Bergin, 1997).

Before implementing a spiritual intervention that uses sacred writings in some way, the clinician should carefully assess his or her clients' beliefs and attitudes about sacred writings, and only utilize such an intervention if it is compatible with clients' spiritual beliefs. Many spiritual seekers believe that sacred writings are a means for helping them communicate with God and know of His will for them. With clients with such beliefs, it would not be unreasonable for clinicians to encourage them to read and reflect on spiritual writings with the purpose of seeking divine insight into their problems and concerns. However, it should also be noted that such an intervention can be misused, as when clients have been advised by ministers or other spiritual leaders that engaging in prayer or sacred reading will effect a magical cure for their problems. If clients do read the sacred writings seeking enlightenment about coping and overcoming their problems and do not realize those outcomes, clinicians "need to be prepared to process such 'failures' with their clients" (Richards & Bergin, 1997, p. 211).

When a clinician believes that a client's understanding of a specific sacred writing is erroneous, referral to an appropriate religious leader for doctrinal discussions and clarification is preferable to discussing the matter in therapy. When client and clinician share the same belief system, it may be appropriate for clinicians to invite clients to explore specific writings that would help clarify their misunderstandings, being careful not to assume the mantle of spiritual authority.

Lectio divina is a time-tested method of praying with Christian sacred writings, particularly scriptural texts. It has been practiced in many forms by monks and other spiritual seekers for over a thousand years. Lectio divina has been described as the "art of letting God speak to us through his inspired and inspiring Word" (Pennington, 1998, p. xi) and then responding, since it is a two-way communication. The method for practicing lectio divina is a relatively straightforward and simple three-step process. The first is to take the sacred text and call upon the Holy Spirit. The second is to listen—read or hear someone else read—to the Lord speaking through the text for about ten minutes, then to reflect on it and respond. Third, choose a word or phrase from the text and take it to reflect on the rest of the day.

Mindfulness

Mindfulness, as noted in the section on meditation, was described as a basic of formal meditation practice, namely, insight or mindfulness meditation. In this section, mindfulness will be described as spiritual practice that can also be practiced outside the formal practice of meditation. As such it has considerably wider applicability since this form of mindfulness focuses on recognizing the sacred in all dimensions of creation in everyday life situations and circumstances. This form of mindfulness is about being fully mindful in the present moment. It is about being fully aware and attentive to the full range of experiences that exist here and now, moment to moment. Mindfulness permits an individual to experience things directly and immediately, seeing for oneself that which is present and true. It brings to bear one's whole personhood, one's entire heart, mind, and attention to each moment.

Mindful awareness is based on an attitude of acceptance. Rather than judging one's experiences as good or bad, healthy or sick, worthy or unworthy, mindfulness accepts all thoughts, feelings, persons, objects, and events exactly as they are in the present moment. Mindful acceptance of difficult thoughts or emotional states can transcend their negativity and defuse aggression. Rather than suppressing emotions or indulging them, a mindful attitude allows one to view them with acceptance (Marlatt & Kristeller, 1999).

A valuable clinical application of mindfulness is the capacity to adopt what Deikman (1982) called an "observing self" which carefully monitors its thoughts and feelings as they occur in the present moment. The observing self is a 'bridge' between meditation and cognitively-oriented psychotherapy techniques such as self-monitoring and cognitive restructuring strategies. While these approaches have some clinical utility, they come with a price. The price is that these strategies conceptualize the individual's thought patterns as 'themselves.' Instead of conceptualizing an individual's identity as a reflection of his or her thoughts, feelings, and actions, mindfulness views an individual's thoughts as 'simply thinking' rather than as personal directives that must be yielded to or followed.

The clinical value of mindfulness is that the process of momentarily stepping back and objectively viewing one's compulsive behaviors and patterns permits individuals to dis-identify themselves from these patterns. That is, "we begin to see that those thoughts and feelings are not us. They come along accidentally. They are neither an organic part of us nor are we obliged to follow them" (Snelling, 1991, p. 55).

How can clients be advised to practice mindfulness in daily life activities? Four steps are involved in the practice of daily mindfulness. First, assist the client in picking a given daily activity, such as eating, walking, watching, or listening and a given time frame. Second, have him or her practice being totally present to the activity for that time frame. Third, the client should observe and reflect on his or her thoughts and feelings about this experience. Fourth, he or she should be instructed to take these thoughts and feelings into the next activity. For example, a client wants to be totally present and mindful during a 20-minute walk in the park. The client is advised to gently look around and find something of beauty such as a child playing, a tree swaying in the wind, or squirrel eating an acorn. Whatever it is, full attention and sensitivity is directed at it. If it is a tree, the different colors are noticed as is the swaying of branches, and the movements of individual leaves. At the same time, the being of thoughts and feelings such as pleasure and appreciation that beauty gives a sense of centeredness, belonging and pleasures. Finally, these pleasant thoughts and feelings are extended to other activities. More specific instructions and guidelines for utilizing the spiritual practice of mindfulness with clients can be found in two books by Jon Kabat-Zinn (1990, 1994).

Service

Service is another type of spiritual practice. Whether called 'altruistic service' (Richards & Bergin, 1997), 'true service' (Foster, 1988) or 'awakened service' (Walsh, 1999), service involves doing something for others. Foster's distinction between 'self-righteous service' and 'true service' is worth noting. Self-righteous service is concerned with making impressive gains and achieving results. It usually requires the reward of recognition by others, picks and chooses whom to serve, and may be affected by moods and whims. True service, on the other hand, makes no distinction between big and small service, is contented with hiddenness (i.e., no recognition), and fosters such virtues as humility and gratitude (Foster, 1988).

Service can take numerous forms, such as providing food to the hungry or clothes and money to the poor, providing emotional support to those who are discouraged or grieving, visiting the sick, or volunteering in one's religious or spiritual community. The expected type and the frequency of service may vary in different spiritual traditions, nevertheless service is an extension of the Golden Rule, "Do unto others as you would have them do to you," or Silver Rule of Confucianism, "Do not do unto others what you would not have them do to you," and is central to all spiritual traditions (Walsh, 1999). It can be formal and planned or informal and spontaneous. In the latter instance it might involve slowing down long enough "to practice the service of listening in a context in which you might normally rush on past while preoccupied with tasks, time constraints, or your own needs and obligations" (Foster & Yanni, 1992, p. 45).

The results of a national survey of volunteers across the U.S. found that individuals who helped others consistently reported better health than non-volunteers and that many believed that their health improved after beginning their volunteer service. Furthermore, the vast majority reported that service provided them a sense of euphoria, greater calm, and relaxation (Luks, 1993).

Not every client will benefit from the prescription for service involvement. Some clients may actually be overcommitted to service in their religious communities, perhaps even to the point of burnout. Instead, they may need help in reducing their service involvement to their communities so they can attend to their own needs and growth (Richards & Bergin, 1997).

How can service be prescribed as a spiritual practice? Advise clients to select an hour, a morning, or a day for the spiritual practice of service. Five steps are suggested: First, begin by dedicating the time and what you will be doing during it. Second, look for ways to serve wherever you are, whoever you are with, and whatever you are doing. Third, try to accomplish the activity in a spirit of service. Fourth, be mindful of the intention to serve in such a way that you learn from each activity while releasing any attachments or bias you may have about those being served. And, finally, reflect on how this experience affects your spiritual journey (Foster & Yanni, 1992; Walsh, 1999).

☐ Concluding Note

The spiritual practices discussed in this chapter are clinically useful adjuncts in the practice of spiritually-attuned psychotherapy and counseling. As activities which foster spiritual balance and a disciplined lifestyle, spiritual practices such as healing prayer, meditation, and forgiveness can be powerful adjunctive treatments which can be directly incorporated into the treatment process or prescribed for intersession homework, such as the relationship dynamics approach case examples in Chapter 6.

☐ References

Bergin, A. (1991). Values and religious issues in psychotherapy and mental health. *American Psychologist, 46*, 394–403.

Carrington, P. (1998). *The book of meditation.* Boston: Element Books.

Cortwright, B. (1997). *Psychotherapy and spirit.* Albany, NY: State University of New York Press.

Deikman, A. (1982). *The observing self.* Boston: Beacon Press.

Ellis, A. (1993). The advantages and disadvantages of self-help therapy materials. *Professional Psychology: Research and Practice, 24*, 335–339.

Enright, R., & the Human Development Group. (1996). Counseling within the forgiveness triad: On forgiving, receiving forgiveness and self-forgiveness. *Counseling and Values, 40*, 107–146.

Foster, R. (1988). Celebration of discipline: *The path to spiritual growth* (Rev. ed.). San Francisco: HarperSan Francisco.

Foster, R., & Yanni, K. (1992). *Celebrating the disciplines: A journal workbook.* San Francisco: HarperSan Francisco.

Kabat-Zinn, J. (1990). *Wherever you go, there you are: Mindfulness meditation in everyday life.* New York: Hypericon.

Kabat-Zinn, J. (1994). *Full catastrophe living: Using the wisdom of your body and mind to face stress, pain and illness.* New York: Delta.

Keenan, J. (1996). *Virtues for ordinary Christians.* Kansas City: Sheed & Ward.

LeShan, L. (1974/1999). *How to meditate. A guide to self-discovery.* Boston: Little, Brown.

Luks, A. (1993). *The healing power of doing good.* New York: Ballentine.

Lipp, M. (1985). *Respectful treatment: The human side of medical care* (2nd ed.). New York: Elsevier.

Marlatt, A., & Kristeller, J. (1999). Mindfulness and meditation. In W. Miller (Ed.), *Integrating spirituality into treatment. Resources for practitioners* (pp. 67–84). Washington, DC: American Psychological Association.

McCullough, M., Worthington, E., & Rachal, K. (1997). Interpersonal forgiving in close relationships. *Journal of Personality and Social Psychology, 73*, 321–336.

McCullough, M., & Larson, D. (1999). Prayer. In W. Miller (Ed.), *Integrating spirituality into treatment. Resources for practitioners* (pp. 85–110). Washington, DC: American Psychological Association .

McLemore, C. (1982). *The scandal of psychotherapy.* Wheaton, IL: Tyndale House.

Meadow, M., & Kohoe, R. (1984). *Psychology of religion: Religion in individual lives.* New York: Harper & Row.

Paloma, M., & Pedleton, B. (1991). The effect of prayer and prayer experiences on measures of general well-being. *Journal of Psychology and Theology, 19,* 17–83.

Pennington, B. (1998). *Lectio divina: Renewing the ancient practice of praying the scriptures.* New York: Crossroads.

Richards, P., & Bergin, A. (1997) *A spiritual strategy for counseling and psychotherapy.* Washington, DC: American Psychological Association.

Sanderson, C., & Linehan, M. (1999). Acceptance and forgiveness. In W. Miller (Ed), *Integrating spirituality into treatment. Resources for practitioners* (pp. 199–216). Washington, DC: American Psychological Association.

Snelling, J. (1991). *The Buddhist handbook.* Rochester, VT: Inner Traditions.

Walsh, R. (1999) *Essential spirituality: The seven central practices to awaken heart and mind.* New York: John Wiley & Sons.

Worthington, E. (1998). An empathy-humility-commitment model of forgiveness applied within family dyads. *Journal of Family Therapy, 20,* 59–76.

IV

THE SPIRITUAL DIMENSION AND THE CLINICIAN

Part IV of the book focuses on the various ways clinicians can incorporate the spiritual dimension in their professional practice. Various levels of incorporation are possible ranging from minimal to maximal. Performing a brief spiritual assessment only would constitute a minimal level of incorporation. At an intermediate level, a clinician might incorporate spiritual assessment and engage in some degree of processing spiritual and religious issues, or possibly making a referral to a minister or spiritual leader. The maximal level of integration would include in-session activities in addition to personal incorporation of the spiritual dimension. This typically includes an integrative philosophy of clinical practice involving the spiritual dimension as well as the integration of the spiritual dimension and spiritual practices into the clinician's own personal life.

Chapter 8, Incorporating the Spiritual Dimension in Personal and Professional Life, offers descriptions of six prominent psychotherapists who incorporate the spiritual dimension in their personal and professional lives. This chapter offers the reader a very candid view of personal and professional convictions and practices that psychotherapists and counselors have about the spiritual dimension and its influence on not only their professional work with clients but also on their personal lives.

8
CHAPTER

Incorporating the Spiritual Dimension in Personal and Professional Life

Clinicians and trainees with the desire to incorporate the spiritual dimension in their personal lives, in their professional practice, or perhaps both, may wonder how psychotherapists actually integrate spirituality in their personal and professional lives. How does one come upon this information? By making inquiries? Possibly, but since the belief that it is inappropriate to discuss religious and spiritual issues in therapy still persists, trainees may not feel particularly comfortable raising the issue if a colleague, faculty member, or supervisor exhibits little or no receptivity to talking about the spiritual dimension in their clinical practice, much less their personal lives. Studies show that although psychologists appear to consider the spiritual dimension of their clients' lives in clinical practice, the extent and manner in which these issues are addressed is primarily determined by their own religious commitments rather than by clinical training (Shafranske, 1996). Furthermore, research indicates that attention to the spiritual dimension in graduate psychology training has been consistently reported as rare or absent, and when it was offered appeared to be related to the personal characteristics of a clinical supervisor (Shafranske, 1996, 2000). Similar findings are noted in psychiatric training (Sansone, Khatain, & Rodenhauser, 1990). Until such time as faculty members and supervisors are more receptive to discussing and disclosing about the spiritual dimension, trainees and practicing clinicians will have to seek other sources of information.

It is for this very reason that I felt it would be useful to devote the final chapter of this book to the various ways in which psychotherapists actually incorporate the spiritual dimension in their lives, professionally and personally. With some trepidation I asked a number of well-known psychologists and psychotherapists about their interest in publically sharing such information about themselves. I was pleasantly surprised that every person I asked agreed to participate.

These individuals were asked to describe how they practice spiritually-sensitive psychotherapy and how they incorporate the spiritual dimension in their lives outside their therapy practice. I asked them to address some or all of the following points. First, they were asked to describe a typical work day, particularly in their psychotherapy practice, from the time they awoke in the morning until they retired in the evening. Did they begin the day with prayer, meditation, or some ritual in preparation for their professional activities of that day? How did they end their day? Did they pray for, with, or about their clients? Second, they were asked to indicate how they approached the spiritual dimension with their clients or patients. Did they perform some sort of spiritual assessment with clients, and if so what type? What did they do with this information? Did they address spiritual issues and concerns or did they refer these clients to a minister, spiritual director, or pastoral counselor? What about interventions related to spiritual issues, such as, what kind of spiritual interventions or practices might they employ? Third, they were encouraged to describe the extent to which the spiritual dimension was incorporated into their theory of psychotherapy and their philosophy of life. Did they have an articulated theory of incorporating the spiritual dimension, and if so, was it incorporated in their own personal philosophy of life?

Following are the responses of six psychotherapists' profiles to these questions. As you will note, these psychotherapists represent some of the diversity of spiritual orientations and faith traditions.

****

☐ P. Scott Richards, Ph.D.

I consider my theory and approach to psychotherapy a theistic, spiritual one. The most important assumptions I make about the world are that 1) God exists, 2) human beings are the creations of God, and 3) there are spiritual realities and influences that can assist us in our efforts to cope, heal, and grow. I also believe that in order to enjoy positive mental health, it is important that we hearken to the quiet influence of God's spirit in our lives, and seek to live our lives in harmony with our understanding of His will for us. Congruence between our religious and moral values and our lifestyle and behavior are thus crucial to healthy personality development and functioning.

My theory and approach is multisystemic and integrative in that I believe that human behavior is influenced by a variety of processes and systems, and that the major enduring psychotherapy traditions each have much to offer as we seek to understand and help our clients. Thus, I incorporate some, but not all, of the insights and therapeutic techniques from the psychodynamic, behavioral, cognitive, humanistic-existential, and family systems traditions.

But my theistic, spiritual perspective and assumptions are the core of my theory of human nature and therapeutic change, and so when I adopt perspectives or interventions from these other traditions, I reframe and remake them so that they are consistent with my theistic view and approach. For example, I accept the behavior therapy notion that environmental influences have a major influence on clients' behavior, but I do not think that such influences act in a deterministic manner. I believe that human beings have agency and the capacity to choose and act on their environment. In therapy, I often explore ways in which clients can make healthier choices and act on their environment so that it does not influence them in unhealthy ways. I also often explore ways that my clients' might allow their religious environment or community to serve as a resource in their lives.

Because I believe in God, I seek to integrate my religious faith in both my personal and professional life. I am active in my religious community and seek to provide service to my church and community. My spiritual beliefs also have a major influence on my family life, and in the ways that I relate to my wife and children. I have learned much more about being a good husband and father from the teachings and influences of my religious community than from my studies and training as a psychologist. Perhaps this is one reason why I believe that the mental health professions could learn much by tapping into the wisdom that exists in the enduring, major religious traditions of the world.

Because of the centrality of my religious faith to my identity and view of human nature, I begin my work days with personal devotions that consist of prayer, scripture reading, and (when I'm not too rushed) private contemplation. Such practices help me keep a more spiritual and eternal perspective in my life, and bring feelings of peace and love into my heart. Such preparations make it easier for me to cope with the pressures and challenges of my day, and help me treat my wife, children, associates, and clients with more patience, understanding, and love. Unfortunately, these preparations do not always help, because I still seem to "lose my cool," or behave thoughtlessly or selfishly, more often than I would like to admit.

During my prayers, I often pray for God's assistance to help me work effectively with my clients (or graduate students) that day. Sometimes I pray for the welfare of specific clients that I am working with—usually those that I feel particularly concerned about. Sometimes I ask for guidance and insight about how I might be more effective in my efforts to help specific clients. At times, I receive impressions and insights about what I can do to better help them. For example, on one occasion after praying for guidance about a client, I felt an impression that it would be helpful to her if I would write down and summarize for her what I perceived to be her "issues" (e.g., her lack of assertiveness with her husband and children; her grief over her father's death) and how she could keep working on them. This is not something I normally do with my clients, but as I gave this woman my typewritten summary and discussed it with her during our next session, she reacted very favorably and it became clear that my summary had helped resolve her confusion and gave her some important insights. During the next 6 months as I worked with her, she commented several times about how helpful this had been to her.

Although I pray for my clients, I rarely pray *with* them because of concerns I have about possible confusion in role boundaries and transference issues. But I use other spiritual interventions with my clients. I begin my work with clients by giving them a written informed consent document that, among other things, informs them that they are welcome to discuss religious and spiritual issues if they wish. It also mentions that I sometimes use or recommend spiritual interventions if I believe it will be helpful to them—but that I only do this if they are comfortable with such interventions.

I do a brief religious and spiritual assessment with all of my clients. I include in the written *Client History and Intake Questionnaire* that I give clients at the start of therapy a number of questions about their religious background and current spirituality. Some clients prefer not to complete a written intake questionnaire, and so with them, I ask questions about their religious background and current spiritual beliefs during my initial clinical intake interviews. Always, I try to be sensitive to my clients' spiritual inclinations and if it becomes clear that religion and spirituality are not important to them, or if they otherwise do not wish to discuss spiritual matters, I respect their wishes.

For some clients, it is clinically indicated to do a more in-depth religious and spiritual assessment to better understand how their religious beliefs are intertwined with, or contribute to, their presenting problems. Occasionally, I ask clients to complete the *Age Universal Intrinsic-Extrinsic Scale* and the *Spiritual Well-Being Scale*. I have also recently developed a brief *Spiritual Outcome Scale* that I have begun using to assess the spiritual outcomes of therapy with my clients. These assessment measures are useful for stimulating discussions and client explorations about their spiritual concerns and issues.

My religious and spiritual assessment helps me determine whether it may be appropriate to use spiritual interventions with my clients. With some of my clients, I feel that it is contraindicated to use spiritual interventions and so I stick with standard "secular" techniques such as cognitive restructuring, assertiveness training, emotional exploration, and so on. When clients are open to it, and when it seems relevant to their presenting concerns and problems, I judiciously use or recommend spiritual interventions in therapy. Perhaps the most common spiritual interventions I use or recommend are discussing spiritual concepts in session with clients, referring clients to their religious leader for guidance and support, encouraging spiritual journal writing, discussing and encouraging forgiveness of self and others, challenging clients' dysfunctional religious understandings, and encouraging clients to pray, meditate, and read sacred writings. With some clients I have found that it is helpful to provide them with self-help materials to help them engage in a more structured process of spiritual exploration and growth. My colleagues in private practice and I wrote a spiritual exploration and growth workbook that we are finding helpful in this regard.

In using spiritual interventions, I seek to apply process guidelines such as 1) make sure a relationship of trust and rapport exists before using spiritual interventions, 2) obtain permission from clients before implementing spiritual interventions, 3) work within clients' value framework, being careful not to use spiritual interventions that are not in harmony with their religious beliefs, and 4) use spiritual interventions in a flexible, treatment tailoring manner. Generally, I find that I use spiritual interventions sparingly with most clients, but when I do, clients usually react favorably and appreciate the fact that I am seeking to respect and honor the healing power of their religious and spiritual beliefs and community.

In my position as a faculty member, I also have the opportunity to teach graduate students about the importance of religious and spiritual diversity and competency. I teach a graduate class to Ph.D. students in counseling psychology called, "Spiritual Values and Methods in Psychotherapy." Almost without exception, graduate students appreciate the opportunity to discuss and examine how they can go about integrating spiritual perspectives into their professional work. Some of them report that in their masters' degree programs at other institutions they were, not so subtly, given the message that any discussion of religious and spiritual issues in therapy was inappropriate. I am grateful for the opportunity to challenge this bias and misperception.

Many clients can only be successfully treated if their religious beliefs and spiritual concerns are sensitively addressed during therapy. I am hopeful that all mental health professionals will grow in their understanding of and respect for religious and spiritual aspects of diversity, and that they will take steps to increase their competency in this domain. As we each do this, I believe that our ability to help our clients will be greatly enhanced.

P. Scott Richards, Ph.D., is a member of The Church of Jesus Christ of Latter-day Saints, and is an Associate Professor at Brigham Young University. He is co-author of *A Spiritual Strategy for Counseling and Psychotherapy* (1997, APA Books), and is a licensed psychologist who provides psychotherapy at the Center for Change.

****

☐ Edward Shafranske, Ph.D.

As I reflect on the intersections of my spiritual life and professional practice, I am reminded of an undergraduate research project. The majority of subjects reported religious experiences as most often occurring when least anticipated—in the setting of the commonplace and ordinary. The finding of the sacred amid the mundane would of course not surprise William James, for whom an inborn religious impulse was an essential human characteristic and had no limits on the form or place of its expression. James once pictured religious sentiment as coming into consciousness through a door that stands ajar. In this view, religious sensibility is always potentially present, albeit, usually outside of our conscious awareness. Moments of faith, of noetic awareness and of piety, come through the kinds of passageways that James suggested in his metaphor. I have found that religious sentiment is emergent in many daily moments and often appears in similar ways in the course of psychological treatment.

In terms of my daily life, I find that my essential religious *practice*, originating in and sustained by the beliefs and sacraments of Roman Catholicism, is *simply allowing* the door to stand ajar. I accentuate *practice* and *simply allowing* to place emphasis on what I consider a particular form of spiritual discipline which involves the conscious intent to allow associations of a spiritual nature to emerge and to take root in consciousness. I am not suggesting a kind of formal meditation, but rather, an intentional receptivity to religious associations, prayer, and reflection within the setting of the commonplace. In the multiple venues of work, my spiritual life is not at a far remove. Although in my professional life I do not integrate formal religious practices, there are moments, for example in teaching or in clinical work, in which recognition of the spiritual foundation that informs my life appears in consciousness. As my schedule permits, this recognition may lead to a brief period of contemplation or simply a conscious "note to myself" of the deeper significance which is embedded in ordinary experience. Such moments are not isolated from formal religious practice; rather, such experiences complement more structured practices of prayer and communal and sacramental worship.

My approach to the religious dimension in the clinical practice of psychology has been influenced by multiple perspectives, including phenomenological-existential, cognitive, and psychoanalytic orientations. In keeping with my earlier comments and reflecting a psychoanalytic vantage, I attempt to be receptive to forms of conscious and unconscious narrative that shape an individual's psychological life and which ultimately result in behavior. Religious narrative, culled from formal religious teaching, denominational beliefs and practices, culturally-supported symbols and traditions, as well as internalized, unconscious God-representations, contribute to the construction of meaning. Both conscious and unconscious, literal and metaphoric systems of attribution create psychological experience. Lying beneath ordinary awareness, religious narrative shapes meaning and, for many, is the predominant cognitive-affective influence that organizes experience, influences emotion, constructs meaning, and governs behavior. I do not assume that spirituality will either predominate nor be absent from a given course of psychological treatment; rather, I attempt to listen to and provide a space for the elucidation of religious sentiment.

During the intake phase of consultation, I include both formal and informal inquiries into the spiritual life of the patient. Formal assessment includes a history of religious participation and education with particular emphasis on the functions religion plays and the salience of spiritual life within the extended family system and local community. I ask for a description of my patients' present perspective on and participation in organized religion as well as private spiritual practice. I also ask patients to describe an event or a period of time in which they felt significantly depressed or anxious and the means by which they sustained hope. This informal assessment often leads to an initial understanding of the contents and salience of religious attributions as well as of my patients' use of religious resources in coping. I listen for the developmental origins of their beliefs and practices, the functions these serve in resilience or conflict, and the salience they ascribe to religiosity. The contributions of early experience in the formation of God representations and the psychic utility of such internal objects is usually not available during the assessment phase. However, a close listening to the patient's narrative often provides a window into the unconscious organizing principles in which identifications with religious objects and internalizations of religious beliefs play a role. Inquiry into the spiritual and religious dimension early in treatment signifies to the patient that this aspect is of equal importance to other constituents of human experience and encourages further associations.

The use of religious and spiritual resources in treatment is dependent upon a number of factors: the salience of spirituality to the patient, the goals and treatment offered, the therapeutic alliance, and the patient's history of the use of religious coping. Individuals differ in respect to religious sentiment. Working with religious material in treatment is most appropriate for clients for whom their spiritual lives play a conscious and central role. I follow the narrative carefully and make interventions based on their free associations; the spontaneous appearance of spiritual content, as if coming through an open door to consciousness, guides my interventions. The treatment that is offered determines as well the kind of integration. In psychoanalytic treatment, my focus is interpretive and the introduction of religious or other directive forms of intervention are contraindicated. Religious ideation is considered in ways similar to other associations drawing upon the principles of unconscious meaning analysis. In focal treatment, religious interventions may be employed, drawing upon the finding of high salience of spirituality for the patient, a well established therapeutic alliance, and a history of the beneficial and naturally occurring use of religious resources in coping. This explicit form of integration comes out of the therapeutic relationship and includes a clear understanding of the role religion has played rather than simply being an introduction of a clinical resource. In my own practice, such explicit use of spiritual resources has been somewhat infrequent and always within the context of providing focal treatment. Implicit integration has been more common, in which the religious dimension has been integrated into treatment through tracking associations and being open to the appearance of spiritual life in conscious attributions and in unconscious symbolism and narrative.

Psychological treatment, although offered in the spirit of neutrality, inevitably includes the irreducible, ever present subjectivity of the clinician. My spiritual orientation therefore impacts my clinical practice of psychology and psychoanalysis whether or not implicit or explicit integration is conducted. That we are made in the image and likeness of God, that we live in a universe larger than what we can apprehend, that we are called to the courage to be, that neither suffering nor ecstasy are pointless, that the construction of meaning supercedes ordinary happiness— each of these personal beliefs orient my sitting with the person across from me. For the patient and myself, the therapeutic process offers a context for the understanding and construction of meaning. By allowing the door to stand ajar, a host of experience, including the religious and spiritual, may stream through, informing our mutual understanding and determining our lives.

Edward Shafranske, Ph.D., is Professor of Psychology, Luckman Distinguished Teaching Fellow, and director of the doctoral program in clinical psychology at Pepperdine University. He also holds a faculty appointment at the Southern California Psychoanalytic Institute. He is a Fellow of the American Psychological Association, past president of APA Division 36, and was editor of *Religion and the Clinical Practice of Psychology* (1996, APA Books) and conducts research on psychoanalysis, psychotherapy, and the psychology of religion. He maintains a private practice in clinical psychology and psychoanalysis in Irvine, California.

****

☐ James Ogilvie, Ph.D.

A kaleidoscopic concept, this notion of the spiritual. A whirl of images arises, a radiant array of meanings: spirituality as opening to something vast, as used in defensive self making, a vestment worn lightly or with the heaviness of the reifying I. And, too, a center is suggested, a still place which emerges in the midst of the surrounding movement.

At times I think of this idea of the kaleidoscope in reference to my daily life. The whirl of work: traveling to the hospital where I work, interactions with patients, families, and staff, then off to my private practice. Staying with the sense of the center, the rising and falling of breath, feeling, mind. After morning meditation I carry into the day an intention to be fully present to all that will arise, to be mindful and non-attached. How easy it is to get caught in the jangle of wishing things could be otherwise when, say, on the phone with the managed care company or in the midst of staff conflicts! How to find the center within the whirl itself; that's the real nitty gritty of my spiritual practice. I would like to describe one way in which I have carried my practice into my work life, a way of tapping into the deep spirituality characteristic of the therapeutic milieu itself.

When I first began working on inpatient psychiatric units I felt a sense of belonging, of being at home, which I found exciting and, at times, somewhat unsettling. I know it was something about the striking spiritual intensity of the ward community, the keen yearning and profound apartness contained there that drew me. I was reminded of the hours I had spent in the woods as a kid, of being captivated by the sharp winter moon shadows, the trance-inducing rhythmic whirr of summer night sounds. These had been moments of expansion, of belonging to something, of safety. How different they had felt from the interpersonal world, whose alleged comforts hid threat, estrangement, and unhappy surprise.

One of the first patients with whom I worked, a slight, intense young woman, would regularly emerge from her hideout within her oversized winter coat and begin to dance ecstatically to the sun as it each day reached a certain position in the sky. She was dancing, I came to learn, in celebration of her imminent wedding to the Son (of Man) who was showing himself to her in the heavenly Sun above. Other patients were encountered kneeling before the alter of the ward water fountain, chanting the rosary, or loosely mumbling on a Biblical theme. The power and nuance of the spiritual language worlds was striking. What other meaning framework could express the vast yet particular range of humanness found, say, in religious exaltation, damnation, and atonement?

Also noticeable was the relative lack of engagement with patients around these themes, at least in a way that did not try to reframe their experiences into less alive psychological categories or, worse, symptomatize them as brain breakdown products. On the other hand, significant curiosity, usually unacknowledged, and some envy were evident in staff responses to the intensity of the patients' religiosity. When I proposed that a spirituality group be started on the unit, the patient and staff response was favorable though qualified. Staff asked that I agree to stay late on the night of the group, lest the patients "act out" as a result of the experience. Administration requested assurance that I was not blurring the church/state divide, while several patients objected to my ecumenicism, wanting a group with a particular, in their case Catholic, point of view. Before turning to some of the specific questions which have arisen for me in the nine years that I have been leading these groups, I would note in general that they have clearly allowed for a more open expression of the spiritual engagements that motivate both staff and patients. The simple acknowledgement of this deep human commonality may indeed be the most significant contribution these groups have made to the development of a sense of community in those inpatient and day treatment settings where they have been held.

In thinking about the exploration of spiritual issues in a psychiatric setting I often recall a remark I heard Ram Dass make a number of years ago. A question regarding the distinction between mysticism and madness had been raised. The madman, said Ram Dass, believes he is Jesus, the one and only Son of God among men; the mystic, too, knows himself to be Jesus—as, he also believes, is everyone else. How often in psychotic states do we encounter a yearning for divinity, specifically a longing to be received as divine, together with a pervasive sense of fundamental nonviability, a basic terror of crumbling, or having already fallen, into nonbeing. The language of divinity allows an attempted self-creation through a joining with the pure, the good; often this carries with it the placing of evil (e.g., the Devil) elsewhere, either outside of oneself, or, in the absence of a more coalesced island of I-sense, in a less clearly defined elsewhere within the sea of goodness and badness from which one may emerge. What we might speak of as the movement from a paranoid-schizoid to a depressive position can be more directly engaged in the transformative religious language of its actual manifestation.

In my initial introduction of the group, each week I describe it as being an open space for discussion of the spiritual aspects of our lives, open for those who are religious and those who are not. I usually make a particular reference to people who may have a more private sense of the spiritual, apart from religion. I often begin by asking what this word "spiritual" means to the group members. The responses range widely, of course, from "it means ghosts" to "it's about love." Sometimes the group opens with one member strongly expressing his or her particular religious point of view, or strongly questioning my spiritual background and authority. Explicit in the group's ecumenical frame is the legitimizing of each individual's inquiry. We can each decide what to believe. This approach extends into the often-raised question regarding the place of treatment with medication for experiences seen as spiritually significant. "If this is the voice of God, why should I get rid of it?" is a question which I encourage. My experience has been that emphasizing the right to think for oneself leads to a more open and balanced reckoning with the pros and cons of medication than is usually seen when our approach is in terms of gaining "medication compliance."

The power of working from within the patient's spiritual frame has shown itself to me in many ways. When the lacerating voices accuse one of evil, they carry an energic charge that can be redirected via, say, invoking the idea of forgiveness. That which sanctions the one also legitimates the other. The "therapeutic turn" allowed by tapping into the dynamics of spiritual language might be likened to moving between heaven and earth. To the expanded I-beyond-all there is the "simply walking on earth" quality of the invoked spiritual identification—Jesus as God become carpenter, the Buddha placing his hand to the earth. To the collapsed most-unworthy-of-all there are the lillies of the field, God's unchoosing love. Often we talk about the idea of incarnation, of being in our lives, our bodies, this group. With the incarnating awareness of both positive and negative valences comes a significant shift in the self-awareness of the group. From projection-fueled estrangement a sense of common humanness can be felt. With this, the experience of a human circle with shared center becomes possible, often manifested by the presence of a quieter, more melancholy feel in the room.

The question of ritual often arises. The group is usually welcoming of prayer, as long as it does not feel imposed or proselytizing. Sometimes we pray for a particular person who may be in the midst of a known suffering. Over the years, one ritual has remained constant. This has involved closing each group with a brief period of silent meditation ended by the ringing of a Tibetan bowl. It would appear that this bowl has become the "concrete" carrier of the group work, often mentioned by patients whom

I have encountered after their discharge from the hospital. "Do you still have the bowl that makes that sound?" The symbolism of the round container that rings forth beautifully is appealing. On one recent evening, a woman wondered how the persecutory voices she had been hearing had managed to go into the bowl and from thence to have been "rung away from me." First, we might say, they needed to find a quiet center within which they could be heard for themselves.

James Ogilvie, Ph.D., is a Senior Psychologist in the Partial Hospitalization Program at North Central Bronx Hospital in New York City. He is a member of the New York City Buddhism and Psychoanalysis Study Group. Dr. Ogilvie has published articles on the treatment of schizophrenia as well as on the philosophy of Ludwig Wittgenstein. He is a candidate in the N.Y.U. Postdoctoral Program in Psychotherapy and Psychoanalysis and maintains a private psychotherapy practice in Manhattan and Westchester County, New York.

****

☐ Paul Giblin, Ph.D.

I was raised as the oldest sibling in an Irish, Roman Catholic, middle class family. I spent five years in seminary studying theology and being "formed" according to Ignatian spirituality. These were wonderful years, dialoguing with the personalities of the scriptures (the margins of my now-tattered Jerusalem Bible attest to the conversations), discovering my contemplative side while on a thirty-day silent retreat, and denying my finitude as a 25-year-old chaplain-in-training working on a cardiac intensive care unit. Fast forward some years, add a doctorate in marriage and family therapy, advanced training in pastoral counseling, a marriage and two children, and a tenured academic position in a major Midwestern Jesuit university. For all that has been both personally rewarding and professionally meaningful and effective, there has been much I have not learned. Spirituality and religion, specifically Catholic faith, were for most of these years synonymous. Together with family-of-origin dynamics, they colluded in my undervaluing and/or mistrusting affect, the body, self care, personal goodness, and the value of one's personal story. Instead they contributed to my overall emphasis on the cognitive dimensions of faith, to a focus on morality, self-sacrifice, unworthiness, guilt, and the collective story. For most of these years I have imaged and sought to relate to the God of creation, the transcendent God. There was not a moment I could say I "came to believe." I always believed, but not in an immanent, immediate God who knew or cared for me intimately. Half a dozen years ago I felt strongly drawn into a new spiritual journey, one that has deepened my original roots and expanded their horizons.

"What can we learn from the East?" For several years I have been part of an American Buddhist meditation group and have committed to daily sitting practice. I regularly include a Buddhist text in my psychotherapy and marriage and family classes (e.g., Jack Kornfield, Mark Epstein, David Brazier, John Welwood, Ondrea and Stephen Levine, and Jon and Myla Kabat-Zinn). Reading the Dalai Lama, Thich Nhat Hahn, Sharon Salzberg, Shunryu Suzuki, has been deeply nurturing. What have I learned from this practice? Whether through sitting or walking meditation, yoga, or body scan exercises, I am invited to engage the ordinary routines of the day with greater attention and intention. Meditation practice moves one toward a non-judgmental, increasingly accepting stance toward all life, beginning with oneself. I have come to value my body as a reliable messenger, signaling through a sense of flexibility and openness that I am on the right path, or conversely, through a sense of constriction and rigidity that some part of me is out of balance and asking for attention. The Four Noble Truths revision suffering—conflict and the feelings that accompany or "co-arise" with conflicts—as an opportunity to engage life at increasing depth, and to learn to be in, but detached from, such feelings (i.e., to accept the affect but detach from immediate interpretation or action). Metta practice, meditation on "lovingkindness," seeks to bring love, compassion, sympathetic joy, and equanimity into the center of one's life and helps counter deeply ingrained patterns of reactivity and resentment.

My maternal grandfather was a brewmaster. Alcohol continues to be a staple of our family get-togethers. Across this extended family system, dysfunctional marriages are frequent, polarized villain–victim, over- and under-functioning arrangements are the norm. There is no shortage of blame and criticism, while emotional distance abounds. Two years ago I began attending Al-Anon in an effort to make sense of this not-so-invisible legacy. This Twelve Step spirituality is challenging and rewarding. Tuesday evening meetings are a form of prayer and practice for the rest of the week. The first three steps have helped me: to own an increased sense of vulnerability and to challenge deep patterns of denial (First Step), to experience an immanent, nonjudgmental, caring God often enfleshed in the community (Second Step), and to discover choices which I did not know existed and to reach out to others for and with love (Third Step). Besides weekly meetings I try to read daily from *One Day at a Time*, *How Al-Anon Works*, or *Paths to Recovery*. I try to make conscious use of the slogans, meet several times a month for coffee or a meal with a co-sponsor, and agree to do the lead talk when invited. Twelve Step, like Buddhist spirituality, calls for a personal conversion, to detach "in love" from blame and obsessive thinking, to take responsibility for one's own growth and healing, and to surrender or "turn over" all that keeps us from living life fully. Both call for an examination of motives and intentions, especially when they come to "helping" others.

Two additional practices help me to empty or clear out space and make time in order to be receptive to the God within, the transcendent God, and the persons and events before me. Trappist Father Thomas Keating is a leading spokesperson for the contemporary (actually ancient) Christian practice of centering prayer. Twice daily one is asked to take twenty minutes to become quiet, rest, and be receptive to God's presence. Use of a "holy word" is recommended for when one is distracted. The practice is very similar to mindfulness meditation with some exceptions. I have been part of a group learning and practicing this prayer form together. The emphasis on silence, simply being not doing, and suspending dialogue, challenges my usual forms of prayer in a complementary way. For Keating, prayer, healing the false selves, and moving toward the true self all go hand-in-glove. I am not there yet!

A final practice I use comes from Richard Schwartz's Internal Family Systems. Where Keating speaks of false selves and the true self, Schwartz speaks of parts and the self or soul. His approach is built on family systems theory, the notion of multiplicity of personality (i.e., subpersonalities), and a self or soul at the core or the personality. I teach his model in family therapy classes and use it at this point less than systematically with clients. A colleague and I meet regularly to facilitate our own and each other's work with parts and self. The boundary between psychological and spiritual work becomes less clear as I come to a better understanding of (a) the parts, false selves, shortcomings within me that get hooked by clients and family members and need to be healed, and (b) the healthy balance of parts and leadership from self, soul, or center from which life is most satisfying and meaningful.

Spirituality and Clinical Practice. We are spiritual beings at our core. We cannot *not* seek to make meaning of our lives, to wonder about where we came from and where we are going, and about the purpose of our lives and our interconnectedness with earth and the cosmos. We cannot not be but awe-struck by the miracle of birth, the beauty of a sunset, power of the sea, and the generosity of those who love, accept, and forgive us. And yet many are the ways we find to "deny death" as well as life, to not live in the present, and to not believe that we can be happy with who we are and what we have. We are an "addictive society."

I seek to assess where a client is on a spirituality-religion continuum, from intrinsic/integrated religious, culturally religious, extrinsically religious, religiously neutral or hostile, to intrinsically spiritual, to spiritually neutral or hostile. Since I am identified as a pastoral marital and family therapist I usually, but not always, find clients are eager to integrate a spiritual/religious perspective. I have made an effort to create two language systems, one of spirituality and one of religion, to speak the language appropriate to each client. Goals of assessment are to determine which language to use, whether the client's spirituality/religion is functional or dysfunctional relative to their presenting problems, and how their spirituality/religion may serve as a resource in therapy. I am continually reflecting on how and where the spiritual is operating in clients' lives. Criteria I use to discern the spiritual: Where is the client being called to grow, stretch, heal, become whole and integrated; where in their thinking and feeling are they experiencing freedom, flexibility, curiosity, acceptance and forgiveness; calm, courage, risk-taking, and responsibility in their actions; and in their bodies constriction, rigidity, closedness, tension and/or expansiveness, openness, at-easeness. The spiritual is often spoken about in terms of paradox, mystery, surprise, and synchronicity.

At the intervention level, spirituality takes diverse forms. I invite clients to listen to and trust their bodies and any shifts in "felt sense." I invite them to identify and access parts through this body sense, and/or through strong feelings, images, thoughts, or "voices." I also invite them to attend to the self or soul, to recognize when they are in it and what that feels like. I lend out tapes by Jon Kabat-Zinn on sitting, walking, and body-scan meditation and by Jack Kornfield on meditation. I have a conspicuous book shelf with authors such as Thomas Moore, M. Scott Peck, Harville Hendrix, John Welwood, Gary Zukav, Kathleen Norris, and Caroline Myss which may serve to introduce the topic of spirituality along with the possibility of bibliotherapy. I let clients know that the spiritual journey is also very important to me.

With clients for whom spirituality-religion is important I share more of my "spiritual clinical theory," including my belief that each of us has a soul which we can access, that this is the point where our deepest wishes and God's dream intersect, along with the belief that a marriage and family has its unique soul, such that Spirit is experienced individually and systemically. For example, when working with a couple I often point with my hands together to the space between them and speak of their marriage as a third party in the room (a spiritual frame), or as the soul-spirit-God's presence (a religious frame) and wonder with them, "what do you think your marriage (or God) is asking or wanting for you at this time?" Or I wonder out loud if their struggles are not in fact a "spiritual crisis."

With more religious clients I make explicit reference to religious imagery and resources and hope they will make the same connections. I will share that I was thinking of them as I listened to Sunday Scriptures and was wondering what they thought of the readings in terms of their life. I have reframed clients' being in very unclear and/or ambivalent spaces as "sacred space," and the "holiness of not knowing," namely, being surrounded by a "cloud of unknowing" and/or being on their own unclear Exodus journey. Client suffering takes on a new meaning when it is viewed in the context of spiritual journey, for which suffering, death, surrender, and new life is normative. To embed our individual stories in a "big story" gives new energy and meaning to the journey. I often invite clients to become curious about the deeper feelings, thoughts, and motivations surrounding their presenting issues. I ask couples to transform their accusations and conclusions into working hypotheses, and to view therapy and this time period as an experiment. Buddhists would refer to putting on "beginner's mind" which is open, curious, and flexible. I may speak from my experience of Al-Anon and/or recommend Twelve Step as a therapeutic adjunct.

Our contemporary times are confusing and paradoxical. On the one hand there is a surge of interest in things spiritual and authors characterize us as entering a new spiritual epoch, a time of increasing cooperation and collaboration, compassion and respect for each other and for the earth, and increased commitment to long-term, broad-reaching values, attitudes, and behaviors. At the same time the culture seems to be dominated by the forces of materialism and consumerism, sexism and racism, speed and productivity, blame and punishment, individualism and competition. Hopefully, psychotherapy will be aligned with the spiritual side of the struggle. In my experience clients are increasingly turning to therapists for help in differentiating from the powerful negative dimensions of the culture. The ritual of psychotherapy may in fact allow for a transformation of time and space, a time for "stopping, calming, and going deeper" (Thich Nhat Hahn's definition for meditation), for client and therapist alike. The therapy hour, like a Twelve Step meeting, centering prayer, or a meditation session, becomes a prayer form, a time of practice that then generalizes to the rest of our life.

Paul Giblin, Ph.D., is Associate Professor of Pastoral Counseling, Loyola University Chicago, the Institute of Pastoral Studies. He teaches courses in marital and family therapy, pastoral counseling, and the integration of psychotherapy, spirituality, and religion. His research focuses on marital spirituality, marital therapy, and enrichment/psychoeducational approaches to marriage. He maintains an ongoing clinical and supervision practice with a particular focus on couples work.

****

☐ Everett Worthington, Ph.D.

The Ph.D. degree in Counseling or Clinical Psychology has undergone a dramatic shift in recent years. The emergence of large PsyD degree programs has provided enormous numbers of practitioners for the field. Master's level programs in Counseling and Clinical Psychology and Social Work churn out the practitioners at a steady rate as well. About five years ago our program at Virginia Commonwealth University in Counseling Psychology (APA accredited) asked the question, What does a Ph.D. provide that PsyD and Master's level degrees do not provide? The answer is research and leadership. We immediately reconfigured our program as a scientist-practitioner-leader training program and sought to change the curriculum to produce scientist-practitioner-leaders. We believe that whether a Ph.D. Clinical Psychologist works in a university setting as a research scholar or in practice as a therapist or a practitioner, the Ph.D. Psychologist will soon be drawn toward executive leadership. He or she will manage large research projects and will manage counseling practices.

I find myself having undergone the evolution toward such a scientist-practitioner-leader. Currently I am serving as Interim Chair for the Department of Psychology in a large state university and spending my spare time serving as Executive Director of "A Campaign for Forgiveness Research" which is a non-profit corporation set up to raise money to fund international projects on forgiveness, and Editor of *Marriage and Family: A Christian Journal*. My practice has not been active for about 12 years. Earlier in my career I saw patients privately, supervised two agencies in Richmond, Virginia, and directed the Mid-Life Counseling Service (a community agency) while serving as a full-time faculty member.

To me, it seems relevant to ask the question, what role does my religion and spirituality serve in my current position? And certainly my "clients" are different from psychotherapy patients. My clients tend to be faculty members and students whom I serve as Interim Chair, researchers whom I serve as Executive Director of "A Campaign for Forgiveness Research," and authors and subscribers of a professional journal whom I serve in my capacity as Editor.

Of course, I still do substantial research and training in my approach to couple enrichment, parenting enrichment, and forgiveness interventions. My training workshops are given throughout the United States and in other countries. I have also been blessed to participate in much public teaching involving media.

My general goal is still the same as it was when I was doing a lot of practice, that is, to help others through disseminating the knowledge that I had accumulated. I find that my spiritual life is every bit as important in carrying out all of these tasks as it ever was in seeing clients. The challenges that I face to living consistently with my Christian beliefs and values are different than when I was seeing clients, but are no less challenging. For example, when I was seeing clients, my struggle was to be able to deal with the dark side of human acts to see the pain and ugliness that humans can descend into and yet be able to not allow the dirt and grime of the world to penetrate into my heart. Without a continual reliance on God and on my community of faith, including my family, I could not have hoped to succeed in that task. Therapists who have a sensitive nature, as I believe I do, are always going to be affected by evil. I quickly found that I did not have the strength within myself to overcome evil. Without relying on a God greater than myself, I could not possibly have coped with the responsibility of helping people in great pain and darkness.

Today I see less of the pain and darkness seeded within my office but I have found that the human spirit is no less tainted with sin in the Chair's Office or in the Executive Director's Office or in the Editor's Chair than in the Therapist's Chair. We all seem to be governed by self-interest, myself included. For example, I recently made a statement in a faculty meeting that cast a negative light on a colleague. I was, of course, reluctant to face that in my own mind, but one of my faculty colleagues was able to confront me about this and exposed the darkness of my own self-interest. That gentle and loving confrontation helped me to be able to publicly apologize to the colleague whom I had put down and thus partially redeemed the damage that I had done. It is my Christian faith that drives much of what I do. I find that faith erodes so easily. The nutrients must be replaced daily to keep the soil productive.

In 1985, I attended a challenging event by traveling with a pastor, Dick Simmons from Oregon. Dick challenged the men in Richmond, Virginia, to meet together for two hours every morning, all week, to pray. And then over 200 men convened, black and white, in approximately equal numbers. We spent the time praying silently. Frankly, I had never, until that time, prayed for two hours at a single time. Most of my prayer had been short petitions or times of group prayer where much of the time was spent listening and little time actually praying. During that week I found it extremely difficult to engage in two hours of continual prayer, but the experience changed my life to such a degree that I have continued to get up at 5:30 every morning for one hour of prayer, study, and reflection. That daily contact with my Lord keeps me grounded in the faith. It provides a framework through which I see the world during my time spent at professional and family activities. Throughout the day, I find that I do not take regular times of prayer, but am driven to pray for various people in my world, mostly by the challenges that come up in the course of the day. Lately, with many executive opportunities, I have been driven to prayer by my inadequacy at meeting all the demands on my time and the challenge of dealing fairly and lovingly with faculty colleagues and other people whose lives I affect with decisions. I am sure that I would be better off if I made it a habit to pray specifically for each person with whom I met but I simply do not seem to have the discipline to carry off such an activity.

Although I teach in a large state university and serve the campaign (which is not a religious campaign), the topics of my research and the questions that I ask in research are all deeply influenced by my Christian values and beliefs. The content that I deal with day in and day out is explicitly Christian and it keeps me thinking in a disciplined way about my faith and how to transmit that faith to others. In that sense, there is a certain stimulus control over my behavior. I attend Christian conventions frequently and speak to audiences of people who are explicitly Christian. They ask me questions that make me integrate my faith, practice, and lifestyle. I am occasionally invited to give talks at Christian universities, which allows me to engage in dialogue with committed Christians and therefore sharpen my integration of Christianity into my research and practice. Those environments and activities where I voluntarily place myself inevitably affect my belief and values. They also determine many of my professional friends and colleagues, thereby placing me in a professional community of other people who are seeking to integrate their faith and professional behavior together.

Outside of work, I am involved in my family's lives, all of whom are committed Christian believers. That intimate day in and day out interaction with people I love and who share a common faith keeps me centered on my Lord. In addition, the local church that I have attended for the 21 years I have been in Richmond has provided a stable, loving community within which my family and I can serve and grow.

There are then a few things that I have attempted to do to maintain my faith in the midst of the professional activities that I do but the real stimulus to remain faithful comes about through the continual challenges that we face. In the words of the cartoon character *Pogo*, "We are overwhelmed by opportunities." M. Scott Peck said, "Life is difficult" and I say, yes, life is difficult. Thank God that it is.

Everett Worthington, Ph.D., is a licensed Clinical Psychologist and is Chair of the Department of Psychology at Virginia Commonwealth University. He has published 16 books and over 100 articles and chapters, mostly on forgiveness, marriage, and family topics. He edits *Marriage and Family: A Christian Journal* and directs "A Campaign for Forgiveness Research" (www.forgiving.org).

****

☐ Lisa Miller, Ph.D.

The Morning. The morning light affirms for me the goodness of life. I quickly turn to my husband to focus on one breath. Then I say a prayer of thanks and a prayer for love in the new day. The morning sun lights the woods as I drive into work. Every day is shocking surprise. The colors change, the hue of the light shifts, the clouds make extraordinary shapes. For a better view I roll back the roof of our Jeep Wrangler—rain or shine. The condition of the land and sky tell a universal message about current influences today. I need to watch carefully to understand myself.

Eight men working at the garage near Columbia University are among the most spiritual people I have met. If I ever feel low, I only need to converse 15 seconds with any single member of the team, I am restored. They love their families passionately, working 60–80 hour weeks in a freezing cold and damp garage. The garage is a place of joy. I approach the building. Time to face the challenge. An emotion of uncertainty confronts me. How am I to engage my responsibility as a teacher, scientist, and colleague? I reach inside myself and know that I must be a source. Everything I teach, every exchange with a colleague, and every insight derived from data will emanate from the condition of my heart. I need to be in place of love if I hope to move closer to G-d,* do G-d's work and achieve greater clarity.

If I can listen to G-d throughout my day, I hear urgent messages, vital to my own development, information I soon will need. An event at the coffee vendor can carry theoretical significance or narratives for a specific student. I must stay alert. People I witness on the subway, the guy at the gas station, my beautiful husband, all sing the voice of G-d.

The Work. The Western world rapidly is evolving towards a post-Newtonian view of time, space, and lately, inner experience or psyche. Academia must evolve to keep-up with the progression of culture, or it will be a hollow shell. Already I see that a new generation of students are bored, as am I, by theories which do not include Soul in Psyche. The Zeitgeist of our time facilitates our bold exploration. Central to our new paradigm in the social sciences will be a recognition of inner life as a source, of what in the past century was called "hard data."

My job, as I take it, is to be part of this vibrant intellectual movement which expands our understanding of the Divinity within us. We in this broadening movement, inside and outside of academia, work to capture and describe that which for some time has been understood by dominant culture as a hunch or vague sense of another dimension of experience.

Author's Note: For religious reasons the author does not write the name of G-d in Full.

For me, the ideal space in which to attempt my contribution is main stream academia. My colleagues, whose work generally does not explicitly involve spirituality, have consistently been interested and quickly engaged in discussion around the topic. Drawing from their own area of specialization, they have offered me tremendous insight on matters of Soul. Into this accepting and intellectually rich environment, I am free to quite fully express my views. I will only know what to say, however, by paying attention to G-d.

Science Professor Scott Richards, a colleague at BYU whom I greatly admire, speaks of the centrality of a Triangle of Love: love of G-d, love of other, and love of self. This road map is my invaluable anchor as I navigate through the messages sent through Life. My observing eye constantly needs to monitor whether I stand inside in the Triangle of Love. If I am in a place of love, then life presents all necessary information. Synchronicity guides. Inner and outer events guide. But I only can perceive these gifts if I am in a place of Love. Our great scientist Einstein wrote, "I want to know G-d's thoughts. The rest are details. Science is for me an attempt to better know G-d. Science gives tools for deciphering order."

G-d's Patterns in the Universe. I search using empirical methods for the development of our relationship to G-d, and how it protects us against self-inflicted harms of misguidedness: alcoholism, depression, or anxiety. Numerical patterns reveal a glimpse into G-d's method. Patterns of thriving versus despair show us how we can grow towards G-d and how we can get derailed. How we lose ourselves suggests how we might be healed—how we might address G-d for help.

Teaching. Teaching is paying close attention and then repeating the information at the right moment. In the course of a classroom experience, we suddenly recall—at crucial moments—valuable books, an aphorism told by my father, that my mother spoke to me about such matters, and significant discussions overheard on the train. Students reach insights I never could have envisioned. As the teacher, I am a facilitator of their path. This I take as an enormous responsibility as I have little certain knowledge of their path. I can only hope to be totally aware of the reality in the room, so that G-d can work through me. To prepare for class I pray that I might be present to the gifts brought to bare by the students. I pray that I might serve G-d in my dealings with my students, to help them to evolve in their path towards Truth. Too many days I fall short; these, of course, are the days that I have not prayed enough or with sufficient intention. On those days when I am in touch with G-d's great love, I see among us in the course such resonance, flow and movement towards Truth. I truly am in awe.

If I take all this quite seriously it means that I must take risks as compared to the dominant myths of teaching. I cannot re-teach the same course year after year. I cannot impose a linear progression to the material. There are multiple connections to be drawn from the constellation of ideas we explore. A class is alive. Life necessitates growth. This means constantly taking the class with me, as students take me with them, on an evolutionary path. The syllabus changes each year. I bring in guest speakers and try new exercises. I lead discussions on central questions that I too am struggling to understand. I want to learn from the students. The students and I join in a spirit of exploration. Rest assured that not every reading or discussion appeals to everybody. But if together we are on this expedition and all of our opinions are worthy, then preferences are expected as part of individuation.

Psychotherapy. Within each of us pushes a powerful trajectory towards health and evolution. A Divine force propels us from within and without along our path. Therapy is collaborating with the client in Love to attend to the screams of Soul. Therapy, like teaching, necessitates being present in the moment. If I can just really listen, then in my mind emerge miraculous images, rich with healing information, and from my mouth burst out the right words, addressing the next step in the client's understanding. To be in such a space, I must pray before a session. I pray to serve G-d by creating the opportunity for human evolution and I ask G-d to work through me. Through praying to G-d I feel love and gain the intention for the client to evolve.

Therapy is about good and evil. The client who attends to their inner Source gains Divine guidance. Therapy can in this way be a process of moral resurrection. For instance, a woman in her early thirties, Claire, came to treatment in severe depression which she felt derived from loneliness. She explained that she had several lovers, most of whom were married. When she spoke of the extreme acts of infatuation on the part of married men, her eyes glimmered with vanity. Pride and arrogance were destroying her life. In treatment Claire listened to her own pain, gradually realizing that such a form of adoration did not truly fill her cup. Next she recognized her desire for real love, and saw her capacity for real love. Several months into treatment, Claire came to session quickly to shift into tears—she had gained empathy for the pain she inflicted of these men's wives and children. By violating a sacred commitment between fellow humans, a tenant of absolute Law which Richards and Bergin (1997) term the Spirit of Truth, Claire had brought herself great torture. Together we created a space for her listening to her Source, from which Claire heard the origin of her pain and that of those she touched, allowing her return to morality.

My only deliberate contributions to therapy are intention and love. If a therapist truly loves the client and believes that the client will heal, the client heals. I recall one of the patients I treated as a novice. Bob was a

56-year-old heroin addict and profoundly depressed homeless man with a prison record. He showed particular hostility towards women; knowing that he had tested HIV positive, he had sexual relations with his former wife. All of his heroin addicted friends from the 1970s were dead. He was alive and seeking treatment, which I take as evidence of the Life Force pushing through him. In our treatment Bob repeatedly portrayed the face of his mother in her coffin when he was but 4 years old, rivaled only by his adult rage, humiliation, and despair for his misspent opportunity on earth.

I did not know what to say to Bob. Strangely I felt for him a deep affection. Despite the data on rates of recurrence among substance abusers, despite dominant therapeutic views on the limits and gradualness of change, and possibly because I was new to the field, I assumed from the second I met Bob that he would kick his heroin addition and find peace. I simply assumed that he would get better. And he did.

Bob never picked up heroin over the course of his year in treatment. He started buying food to keep in his SRO residence and with dignity explained in one session about ordering a chicken dinner in restaurant, rather than buying drugs. He apologized to his former wife, who did not accept the apology but appreciated that he recognized his transgression.

In our final session, Bob emphasized that he could continue improving without our sessions. He certainly was right, but as he spoke he shot darts from his eyes. We reviewed his progress and shook hands. Then as he got up to leave and I uncontrollably blurted out into tears. Bob broke into a huge smile, headed towards the door, looked back over his shoulder with great light in his eyes. We are part of the Universe, so upon it we must rely. Intention and love we actively can do, so that they might take on a life of their own.

Sticking to It. In both teaching and research I want to take my cues from life, not from so-called precedents. I regret when I do not listen to life. I regret when I am too busy or preoccupied to have respected life. This means that I need much prayer to stay focused. I pray when I rise. I pray before entering a class. I pray before speaking. If can be in a place of Love, I hear the questions of students or comments people and in turn respond based upon an inherent goodness. Value flows right through me and them. Together we are on the same wavelength of creation.

Perhaps the most healing and guiding forces in my life come from living on a river stream. I see ducks survive the winter and in the spring lead new offspring. Geese loyally stay in ganders month after month. A doe wakes before me and greets me when I rise. The land absorbs the winter ice. These things are Real. Obsessions about publications, tenure, or offhanded transgression from a colleague are not Real. G-d is in the land. If I lose my feeling of unity with this force, then nothing I do or say can have value.

Lisa Miller, Ph.D. is an Assistant Professor in the Clinical Psychology Program at Teachers College, Columbia University. Her research focuses on the developmental path of spirituality and its association with resilience in adolescents and adults, for which she has received the 1998 Outstanding Paper in Humility Theology from the Sir John Templeton Foundation and the W.T. Grant Faculty Scholars Award. She teaches a course on spirituality and psychotherapy, as well as courses on short-term psychotherapies.

☐ Concluding Note

These first-hand accounts portray the daily lives of six psychotherapists from several faith traditions—Jewish, Roman Catholic, Buddhist, Mormon, and Evangelical Christian—who incorporate the spiritual dimension into their professional practice and their personal lives. My hope in including these self-descriptions is that readers can appreciate the various ways in which the spiritual dimension can be incorporated into clinical and psychotherapeutic practice.

☐ References

Richard, S., & Bergin, A. (1997). *A spiritual strategy for counseling and psychotherapy.* Washington, DC: American Psychological Association.

Sansone, R., Khatain, K., & Rodenhauser, P. (1990). The role of religion in psychiatric education. A national survey. *Academic Psychiatry, 14*(1), 34–38.

Shafranske, E. (1996). Religious beliefs, affiliations, and practices of clinical psychologists. In E. Shafranske (Ed.), *Religion and the clinical practice of psychology* (pp. 149–162). Washington, DC: American Psychological Association.

Shafranske, E. (2000). Religious involvement and professional practices of psychiatrists and other mental health professionals. *Psychiatric Annals, 30*(8), 525–532.

EPILOGUE

This book has attempted to overview theoretical and clinical developments in a new and exciting field. It has emphasized spiritual development in light of personality development and functioning, with attention to the psychoanalytic, the developmental research and the transpersonal perspectives, as well as spiritual practices from both the Eastern and Western religious and spiritual traditions. Its purpose was to integrate these various theoretical perspectives and insights for use in the clinical practice of spiritually-attuned psychotherapy and counseling.

This Epilogue describes likely future trends and developments regarding spiritually-attuned psychotherapy and counseling. While forecasting future trends and likely scenarios is fraught with certain dangers, strategic thinkers in business and government regularly engage in the visioning process in order to anticipate future threats as well as opportunities. Clinicians might do well to engage in a similar kind of forecasting regarding the future of psychotherapy, particularly spiritually-attuned psychotherapy and counseling. With some hesitation, I'll briefly describe my vision and forecast for the future of spiritually-attuned psychotherapy.

First, there is no reason to believe that the present trend of seeking to incorporate the spiritual dimension in daily life will diminish soon. Rather, the trend is likely to increase in intensity as our personal and work lives become more complex and harried, along with growing community sentiment that character and virtue does matter. As a result more clients will actively seek assistance from clinicians regarding various spiritual emergencies and concerns about spiritual practice, complex ethical dilemmas, and so forth.

Second, the high level of interest and increasing number of publications in the past two years in the relatively new field of "positive" psychology—wherein the emphasis is on strengths and health rather than weakness and pathology—is quite heartening. Research protocols on virtues such as optimism, resilience, wisdom, and gratitude, to name a few, are now being planned and implemented by some of the best and brightest researchers today. This trend reflects a retrieval of psychology's early experimental studies on character and implies that the field is maturing. It also suggests that clinical implications and applications will be forthcoming.

Third, funding for applied research involving a variety of spiritually-oriented topics, such as forgiveness, spirituality and health status, and healing prayer seem to be increasing. Both federal funding and private foundation grants in this area have increased significantly in the past five years, and is likely to continue for the foreseeable future. Funds for training and demonstration projects involving the spiritual dimension have also become available. The Templeton Foundation was one of the first to fund training programs involving the spiritual dimension for medical students and psychiatry residents.

Fourth, clinical practice is, of necessity, becoming increasingly sensitive to multicultural issues and diversity. At least two factors account for this. First is the changing demographics of America and the clinician's ethical responsibility to address issues of diversity within their clinical practice. The second is the fact that religion and spirituality have been conceptualized by professional organization such as the American Psychological Association and the American Counseling Association as major components of diversity. Accordingly, graduate education program in psychology and counseling, along with psychiatry, family therapy, pastoral counseling and nursing, are obliged to expose their trainees to understanding and utilizing interventions appropriate to the spiritual dimension.

Finally, clinicians themselves are increasingly interested in incorporating the spiritual dimension in their own personal lives. Many are involved in their own spiritual development and utilize various spiritual exercises such as prayer and meditation. Those who are pioneers in this emerging field will experience more support and less resistance from colleagues when they share—like the six psychotherapists and counselors profiled in Chapter 8—their experiences with clients, trainees and colleagues. Many will seek additional knowledge and training which will further increase their capacity to respond to the concerns of their clients. In other words, the prospects for incorporating the spiritual dimension in clinical practice are great. Hopefully, this book has sparked interest or re-affirmed and reinforced your interest and involvement with this dimension and its interrelationship with the psychological dimension. I trust that your journey into the heart of the spiritual dimension will be fruitful and gratifying.

INDEX

('f' indicates a figure; 't' indicates a table)

A

Adoration prayer, 152
Affection, human need, 70–71
Affective conversion, 45–46, 47, 75t
Affective dimension
    self-transcendence, 39
    spiritual counseling assessment, 15
Affective self-transcendence, 39–40
Age Universal Intrinsic-Extrinsic Scale, 172
Allport, Gordon, 27
"Altruistic service," 163
American Psychological Association, biopsychosocial model, 24
Analytic psychology, concepts of, 35–36
Anger, guideline for letting go of, 156–157
Aquinas, Thomas, 35
Archaic stage, developmental spectrum model, 65
Archetypes, analytic psychology, 35
Assagioli, Roberto, 36
Assessment
    relationship counseling, 136–138, 140–141
    spiritual counseling, 14, 15–16, 109–118
Association of Pastoral Counselors, 12
Attachment
    exercise, 153
    God representation, 126
    self psychology, 61–62
Attention, 159
Authentic self-transcendence, human development, 63
"Autonomous self," 27
Autonomy,
    self psychology, 61–62
    versus doubt/shame, psychosocial development, 55
"Awakened service," 163
Awareness of the holy, key category, 137, 140

B

Behavior modification, 124
Beliefs, spiritual assessment, 112, 114
Belonging, self psychology, 61
Bibliotherapy, 143, 183
Biological dimension, human experience, 23, 24, 24f
Biological/somatic factors, spiritual counseling assessment, 15
Biopsychosocial model, human behavior, 24
Bipolar-spectrum disorders, 99
Borderline personality, 17, 22, 31
    description of, 93–94
    spiritual dynamics of, 93–94
Boundary issues, relationship dynamics, 134–135
Brief spiritual assessment, performing, 111–112

C

"Campaign for Forgiveness Research, A," 156, 185
Carrington, Patricia, 159
Case example
    experiential focusing method, 131–133
    psychodynamic interventions, 128–129
    relationship therapy, 140–143
    religious cognitive therapy, 124
Case formulation, spiritual assessment, 114–115
Causal stage, developmental spectrum model, 66
Centering prayer, 73–74, 160–161
Channeling, spiritual emergency, 82t, 83
Character
    concept of, 26–27, 30
    moral development, 58
    psychosocial development, 55
    three dimensions of, 31–34

Character perspective, 21, 29t, 30–34, 75t, 76t
Christian spiritual tradition, three-stage approach, 53, 53t
Christianity
  conversion in, 46–47
  early childhood conceptions, 43
  moral-spiritual split, 28–29
  spiritual direction practice, 9
Client History and Intake Questionnaire, 172
Clients
  in pastoral counseling, 11, 13t
  in psychotherapy, 9, 13t
  spiritual counseling, 14
  in spiritual direction practice, 10, 13t
  spiritual search, 5, 126
Climacus, John, 53
Clinical depression, 84–85
Clinical practice
  faith development model, 60–61
  God representations, 44–45
Clinical social workers, spiritual interventions, 7
Cloninger, Robert, 30–31
Cognitive behavioral strategies, spiritual dimension, 104, 120, 122–125
Cognitive dimension, self-transcendence, 39
Cognitive restructuring techniques, 123–124
Cognitive self-transcendence, 39–40
Collective unconscious, analytic psychology, 35
Colloquial prayer, 152, 153t
Communion, key category, 137, 141
Compassion, 32, 33, 148
Compassionate stage, spiritual development, 63
Confession, 152
Conformist stage, spiritual development, 63
Conjunctive faith, faith development model, 59
Conscientious conformist stage, spiritual development, 63
Conscientious stage, spiritual development, 63
Consciousness, transpersonal psychology, 37–38
Contemplation
  in spiritual direction, 10
  spiritual discipline/practice, 104

Contemplative prayer, 159–160
Conventional level, moral reasoning, 57
Conversion
  definition of, 45
  dimensions of, 75t
Conversion perspective, 21, 29t, 45–47, 76t
Cooperativeness, character dimension, 31, 32–33, 34
Cosmic stage, spiritual development, 63–64
Countertransference
  issues, spiritual dimension, 103
  managing, 106–107
  spiritual counseling, 106, 118
Couples
  assessment categories, 137
  relationship dynamics, 133–135
  spiritual belief's impact, 135–136
Crisis, definition of, 80
"Cultural conditioning," 71–72
Cultural dimension, spiritual counseling assessment, 15
Cushman, Philip, 27

D
Dalai Lama, 148, 181
Dark night of the senses stage, spiritual journey, 68
"Dark night of the soul," 17, 22, 67, 68, 85–86
Dark night of the spirit stage, spiritual journey, 68
Dass, Ram, 178
Defense mechanisms, character, 30
Depression, diagnosis of, 17, 22, 84–85
Depressive personality
  description of, 97–98
  spiritual dynamics of, 98
Development strategy, spiritual counseling, 16
Developmental crisis, 52
Diagnostic and Statistical Manual of Mental Disorders, 4th edition (DSM-IV), religious/spiritual problems, 79
Differentiation, self psychology, 61
Dissociative disorders, 17, 22
Divine therapy, 74–75
Dreams, relationship therapy, 141–142

E
Early childhood development, three phases of, 40–44

Ellis, Albert, 6, 161
Empathy, 32, 33
"Empty self," 27
Engagement strategies, spiritual counseling, 105–109, 118
Engel, George, 24
Erikson, Erik, 51–52, 53–54
"Essential spiritual practices," 147, 148t, 148–151, 151t
Essential Spirituality: The Seven Central Practices to Awaken Heart and Mind, 147
Ethical living, essential spiritual practices, 148t, 149, 151t
Ethical perspective, 21, 29t, 34–35, 75t, 76t
Evolutionary spectrum model, 64
Evolving Self, The, 61
Existential transpersonal psychotherapy, 36
Exorcism, spiritual intervention, 7
Experiential focusing method, 130–131, 139–140
External Locus of Control, 31

F
Faith
    key category, 137, 140
    in spiritual direction, 10
Faith community, in spiritual direction, 10
Faith development model, 22, 48t, 54
    critique of, 60
    spiritual dimension, 54t, 58–60, 75t
False self, 38–39, 70–73, 74t, 182
Family dimension, spiritual counseling assessment, 15
Family therapy, 182
Fasting, spiritual discipline/practice, 104, 147, 154–155
Fellowship, spiritual discipline/practice, 104
First consent, spiritual journey, 69
Five-Factor Model of Personality (FFM), 118
Focusing strategies, spiritual dimension, 104, 120, 130–131, 139–140
Forgiveness
    guideline for requesting, 157
    relationship therapy, 142–143
    research on, 187
    spiritual discipline/practice, 104, 147, 155–157
Four Noble Truths, 181
Fourth consent, spiritual journey, 69
Fowler, James, 46, 51, 54, 58–60

Frank, Jerome, 27
Freud, Sigmund, 6, 30, 51, 65
Freud: The Mind of a Moralist, 27
Full spectrum model, 22, 64–67, 75t, 75–76
Full spiritual assessment, performing, 112–114

G
Gandhi, Mohandas, 60
Gelpi, Donald, 45, 46
Gendlin, Eugene, 130
Generativity versus stagnation, psychosocial development, 56
Giblin, Paul, 180–184
Gilligan, Carol, 57–58
Goals
    in psychotherapy, 9
    in pastoral counseling, 11, 13t
    in relationship therapy, 137
    and self-transcendence, 40
    in spiritual counseling, 14–15
    in spiritual direction practice, 10, 13t
    in spiritual psychotherapy, 16
God Image Inventory, The, 113, 117
God representations, 22. *See also* Image of God
    clinical implications, 44–45
    formation of, 40–44, 126, 175
    relationship therapy, 139
    spiritual assessment, 112, 113
    transformation of, 127–128
Goodness, moral dimension, 29
Grace, key category, 137, 140
Gratefulness, key category, 137, 140
Grof, Stanislav, 36
Growth, spiritual dimension, 139
Growth strategy, spiritual counseling, 16
Guilt, obsessive-compulsive personalities, 90, 91

H
Hallucinations, 85
Happiness, concept of, 71
"Hardened heart," 86
Healing prayer
    research on, 187
    spiritual practice, 147, 151, 152, 153t
Healing strategy, spiritual counseling, 16, 105
"Healing" touch, spiritual intervention, 7
Health, spiritual impact on, 23, 25–26, 79

"Heart of flesh," 86
Helminiak, D., 51, 52, 63
Hendrix, Harville, 183
Hillman, James, 27
Holding environment, 41
    borderline personalities, 96
Holiness, spiritual dimension, 29
How to Meditate, 159
Human behavior, biopsychosocial model, 24
"Human condition," 70
Human development
    four factors of, 63
    stage model overview, 51–52
Human experience, five basic dimensions,
    21, 23–24
Hynotherapy, 83
Hypomanic personality
    description of, 98–99
    spiritual dynamics of, 99–100

I
"Identity neurosis," 67
Identity versus diffusion, psychosocial de-
    velopment, 55
Illuminative approach, Christian spiritual
    tradition, 53, 53t
Image of God. *See also* God representations
    borderline personalities, 95
    depressive personalities, 98
    hypomanic personalities, 100
    narcissistic personalities, 87–88
    obsessive-compulsive personalities, 90
    passive-aggressive personalities, 93
"Imaginary companion," 42–43
Imperial stage, self-development, 62
Impulsive stage, self-development, 62
In a Different Voice, 58
Index of Core Spiritual Experience (INSPIRIT),
    117
Individualism, in psychology, 27–28
Individuation process, analytic psychology,
    35, 36
Individuative-reflective faith, faith devel-
    opment model, 59
Industry versus inferiority, psychosocial
    development, 55
Initial contemplation stage, spiritual jour-
    ney, 68
Initiative versus guilt, psychosocial devel-
    opment, 55
Insight, self-transcendence, 33
Institutional stage, self-development, 62

Instrumental relativist orientation, 57
Integrity
    human development, 63
    versus despair, psychosocial develop-
        ment, 56
Intellectual conversion, 46, 75t
Intellectual dimension, spiritual counsel-
    ing assessment, 15
Intention, 159
Intercessory prayer, 152
Interdependence, self psychology, 62
Interindividual stage, self-development, 62
Intermediate contemplation stage, spiritual
    journey, 68
Internal Family Systems, 182
Internal locus of control, 31
International Classification of Disease
    (ICD–9), hypomanic personalities, 99
Interpersonal stage, self-development, 62
Interventions
    contraindications to spiritually-oriented,
        121t, 121–122
    Giblin, Paul, 183–184
    Miller, Lisa, 190–191
    Ogilvie, James, 179–180
    in pastoral counseling, 11, 13t
    in psychotherapy, 9, 13t, 104
    relationship therapy, 138–140
    Richards, P. Scott, 173
    Shafranske, Edward, 176
    spiritually-oriented 7–8, 104, 120–121
Intimacy issues, relationship dynamics,
    134–135, 137
Intimacy versus isolation, psychosocial
    development, 55–56
Intuitive consciousness, evolutionary spec-
    trum model, 65
Intuitive-projective faith, faith develop-
    ment model, 59

J
James, William, 35, 174
Jung, Carl, 35–36, 51
Justice perspective, 58

K
Kabat-Zinn, Jon, 163, 183
Keating, Thomas, 51, 52, 67t, 67–75, 160,
    182
Kegan, Robert, 51, 52, 54, 61–62
Kohlberg, Lawrence, 51, 52, 54, 56–58, 65,
    66, 75

Kornfield, Jack, 183
Kundalini awakening, spiritual emergency, 82t, 84

L

Ladder of Divine Ascent, 53
LeShan, Lawrence, 159
Lesser, Elizabeth, 3
"Lex talionis," 95
Loevinger, Jane, 61, 65, 66
Lonergan, Bernard, 45

M

Magic stage, developmental spectrum model, 65
Major depressive disorder, 97
Managed care, and spiritual dimension, 6–7, 18
Mania, 17, 22
Marriage and Family: A Christian Journal, 185
Maslow, Abraham, 65, 66
Masterson, James, 95
Meditation, 7, 10, 147
  Giblin, Paul, 181
  self-transcendence, 33
  spiritual assessment, 112
  spiritual discipline/practice, 5, 17, 104, 158–161
  spiritually-oriented intervention, 7
Meditative prayer, 152, 153t
Mental egoic consciousness, evolutionary spectrum model, 65
Merton, Thomas, 39
Mesmer, Franz Anton, 6
Miller, Lisa, 188–192
Mind, essential spiritual practices, 148t, 149, 151t
Mindfulness, 150, 153, 162–163
Modes and Morals of Psychotherapy, The, 5
Moore, Thomas, 183
Moral conversion, 46, 47, 75t
Moral development model, 22, 48t, 54
  critique of, 57–58
  spiritual dimension, 54t, 56–57, 75, 75t
Moral dimension
  human experience, 21, 23, 24, 24f, 75
  relation to spiritual dimension, 28–29
  self-transcendence, 39
  spiritual counseling assessment, 15
  spiritual impact on, 26–28
Moral instruction, spiritual discipline/practice, 104, 147, 157–158

Moral judgement, moral development, 58
Moral reasoning, three levels of, 56–57
Moral self-transcendence, 40
Moral sensitivity, 58
Moral virtues, concept, 35
Mother Teresa, 60
Motivation
  essential spiritual practices, 148t, 148–149, 151t, 152–154
  moral development, 58
Mutual engagement, in spiritual direction, 10, 13t
Mutuality, self psychology, 62
Myss, Caroline, 183
"Mystical voices and visions," 17, 22, 85
Mythic consciousness, evolutionary spectrum model, 64
Mythic-literal faith, faith development model, 59
Mythic stage, developmental spectrum model, 65

N

Narcissistic personalities
  description of, 87
  spiritual dynamics of, 87–88
Near-death experience, spiritual emergency, 82t, 82
Needs, basic human, 70–71
"Neglected dimension," morality, 23, 26
Noncooperation, passive-aggressive personalities, 92
Norris, Kathleen, 183

O

Object constancy
  early childhood development, 40
  God representation, 40–44
Object-relations perspective, 21, 29t, 40–45, 61, 75t, 76t, 125–126
"Observing self," 163
Obsessive-compulsive personality
  description of, 88–90
  spiritual dynamics of, 90–91
Ogilvie, James, 177–180
One Day at a Time, How Al-Anon Works, 181
Ongoing conversion, 45
Openness, human development, 63

P

Passive-aggressive personality
  description of, 91–92

Passive-aggressive personality (*continued*)
  spiritual dynamics of, 92–93
Past-life experience, spiritual emergency,
  82t, 83
Pastoral counseling, practice of, 11–12, 12,
  13t, 14f
Pastoral psychotherapy, practice of, 11, 12,
  13t
Paths to Recovery, 181
Peak experience, spiritual emergency, 82t,
  82
Peck, M. Scott, 183, 187
Personal level, transpersonal spectrum
  model, 66–67
Personality, 86
  contrasted with character, 26–27, 30
  style, 86
  types, spiritual characteristics, 22
Personality disorder, 86
Petitionary prayer, 152, 153t
Piaget, Jean, 51, 52, 54, 56, 65, 66
Possession states, spiritual emergency, 82t,
  83
Post-conventional levels, moral reasoning,
  57
Power
  human need, 70, 71
  relationship dynamics, 134–135
Prayer
  protocol for use, 109, 118
  relationship therapy, 141
  Richards, P. Scott, 171, 172
  spiritual assessment, 112, 113–114
  in spiritual direction practice, 10, 152
  as spiritual discipline/practice, 5, 17, 104
  in treatment process, 7–8, 107–108
  types of, 152, 153t
  Worthington, Everett, 186–187
Prayer styles, 22
  borderline personalities, 95
  depressive personalities, 98
  hypomanic personalities, 100
  narcissistic personalities, 88
  obsessive-compulsive personalities, 90–
    91
  passive-aggressive personalities, 93
Precognition, 84
Pre-conventional levels, moral reasoning,
  56–57
Pre-personal level, transpersonal spectrum
  model, 66
Problem-solving methods, PC, 11

Providence, key category, 137, 140
Psychiatrists, spiritually-oriented interven-
  tions, 7, 152
Psychic opening, spiritual emergency, 82t,
  84
Psychic stage, developmental spectrum
  model, 66
Psychodynamic strategies, spiritual dimension, 104, 120, 125–128
Psychodynamic theory, human develop-
  ment, 51–52
Psychological dimension
  human experience, 21, 23, 24, 24f, 75t
  spiritual impact on, 25–26
Psychological factors, spiritual counseling
  assessment, 15
Psychological renewal, spiritual emer-
  gency, 82t, 84
Psychosis, diagnosis of, 17, 22, 85
Psychosocial development model, 22, 48t,
  75t
  spiritual dimension, 54t, 54–56
Psychotherapy, practice overview, 9, 12,
  13t, 14f
Psychotherapy and the Human Predicament, 27
Psychotropic medication, in PY, 9
Punishment/obedience orientation, 57
Purgative stage, Christian spiritual tradi-
  tion, 53, 53t
Purposefulness, self-determination compo-
  nent, 31, 32
Pyramid model of forgiveness, 156

R
Rational stage, developmental spectrum
  model, 66
Real self, self-transcendence perspective,
  39
Rebirthing, 83
Reconciliation, 157
*Re-envisioning Psychology: Moral Dimensions
  of Theory and Practice*, 28
Rehabilitation psychologist, spiritually-oriented interventions, 8
Relationships
  dynamics of, 133–135
  self psychology, 61
Religion
  mental health practitioners, 7–8
  traditional psychoanalytic view, 6
  spirituality, contrast, 4
"Religious assessment," 127

Religious beliefs/practices
    Giblin, Paul, 180–182
    Miller, Lisa, 188–190
    Ogilvie, James, 177
    Richards, P. Scott, 170–171
    Shafranske, Edward, 174–175
    Worthington, Everett, 185–187
Religious cognitive therapy, 122–125
Religious conversion, 46–47, 75t
Religious dimension
    human experience, 24, 24f
    self-transcendence, 39
    spiritual counseling assessment, 15
Religious features
    borderline personalities, 95–97
    depressive personalities, 98
    hypomanic personalities, 100
    narcissistic personalities, 88
    obsessive-compulsive personalities, 91
    passive-aggressive personalities, 93
Religious narrative, 175
"Religious or Spiritual problem," V-Code,
    17, 22, 80
Repentance
    key category, 137, 140
    spiritual discipline/practice, 104
Resourcefulness, self-determination com-
    ponent, 31, 32
Richards, P. Scott, 170
Rieff, Philip, 27
Ritual, 179–180
Ritualistic prayer, 152, 153t

S
Sacred writings
    relationship therapy, 142
    spiritual discipline/practice, 104, 147,
    161–162
Sacredness, essential spiritual practices,
    148t, 149–150, 151t
Salzberg, Sharon, 181
Schwartz, Richard, 182
Second consent, spiritual journey, 69
"Secular priests," 5
Self, analytic psychology, 35
Self-determination, components of, 31–32
Self development model, 22, 48t
    spiritual dimension, 54t, 61–62, 75t
Self-directedness, character dimension,
    31–32, 3
Self-efficacy, self–determination compo-
    nent, 31, 32

Self-esteem, self–directedness develop-
    ment, 32
Self-fulfillment, 39
Self psychology, 61
Self-responsibility, human development,
    63
"Self-righteous service," 164
Self-sacrifice, 39
Self-talk, relationship therapy, 142
Self-transcendence
    character dimension, 31, 33–34
    couple therapy, 139
    perspective, 21, 29t, 38–40, 75t, 76t
    spiritual psychotherapy, 16
Self-transformation
    God representation, 127–128
    perspective, 21, 75t
    process of, 74t
Separation
    God representation, 126
    self psychology, 61
Separation-individuation
    early childhood development, 40
    God representation, 40, 41–42
Service, spiritual discipline/practice, 104,
    147, 148t, 150–151, 151t, 163–165
Shafranske, Edward, 174–177
Shamanic crisis, spiritual emergency, 82t,
    84
Simmons, Rick, 186
Social contract orientation, 57
Social dimension
    human experience, 21, 23, 24, 24f, 75t
    spiritual impact on, 26
Social factors, spiritual counseling assess-
    ment, 15
Sociopolitical conversion, 47, 75t
Sociopolitical dimension, spiritual counsel-
    ing assessment, 15
Somatic conversion, 47, 75t
Somatic dimension
    human experience, 21, 23, 24, 24f, 75t,
    75–76
    spiritual impact on, 25
Spectrum model, 22, 64–67, 75t
Spinoza, Baruch, 66
Spirit guide communication, spiritual
    emergency, 82t, 83
Spiritual assessment, 103, 109, 111–112,
    114, 118. *See also* Assessment, Spiri-
    tual counseling
    Giblin, Paul, 182–183

Spiritual assessment (*continued*)
  psychodynamic interventions, 127–128
  questions, 115t
  Richards, P. Scott , 173
  Shafranske, Edward,, 175
Spiritual bibliotherapy, 143, 183
Spiritual community, spiritual assessment,
  112, 113
Spiritual counseling
  assessment, 14, 15–16, 103, 109–118, 115t
  practice of, 14–16
  prayer in, 14–15, 16, 107–109
Spiritual crises, 17, 22, 79, 80–81, 81t
Spiritual development
  developmental models, 22, 48t, 54t, 75t
  dimensional perspectives, 21, 23
  historical models, 52–53
  stages of, 54t, 63–64
*Spiritual Development: An Interdisciplinary
  Study*, 63
Spiritual dimension
  centrality of, 23, 24–25
  human experience, 21, 23, 24, 24f, 75t
  and moral dimension, 28–29
  self-transcendence, 39
  six perspectives of, 23
Spiritual direction practice, 9–11, 12, 13t, 14f
  clients spiritual search, 5
  spiritual discipline/practice, 104
Spiritual Directors International, 10
Spiritual disciplines, 72–73, 104, 147–151
Spiritual emergencies, 17, 22, 67, 79, 81–84
  criteria for, 85
Spiritual Emergency, 81, 82
Spiritual Experience Index, The (SEI), 118,
  137
Spiritual features
  borderline personalities, 95–97
  depressive personalities, 98
  hypomanic personalities, 100
  narcissistic personalities, 88
  obsessive-compulsive personalities, 91
  passive-aggressive personalities, 93
Spiritual genograms, 115–116
Spiritual growth model, 22, 48t
  spiritual dimension, 54t, 64–67
Spiritual Health Inventory, 116–117
Spiritual history, spiritual assessment, 112–
  113
Spiritual intelligence, essential spiritual
  practices, 148t, 150, 151t
Spiritual interventions. *See* Interventions

Spiritual journey, 1, 17, 29, 40, 183
  dangers of, 79
  dynamics of, 69–75
  stages of, 48t, 54t, 67–69
  stages of consent, 69
Spiritual maps, 116
Spiritual Outcome Scale, 172–173
Spiritual practices/disciplines, 72–73, 104,
  147–151
  essential, 147, 148t, 148–151, 151t
  spiritual assessment, 112, 114
Spiritual psychotherapy, 16, 143
"Spiritual seekers," 94, 133, 140, 161
Spiritual traditions, human development,
  51, 52
Spiritual transcendence, definition of, 117
Spiritual Transcendence Scale, 117–118
Spiritual values, clients, 5
"Spiritual Values and Methods in Psycho-
  therapy," 173
Spiritual well-being, concept, 116
Spiritual Well-Being Scale, 116, 117, 137, 172
Spirituality and Personal Maturity, 11
Spirituality
  current practice of, 1, 3, 17–18
  mental health practitioners, 7–8
  and psychotherapy, 2, 3–4, 18
  and religion, 4
Spiritually-attuned psychotherapy and
  counseling, 8–9, 12, 13t, 14, 14f, 17
  future of, 193–194
  sacred writings, 161–162
"Spiritually homeless," 5, 6
"Splitting," borderline personalities, 94,
  95–96
Stage models
  incorporating spiritual dimension, 48t
  overview of, 51–52
  spiritual dimension, 54t
Structural-developmental theory, human
  development, 51, 52, 56
Subtle stage, developmental spectrum
  model, 66
Survival, human need, 70, 71
Suzuki, Shunryu, 181
Symbiosis
  early childhood development, 40
  God representation, 40, 41
Synthetic-conventional faith, faith devel-
  opment model, 59
Systemic strategies, spiritual dimension,
  104, 120

T

"Talionic principle," 95
Temperament Character Inventory (TCI), 31, 32
Thanksgiving prayer, 152
Therapeutic alliance,   PY, 9
Therapeutic alliance, spiritual counseling, 15, 105, 108
Thich Nhat Hahn, 181
Third consent, spiritual journey, 69
Three Ways, Christian spiritual tradition, 53, 53t
Tillich, Paul, 66
Time-out strategies, relationship therapy, 142
Training
  pastoral counseling, 11–12
  for spiritual direction practice, 10
  spiritually-oriented therapy, 187, 194
Transcendental Meditation (TM), 159
Transference, spiritual counseling, 106
Transformation, process of, 74t
Transforming union stage, spiritual journey, 68–69
"Transitional figure method," 128
"Transitional modes," 41–42
Transpersonal perspective, 21, 29t, 35–38, 75t, 76t
Transpersonal Psychoanalytic Psychotherapy, 36
Transpersonal psychology, 35–38
Transpersonal theory, human development, 51, 52
"Transpersonal" identification, 33, 34
Triumph of the Therapeutic, 27
True self, 38, 39, 70, 182
"True service," 164
Trust versus mistrust, psychosocial development, 55
Twelve Step Program, Paul Giblin, 181–182
21st Century Spirituality, 3
Typhonic consciousness, evolutionary spectrum model, 64

U

UFO experience, spiritual emergency, 82t, 83
Unitive approach, Christian spiritual tradition, 53, 53t
Unitive consciousness, evolutionary spectrum model, 65
Unity stage, spiritual journey, 68
Universal ethical principles orientation, 57
Universalizing faith, faith development model, 59–60

V

V code (DSM-IV), "Religious or Spiritual problem," 17, 22, 80
Values
  in psychotherapy, 28
  spiritual assessment, 112, 114
Ventura, Michael, 27
Virtue ethics, 34–35
Virtues, psychosocial development, 55–56
"Virtuous" therapist, 34, 35
"Vision logic," 66
Vocation
  key category, 137, 141
  relationship therapy, 142

W–Z

Walsh, Roger, 147–151
Welwood, John, 183
Wholeness
  clients, 5
  human development, 63
Wilber, Ken, 36, 51, 52, 64–67, 67t, 67–68
Will, 55
Wisdom, 56
  essential spiritual practices, 148t, 149, 150, 151t
Workaholism, obsessive-compulsive personalities, 89
Worship/ritual, spiritual discipline/practice, 104
Worthington, Everett, 184–187
Zukav, Gary, 183

DATE DUE

AG 6 '02		
AP 2 '03		
AG 5 '03		
9/11/03		
MY 16 '04		
MY 04 '06		

#47-0108 Peel Off Pressure Sensitive